THE DOLPHIN GUIDE TO NEW ORLEANS

K - Pauls
416 Chartres

Preservation Hall
726 St Peter

Brewery
Decatur @ St Peter

Ferry
Foot of Canal

Trade Mart
Foot of Canal

Info
334 Royal

Tony's
212 Bourbon

THE DOLPHIN GUIDE TO
NEW ORLEANS
New, Revised Edition

Carolyn Kolb

DOLPHIN BOOKS
DOUBLEDAY & COMPANY, INC.
GARDEN CITY, NEW YORK
1984

Library of Congress Cataloging in Publication Data
Kolb, Carolyn, 1942–
    The Dolphin guide to New Orleans.

    Rev. ed. of: New Orleans. 1st ed. 1972.

    Includes index.
    1. New Orleans (La.)—Description—Guide-books.
I. Title.   II. Title: Guide to New Orleans.
F379.N53K6 1984   917.63'350463   82-45858
ISBN 0-385-18067-5

ACKNOWLEDGMENTS

So many people contributed to the writing of this guidebook. I can best explain that by admitting I could never have done it alone.

My husband, Ken, patiently clocked mileage on the plantation tour and revisited innumerable sights with me. Our children, Pherabe and Kenneth, turned out to be great travelers and added so much to our enjoyment of New Iberia, as well as being very willing guinea pigs when it came to restaurant testing. To my parents, Mr. and Mrs. Joseph Hugh Goldsby, Jr., of Bogalusa, Louisiana, I still owe a debt of gratitude for giving me such an appreciation of Louisiana and New Orleans.

Researching this book was made pleasant by the staffs of the Historic New Orleans Collection, the Louisiana section at the New Orleans Public Library (with a special thank-you to all the folks at the Latter Branch), and, at Tulane University, Bill Meneray in Special Collections. Also helpful was Father Robert Stahl at the library of Notre Dame Seminary. In the Louisiana Collection at Tulane I must mention Jane Stevens and, on her staff, Gay Craft, Cathryn Marchese, and Clemencia Molina: they lent me pencils, helped check spelling, and probably took out every vertical file in the cabinets. I heartily thank them all.

To all those people I called on with questions: Frank Davis, Paul Prudhomme, Bob Marshall, Roger Green, Nat and Frances Belloni, Betty Wisdom, Mrs. Louis Pfister, Patricia Chandler, Dr. George Reinecke, Rosemary James De Salvo, Sally Reeves, Roulhac Toledano, Don Lee Keith, Councilman Mike Early, Mary Lou Christovich, Leonard Huber, Missy Lueg, Helène Crozat, Jeff Hannusch, Errol Laborde, Tony Gagliano, Dick

Allen, George Schmidt, Patty Gay, and Tom Fitzmorris—I thank you all.

And I thank Tommy and Barbara Lemann for their good information, and State Representative John Hainkel for making our trip to Baton Rouge extra special.

Beverly Gianna of the Greater New Orleans Tourist and Convention Commission was a great help, as was Bob Rintz of the Louisiana Office of Tourism and their New Orleans staff.

All the personnel at hotels, museums, parks, shops, and restaurants were very gracious. Every organization I contacted was willing and helpful. I feel that visitors to New Orleans are in very good hands.

I must also note the help and encouragement I received from my editor, Roy Wandelmaier of Doubleday & Company, Dolphin Books. Roy, I appreciated it. Thanks also to Jennie McGregor and Jim Fitzgerald at Doubleday.

To Mary Upton, who was ever so much more than a typist, I owe a great deal. And Cora Lee Larks, who kept my house running, also deserves thanks.

But most of all, I am grateful to Ken and Pherabe and Kenneth, who had to live through it. I could not have done it without them.

All the errors, of course, I can claim as my own.

Carolyn Kolb

CONTENTS

INTRODUCTION	ix
NEW ORLEANS HISTORY	1
NEW ORLEANS FOOD	11
MARDI GRAS	24
NEW ORLEANS JAZZ	34
RHYTHM AND BLUES	42
HOW TO SPEND YOUR TIME IN NEW ORLEANS	44
THE FRENCH QUARTER	48
THE GARDEN DISTRICT	95
UPTOWN	107
THE BUSINESS DISTRICT	117
THE IRISH CHANNEL	129
DOWNTOWN	138
ESPLANADE, BAYOU ST. JOHN, CITY PARK, AND THE LAKEFRONT	147
PLANTATION TOUR	157
BATON ROUGE	177
NEW IBERIA	183
CALENDAR OF EVENTS AROUND LOUISIANA	190
EMERGENCIES	201
TRANSPORTATION	204

CLOTHES AND SHOPPING	208
WHERE TO STAY	210
CAMPING	224
RESTAURANTS	226
NIGHTLIFE	244
ENTERTAINMENT	249
FREEBIES!	253
SPORTS	262
SIGHTS TO SEE	276
TOURS—SIGHTSEEING	282
SOUVENIRS	286
WHAT TO READ	289
THE WORLD'S FAIR	291
INDEX	294
ABOUT THE AUTHOR	309

INTRODUCTION

You have to be in a certain frame of mind to truly appreciate New Orleans.

Picture yourself lounging on an upstairs balcony. There's an open french door behind you, and you can hear the whirr of a ceiling fan. It's just at the moment of sunset when everything takes on a rosy glow. The clouds you can see through the branch of the live oak have tinges of pale green and lavender. You can catch the scent of sweet olive in the air, or is it jasmine? Can you faintly hear a jazz band playing in the distance? Or is that the clacking of the streetcar along its tracks? Do you smell the aroma of bay leaves and spices in the gumbo pot? Relax. Close your eyes. Breathe in deeply and wish very hard.

That's what New Orleans feels like.

It's a sensual town. Like an aging coquette, it has a spicy past. It's like the Caribbean; it's a little like France; it's not really like anyplace else.

New Orleans can charm you. It can captivate you. It can startle you.

New Orleans is not another Houston, or another Atlanta, or another New York. It has its own bewitching aura, jealously and parochially cultivated by a city that has never truly been part of the mainstream of American life.

So that you can be at ease here and enjoy yourself, this book will try to explain New Orleans to you: how and why this city is the way it is. You will also find here all the information you will need to make your life in New Orleans simpler: how to go places, where to sleep and eat and sightsee.

No guidebook can "sell" a town, since an exaggeration or

falsehood will be obvious to a visitor on the scene. But a good guidebook should add an extra dimension to what is at hand. This book will attempt to do that.

New Orleans needs only to exist to win you over.

NEW ORLEANS HISTORY

To understand the personality of New Orleans you have to go to the very beginning, back to the first white men who came here.

Spain in the sixteenth century was hungry for gold. Explorers were endlessly wandering wherever their ships could take them. Spaniards who reached the Gulf of Mexico set out on foot; from the Indians they learned of a great river, wide and deep, that poured fresh water into the Gulf. The Spaniards sought the river as a trade route for the riches they hoped to find.

Hernando de Soto perished during one of these expeditions, but his men escaped hostile Indians by sailing down the river to the Gulf. On their way they passed the present site of New Orleans, but they took no notice. That was in 1543.

THE FRENCH YEARS

For over a hundred years the lower Mississippi Valley was ignored by Europe. Finally France stepped in. Cavalier de La Salle descended from the Great Lakes and made a stop in 1682 at an Indian settlement located where New Orleans is now. Farther down the river, in what is now Plaquemines Parish, La Salle planted a cross and claimed the territory for Louis XIV, King of France.

Naturally France wanted to protect her new possession with a settlement. The French maritime minister sent Pierre le Moyne, Sieur d'Iberville, who arrived at the river on Mardi Gras Day, March 3, 1699.

Iberville planted a cross at the site of New Orleans, then went back to his base camp on the Gulf, where Ocean Springs, Mississippi, is now.

Iberville's brother, Jean Baptiste le Moyne, Sieur de Bienville, set out from the base camp the next year. On his way back down the river he met an English ship, but he turned away the English by convincing them he was the vanguard of a French fleet. That point in the river is called English Turn. Only by chance did New Orleans become a French city.

THE FOUNDING OF THE CITY

The site of New Orleans attracted the French for two reasons: the river was deep and swift and there was an easy portage route from the river to a little stream (Bayou St. John) that led into the immense Lake Pontchartrain. Although New Orleans was some 110 miles by river to the Gulf, the portage trade route made it an important crossroads.

From 1712 to 1717 the entire territory had belonged to a French businessman, Antoine Crozat. Even by importing slaves he could not make his investment pay, so the land returned to the King.

Iberville and Bienville were Canadians, exploring and holding territory for France. To Bienville fell the task of founding New Orleans and getting profit out of the colony.

The plan was laid out by Adrien de Pauger, one of Bienville's engineers. The city would be a late French medieval town, containing a central square on the river (the Place d'Armes, now Jackson Square) with a church, a government office, a priest's house, and official residences fronting the square. The streets were laid out in a grid from the square with forts and earth ramparts on the outskirts. The French Quarter of today includes the area of Bienville's first town. He named the city for the Duc d'Orléans, the Regent of France. Lake Pontchartrain and Lake Maurepas were named for the French maritime minister and his son.

Bienville faced immense problems. France wanted gold. There was none. Bienville wanted hardworking colonists to farm, trap for furs, and fight Indians. France sent him only prisoners, slaves, and bonded servants.

Until 1731 the colony was under the control of the Company of the Indies. This began as part of the "Mississippi Bubble" of John Law, a financier who wrecked the French economy with worthless stock. The Company of the Indies convinced Europe that Louisiana was full of riches. The arriving colonists were embittered when they saw the truth.

EARLY NEW ORLEANS

The European nations that colonized America did so in different ways. The English mostly sent families and religious dissenters. The Spanish and French sent military missions and priests. Out of these early differences would grow the characteristics that would set apart states like Massachusetts and Louisiana.

Women for the French colonists had to be sent from France. First they sent the dregs of society, inmates from correctional institutions; then, in 1728, the *"cassette* ("casket") girls" began to arrive. Poor but of good reputation, they were given a dowry of clothes and housed with Ursuline nuns in New Orleans while they were courted by their future husbands.

Later Louisiana wits have remarked how prolific those casket girls were—the fallen women seem to have left no descendants.

Both women and men found life hard in the colony. Houses were built of cypress and filled in with moss and clay. Streets were rivers of mud. Water came from shallow wells or the Mississippi River.

For the spiritual life of the colony, France sent Ursuline nuns, Capuchin monks, and Jesuits.

All business and civic life was controlled by the King's representative, the governor. One of these governors, the Marquis de Vaudreuil, gained fame for his lavish parties and balls.

From the beginning New Orleans loved music, dancing, and nightlife. Old records show that the colonists were high-spirited and much given to gambling, drinking, and other social vices.

UNDER THE SPANISH

By a secret Bourbon family pact, Louisiana was passed to Spain in 1763. Since the colonists thought of France as their home country, they did not take kindly to the change. Spain's first governor gave up and went home. The town seethed with rumors and anti-Spanish plots.

The next governor, Don Alexander O'Reilly, found out the names of some dozen of the conspirators and imprisoned or executed a few in 1770. Spanish rule was harsh at times, but the colony began to prosper.

New immigrants arrived. French colonists of Nova Scotia came to Louisiana when the English occupied their homes. Called Acadians or Cajuns, they moved on to settle the bayous of what is now southwestern Louisiana.

Spain wanted no trading by the American colonies on the river. Laws were passed to that effect, but often they were not enforced. The American population began to grow.

In 1788 and in 1794 giant fires swept New Orleans, destroying all but a few French buildings. The Spanish immediately began rebuilding, and as a result the French Quarter today with its hidden patios and shuttered windows has a definite Spanish look.

The agriculture had depended on indigo as a cash crop for some time. But in the 1790s a way was found to make granulated sugar from sugarcane and a new crop took over.

In 1803 Spain transferred Louisiana back to France amid rumors that France had sold the whole territory to the United States. The French governor had only a month to set up a government. Then, as his last official act, he signed the papers transferring Louisiana to the United States.

UNDER AMERICAN RULE

The Louisiana Purchase was a $15 million bargain. The United States doubled its territory and gained a major river route. In return, New Orleans got the Americans. The Creoles (descendants of French or Spanish parents born in the colonies) considered it a mixed blessing. The "Kaintocks," as they called all Americans, seemed rude and boisterous.

Nevertheless, New Orleans loved parades and ceremonies, and the whole town turned out for the formal transfer in the Place d'Armes. The signing took place in the Cabildo, the Spanish city hall next to the cathedral.

New Orleans attracted other immigrants besides Americans. French settlers from Santo Domingo fled slave uprisings and nearly doubled the population of New Orleans in a few years. They brought with them a languid life-style suitable mostly to the tropics, a mixture of African and Catholic superstition and religion called voodoo, and black priestesses to practice it.

In 1812 Louisiana was admitted to the Union as a state, and in that year the first steamboat came down the river. Trade became easier and cotton became the main crop.

In 1814 the city was shaken by news that the British were downriver and ready to attack. A treaty ending the War of 1812 had already been signed in Belgium, but no one knew. Under General Andrew Jackson a force went out to fight. Kentucky and Tennessee men with long rifles, free blacks, plantation dandies, Creole aristocrats, and a sprinkling of adventurers under the pirate (or smuggler) Jean Lafitte—the American forces met the British downriver at Chalmette.

The Americans won a resounding victory, with only 7 dead to the British 289. The Battle of New Orleans (January 8, 1815) won no war, but it was a big step toward the Americanization of the old French colony.

The Creoles still stayed aloof. American merchants avoided the French Quarter and began settling upriver, in what is now the Garden District. English was spoken more and more. New Orleans was changing.

Immigrants came in: Irish and German, moving on to farms in the American West or dying of yellow fever and cholera as they dug the canals and built the levees that kept New Orleans alive.

In the first half of the nineteenth century the city prospered. Cotton was king, the port flourished, public buildings went up, residential housing with delicate wrought- or cast-iron balconies appeared on more and more new streets. Politics was a consuming interest—at one point the Creoles and Americans disagreed so much that they split the city into three separate municipalities, each with its own mayor.

The slavery question rocked the nation. New Orleans depended on crops that in turn depended on slave labor. In the city itself there was a whole class of free black tradesmen, and, in general, slaves received better treatment than Irish immigrants. But both the city and the state decided to stand with the South. Louisiana seceded from the Union on January 26, 1861, and New Orleans prepared for war.

THE WAR YEARS

New Orleans readied for battle with fanciful uniforms and gala parades and bazaars. But for the city the war was short. U.S. Admiral David Farragut occupied the city for the Federal government in May 1862.

General Ben Butler (known locally as "Silver Spoons," for his reputed fondness for commandeering silverware) was named military governor of New Orleans. He set the unemployed to cleaning the streets and docks, he provided food for the needy, and he tried to improve the primitive drainage and sanitation system. But his was a harsh rule. A boy was hanged for lowering the American flag over the U.S. Mint, women were arrested for being "disrespectful" to U.S. soldiers. When Butler was replaced, some said it was because world opinion had turned against him.

The city and the state were occupied by Federal forces of one kind or another until 1877.

Much has been said—most of it unprintable—about the Reconstruction period. During that time former Confederate leaders were disenfranchised. Scalawags (local whites supporting

Reconstructionist policy) and carpetbaggers (outsiders coming in to take advantage of the political climate) caused much bitterness.

Still, the economy and government improved. Railroads had already taken away the bulk of the immigrant traffic. Labor problems, floods, and droughts complicated the economic situation.

But by 1884 New Orleans was ready to host the grand Cotton Exposition Centennial, celebrating one hundred years since the first commercial shipment of cotton from the United States.

The exposition took place in what is now Audubon Park, and from a financial standpoint it was a disaster. But it gained the city national notice and the port continued to grow.

In 1897 New Orleans took a strange step and set up a legalized prostitution district on the edge of the French Quarter. Storyville (nicknamed for the councilman who introduced the law) was in existence until 1917, when the city closed it rather than lose a U.S. Navy post.

Many pretty stories have been told of Storyville, but the fancy houses were few. Most girls worked out of "cribs" or single rooms, and the gleam in their eyes might have come from cocaine (or "nose candy").

The three New Orleans specialties—food, jazz, and Mardi Gras—had already developed by this time and the city was well known as an enjoyable spot.

New immigrants arrived, the Italians. With them they brought the Black Hand, the Mafia, from Sicily. In 1890 the New Orleans police chief was murdered by Mafia henchmen. When the jury was successfully bribed by other mafiosi, the suspects were lynched by the citizens. The incident was the subject of much discussion and disagreement all over the country. Finally the United States had to pay a tribute, a reimbursement, to the Italian government.

The Italians moved into the French Quarter, where the old buildings were falling into disrepair. Although during the artistic revival of the 1920s in New Orleans many writers and painters lived in the French Quarter, it was only after World War II that the French Quarter received the attention, and the renovation money, it deserved.

HUEY LONG

Elected Louisiana governor in 1928, Huey P. Long was a tremendous personality and a vivid and persuasive speaker.

His topics—"Every Man a King" and "Share the Wealth"—and his populist philosophy divided the state. The urban Catholic leadership of New Orleans lost control of state government to rural northern Louisiana Protestants.

Huey Long was a United States senator from 1932 until his assassination in 1935 (a confusing incident: whether he died from his assailant's bullet or from one of his own guards' has still not been proven to everyone's satisfaction). During his Washington years he was a major political figure and planned on being President. He even wrote a book about it, saying he could keep FDR on as Secretary of the Navy.

Huey Long's public works programs put a bridge over the Mississippi at New Orleans and added numerous other buildings and projects. After his death, and the scandals that followed, many people, including New Orleanians, went to federal prisons. The Huey Long "good ole boy" mystique is still a major force to be reckoned with in Louisiana politics.

After struggling through the Depression, New Orleans prospered during World War II. Shipbuilding and port activity enlivened the city's economy.

NEW ORLEANS TODAY

City politics is much more intriguing to the people of New Orleans than state events. So the "clean sweep" of deLesseps Morrison in 1946—when he was elected mayor by running against the old party machine—affected the city tremendously. Morrison was not only attractive, he was socially acceptable. He served as mayor until 1961 and was responsible for much building and renovation.

Until 1970 the mayor of New Orleans was Victor H. Schiro, who became acting mayor when Morrison resigned to become an ambassador to the Organization of American States. Morrison was killed soon after in a plane crash. Mayor Schiro's favorite saying was "If it's good for New Orleans, I'm for it," and he continued Morrison's modernization plans for the city.

In 1970 Moon (his name was legally changed from "Maurice") Landrieu became mayor. Landrieu made a massive effort to involve blacks in city government and continued with building programs that saw the development of the Poydras Street corridor and its filling with high-rise buildings between the Superdome and the river. Landrieu's administration brought the renovation of Audubon Zoo, set historic districts, and rebuilt the French Market complex. The Theatre of the Performing Arts and Armstrong Park were put next to the Municipal Auditorium on North Rampart Street.

After his term as mayor, Moon Landrieu served for a time on the cabinet of President Jimmy Carter as Secretary of Housing and Urban Development. This was a fitting tribute to the work he had done for his home city.

In 1978 New Orleans elected its first black mayor, Ernest "Dutch" Morial. With his record as a former judge and member of the state legislature, Morial came into office with excellent credentials, as well as a feisty personality. The black population majority began to be reflected in the makeup of the city council. The downtown building boom continued: at one point in 1982 more than half the office space in downtown New Orleans was newly constructed. Plans for the 1984 World's Fair saw warehouse space and vacant land on the riverfront being rapidly developed. With decreased federal funding and increased operating costs, Dutch Morial managed to combine growth with economy—and he got results.

New Orleans has problems in common with any American city: a large population of the poor, much substandard housing, difficulty in pleasing everyone with city services such as crime prevention and street repair. The charm of New Orleans, for those who live here, lies in its uniqueness and in its past. A large number of us were born here, and we share roots and memories. No one is going to mistake New Orleans for Houston, and that's fine with us. Newcomers are attracted by the city's amenities and by its potential. New Orleans' key location, which made Bienville choose this site, is still its finest asset.

New Orleans seems to have hit on a winning combination: keeping the best of the old and integrating the new. The heart of the city, the French Quarter, is perhaps the best central city residential area in the country. Even the boom in the business district has produced the Julia Row renovations and the sprightly Italian Piazza on Poydras Street as well as conventional skyscrapers. In addition, the World's Fair will leave a newly refurbished waterfront. The picture of New Orleans' future seems bright.

But best of all, New Orleans has an indefinable something about it, a sort of atmosphere or feeling that can't quite be put down on paper.

You will just have to explore it for yourself.

NEW ORLEANS FOOD

It would be impossible to talk about New Orleans without discussing food. Mention New Orleans anywhere, and you conjure up three images: jazz, Mardi Gras, and Creole cooking.

Now, Creole cooking, like everything else Creole, usually means homegrown, or indigenous. "Creole" also means of French or Spanish descent.

Creole cooking includes not only the poetic creations of restaurants but also the prosaic food that people in New Orleans eat every day. It is a blend of French provincial cooking, with some Spanish, Indian, African, and American Southern thrown in.

The better New Orleans restaurants will have Creole dishes on the menu and offer gourmet creations using Creole foods, but a cook's tour of New Orleans should also include the kind of home cooking found at little lunchrooms, oyster bars, and sandwich shops.

This guide to Creole cooking should make your mouth water and give you a few ideas on what you ought to be eating in New Orleans.

And don't forget the spicy country cousin of Creole cuisine: Cajun cooking. The French peasant settlers of Nova Scotia came to Louisiana's bayou country when exiled by the English from their settlements in Acadia in the eighteenth century. "Cajun" is short for "Acadian." Although Cajun food has more pepper and Cajun sausage is smokier, the main ingredients are the same as for Creole food. The one Cajun dish that did not catch on in the city is cushcush—cornmeal mush.

COFFEE

New Orleanians like their coffee strong, hot, and black on the order of European coffee. You can get coffee pure or with chicory (the added chicory gives a bitter-tasting tang and supposedly was first added to stretch the scant coffee supply during the Civil War). You can take your coffee black or "au lait" (oh lay) which means mixed half and half with hot milk. It is said that at the French Market coffee stands they mix in one or two chocolate beans when grinding coffee to get added flavor.

BREAKFAST FOODS

Creole cream cheese used to be made at home with a cheese-cloth hanging on the back porch or in a wooden mold. It is a sort of farmer cheese or pot cheese and is very like curds and whey. Creole cream cheese is served with milk and sugar or perhaps vanilla extract or with fruit. It is very rich.

Grillades (gree-AHDS) are made from round steak of beef or veal cooked in a brown gravy and are very flavorful. To make grillades, you begin by making a roux (roo): brown flour in some fat in a pan until the flour is dark brown, the color you want your gravy to be. Then you add meat juices and (in the case of gril-lades) onions and tomatoes and spices. The meat will have to cook long enough to make it tender. Grillades may be served, usually with grits, at any meal, but they are best at breakfast, preferably after a long night of partying.

MEATS

Daube (dohb) can be beef, but it should be veal. Besides being used to prepare grillades, it appears as panéed meat (pahn-AYED), which is really breaded veal cutlets, as spaghetti and daube with tomato sauce over spaghetti, or in a daube glacée.

Daube glacée (dohb gla-SAY) is a very spicy gelatin with pieces of meat in it. It may be served as a luncheon dish or an hors d'oeuvre, but it most often appears on canapés. Making it involves boiling calves' feet and other laborious details, none of which make it sound appetizing. It is similar to hog's head cheese, another dish that tastes better than it sounds.

Many kinds of sausage are available in New Orleans, some only in the fall after butchering time. Smoked sausage is available hot or mild and is usually cooked until crusty and served with red beans. Boudin (boo-DAN) is available in white or red and contains onions and spices and rice and pork in a sausage casing. Red boudin has blood also. Chaurice (cho-REECE) and andouille (ahn-DEW-ee) are hard sausages and are mostly used for flavoring beans or soups. Andouille has bigger pieces of meat and is saltier. Tasso is dried smoked ham or beef and is used to flavor beans or gumbo.

CRABS

Since there are over 3,000 square miles of water in Louisiana and countless miles of winding Gulf shoreline, fishing has always been both a means of livelihood and a cheap and easy way of getting fed for many Louisiana people.

About the simplest things to fish for are crabs. No matter where you stay in New Orleans, crabbing will provide you with an easy and inexpensive family outing. After all, you don't have to keep and cook them—you can always throw them back in. Louisiana crabs are blue crabs, but they redden with cooking.

Crab nets usually cost a little over a dollar. You will need perhaps three nets, some extra line, and some bait, either chicken backs or beef melt. The worse the bait smells, the more the crabs like it. You find crab nets in fishing supply or hardware stores.

You can go to any number of places in or near New Orleans to crab. It is probably best to ask the sales clerk you buy the net from where to go. The shores of Lake Pontchartrain and small salt bayous are good spots.

Set out your nets so that they rest on the bottom of the lake or bayou. When you feel a tug on the net, pull it in quickly. Or just check them occasionally. Put your crabs in a round wooden apple crate or an old ice chest. Cover them so they don't run off. When you get home, rinse them well, and then boil them in a pot with crab boil mix (mostly peppers and allspice and available where you bought the net or in any grocery).

Eating a boiled crab is an adventure in itself and must be seen to be believed. Put the crab in front of you, red-shell side down and eyes toward you. There is a white triangular flap on top. Grasp the small end and, holding the crab, pull it toward you. When that is off, you will see a place to get a thumb hold to pull off the red crab shell. Pull it off and don't worry about the legs yet. Now take off the gray spongy fingers (the "dead man") and scoop out any pasty yellow stuff from the middle. (This is crab fat and is good on crackers. The bright orange eggs are good eating, too.) Now the problem is to get the white shell off the lumps of crab meat. Try breaking the crab in half down the middle using a knife. Use a nutcracker on the fat red claws.

Better yet, go to a restaurant out by the lake and watch the other tables.

Besides being boiled or hard-shell, crabs can be busters and soft-shell. For reasons mainly of interest to other crabs, the crab will shed its shell every time it grows bigger. When it breaks out of its shell, it is a buster and is very rich and totally edible (usually broiled and served with lemon butter on toast). When it begins growing a new shell, the shell is soft at first, so the crab is a soft-shell. Then it can be broiled, but it is most often fried and is delicious in a po' boy sandwich. Crabs can also be used, shells and all, in gumbo. (Po' boy and gumbo explained in a moment.) Crab meat makes delicious salads and casseroles.

SHRIMP

Shrimp and crabs are not red when you catch them—they get that way when they are boiled. Boiled shrimp (using the same spices as for crabs) are easily peeled and are delicious. Shrimp can also be crisply fried, or shelled and mixed with ham, tomato, spices, and rice to make jambalaya. Shrimp in their shells can be marinated in a spicy sauce for barbecued shrimp. Shrimp Creole is prepared with a tomato sauce and served over rice. River shrimp are tiny little shrimp and true river shrimp are available only in summer.

OYSTERS

There are bumper stickers available in New Orleans that read EAT OYSTERS—LOVE LONGER. That may or may not be true. The thing about oysters being edible only in "R" months was *very* true before refrigeration and not so true now. Oysters can be eaten raw (on the half shell) and are good if dipped in a mixture of horseradish, lemon, ketchup, and Tabasco ® or other hot sauce (or just eat them with a little lemon juice). At stand-up oyster bars all the fixings are available; they will be brought to your table in a restaurant.

Fried oysters can be a main dish or can be served on long French bread as po' boys or oyster loaves. A "half loaf" means "a half dozen oysters."

Oyster soup can be either a clear broth with oysters, celery, and onion or a broth with milk. Oyster stew uses more oysters and creamier stock. Oysters also appear in gumbo, either with other seafood or with chicken.

Oysters also lend themselves well to casseroles. Turkey with oyster dressing, oysters and artichoke hearts, and oysters with bread crumbs and Italian seasonings (and lots of garlic) are standard oyster dishes.

Oysters can also be served hot on their shells with sauces on top. Rockefeller is a green, spinachy sauce with absinthe flavor; Bienville is cheese-tasting. Oysters brochette are on skewers with bacon.

Even oyster shells get used. They are ground up for road construction material.

CRAWFISH

Pronounced CRAW-fish but sometimes spelled "crayfish," these tiny little lobster-looking things are best when they are in season—usually early spring. They can be boiled (like shrimp and crabs), and in this case the curled tail conceals the meat. You are supposed to suck the goody out of the head.

Crawfish also appear in étouffée (a-too-FAY), which is a sort of smothered stew served with rice. Crawfish stew, which is almost the same as étouffée, sometimes has more tomato. Crawfish bisque is a rich thick soup made of crawfish stock with crawfish shells stuffed with crawfish meat, bread, and spices floating in it. Crawfish tails can be fried and crawfish filling makes a good pie.

POMPANO

Pompano is the best fish around, anywhere. It is delicate, not fishy-tasting, and tender. Served with a sauce baked in a paper sack, it is called pompano en papillote (onh pop-ee-YOT; supposedly it was invented to honor a balloonist, as the bag balloons out). Pompano can also be broiled and served with lemon butter. Its main season is in cold weather. Be sure to try it.

There are many other varieties of fish served in New Orleans, because just about anything that can be caught can be eaten by someone. Louisiana clams occasionally appear at seafood stores and, if you insist, you can locate imported lobsters, scallops, and mussels. Frogs' legs are local and are larger than the French variety. Even alligator meat is often used now. It tastes like turtle.

CREOLE TOMATOES

Homegrown tomatoes are a necessity for good eating in New Orleans. They are best in hot weather, and you will find them in the market stalls at the French Market. The misshapen ones with the horny skins are the best. Let them ripen to a rich red, and then dip them in boiling water or hold them over a flame to loosen the skin. Peel and eat. Heaven must taste like that.

Tomatoes when fresh are good served with breakfast, lunch, and dinner. They can also be broiled or stuffed with bread crumbs, and they make the base for many Creole sauces.

RICE

Rice is, of course, grown in Louisiana. It is available in long grain or short grain (there is not really much difference) and sometimes it can be called "head" rice if it is especially long and good. The Konriko rice mill in New Iberia sells a variety called Wild Pecan that has a nutty flavor. Dirty rice is rice cooked with meat juice and mixed with onions, spices, and pieces of chicken giblets or meat. Rice is served often with gravy, usually brown gravy thickened with flour. Rice is put in gumbo when it is served and forms the base for jambalaya (usually made with tomato, pepper, shrimp, and ham). When left over, rice makes rice pudding or custard, and a batter with rice and leavening can make fried cakes called calas, which are served with sprinkled sugar. Calas used to be sold on the streets by vendors.

FRENCH BREAD

New Orleans french bread is not the firm-textured variety or the sourdough type. It has a crisp crackly crust and a feathery light inside. Loaves made for po' boys are thin and long. Fat and long loaves are ideal for making garlic bread. Round loaves are "cap loaves." Little rolls of french bread are sometimes called pistolettes. French bread crumbs and french bread pieces are also sold and when soaked in liquid become the base for dressings and pudding.

RED BEANS

If New Orleans has one typical dish, it is red beans and rice. A filling, tasty staple, red beans and rice is always eaten on Mondays. This is supposed to be because before washing machines, the stove had to be used to boil wash water on Mondays and the red beans could be soaked overnight and would use only one burner to cook. Red beans are kidney beans. They are boiled with onions, garlic, bay leaves, and some salt meat or ham or sausage. They are cooked until soft. The creamy gravy is made by mashing a few beans and stirring them in. Sometimes a lump of butter is added. Red bean soup is made of pureed red beans.

SOUPS

Turtle soup—with hunks of turtle meat, egg, and a lemony flavor—and crawfish bisque—with stuffed crawfish shells on top—are New Orleans standbys. A good bouillabaisse is also made from local seafoods.

The word "gumbo" comes from an African word meaning "okra." A gumbo can be any thick soup, but it usually means one that is thickened with either okra or filé (FEE-lay: powdered sassafras leaf).

Okra gumbo is usually seafood gumbo with pieces of crab, shrimp, and sometimes oysters in a tomato base. Bay leaf and thyme are important flavorings. Gumbo is always served with rice.

Filé gumbo is usually a clear chicken stock with pieces of chicken, salt pork, or sausage and oysters. The filé is the thickener. Some people sauté the filé powder with their onions when starting the gumbo. Some sprinkle it on the soup at serving. But it gives best results when mixed with a little of the hot stock and added just before serving. Filé is never boiled; if it were, it would be gummy. "Filé" means "thread," and improperly cooked filé makes a stringy mess.

Gumbo z'herbes (zairb) is really soul food. As many different greens as possible—usually the number is twelve—are boiled with salt meat and served with their liquor as a soup. Gumbo z'herbes is often served on Good Friday. The twelve greens stand for the twelve apostles.

PO' BOY

The po' boy sandwich presumably began as a poor boy's lunch, and it used to cost a nickel. Today it costs more but tastes the same. The oyster loaf is a typical po' boy, but roast beef and gravy, ham and cheese, sausage, fried trout, shrimp, soft-shell crabs, or tuna fish salad can also make po' boys. The loaf is long and only about two inches wide. It is sliced in half lengthwise and the filling is put in. Chowchow is a mustard with pieces of cauliflower pickle mixed in and is often served on po' boys. Mayonnaise is always used, except in the case of oysters, where hot sauce suffices. If you want lettuce and tomatoes, order your po' boy "dressed."

BEIGNETS

Beignets (bay-NYAYS) are square fried doughnuts sprinkled with powdered sugar and served most often at the French Market coffee stands. They are made from deep-fried squares of yeast dough. If you know Southwestern food, you will recognize beignets as light sopaipillas.

SPICES

The main spices in Creole cooking are onion, both green and regular, garlic (a hint), parsley, bay leaf, thyme, celery, and green (or bell) pepper. This would make up a Creole bouquet garni, a collection of herbs for flavoring. Sassafras, as powdered filé, is used, as are cloves (as in turtle soup) and allspice (as in crab boil). Since almost every dish begins with sautéed onion, celery, and bell pepper, these three are sometimes called the "Holy Trinity."

Besides regular black and white pepper, Creole cooking makes use of powdered red cayenne pepper and a variety of hot-pepper sauces. Tabasco is probably the best known, but Louisiana Red Hot is another brand and there are many more. The ingredients are hot red peppers fermented in brine and vinegar. On restaurant tables you will also see bottles of little green peppers pickled in vinegar. New Orleans gardens often contain tiny hot cherry peppers. And, of course, the bell pepper (sweet green pepper) is an absolute necessity to a Creole cook.

Vegetables grown locally and used often in New Orleans include eggplant, mirliton (vegetable pear), alligator pear (avocado), plantains (starchy, large bananas), and yams.

SNOWBALLS

Probably the most typical New Orleans summer dessert is the snowball. Shaved ice is put into a cone with an ice-cream-shaped scoop on top or served on a flat paper plate or piled into a pint-sized box. Then sweetened syrup is poured over it. Sometimes condensed milk is used. For a different snowball, try a little bourbon added to a mint-flavored one. Undoctored snowballs are sold at stands all over town, mostly in residential neighborhoods.

PRALINES

Sugar plus pecans makes pralines (prah-leens). Round and thin, they often have a creamy texture and a chocolate or rum flavor. Pralines are very sweet, keep well, and are easily mailed. Usually the mixture is cooked and then poured by spoonfuls onto a marble countertop.

Pecans are a Louisiana product, as are the succulent Louisiana oranges that appear in time for making that Christmas dessert favorite, ambrosia—orange sections and other fruit sprinkled with coconut and served cold.

CAFÉ BRÛLOT

Café brûlot (cah-fay brew-low) is a lovely flaming way to serve coffee mixed with spices and liqueurs. Café brûlot requires its own special cups, ladle, and chafing dish, all readily available at New Orleans' jewelers.

DRINKS

Since the cocktail was supposedly invented in New Orleans, drinks cannot be ignored. As the tale goes, a Monsieur Peychaud had a place in the 400 block of Royal Street and served a little drink there out of eggcups *(coquetiers)*. Since the Americans spoke little French, they just pronounced as best they could and called the drink a cocktail.

Ramos gin fizz is a sort of gin soda, creamy with egg whites and delicately flavored with orange-flower water.

The sazerac is a concoction of rye whiskey and bitters served best at the Sazerac Bar of the Roosevelt Hotel.

A hurricane is really rum and passion-fruit punch in a hurricane-lamp-shaped glass, served best at Pat O'Brien's bar in the patio.

The absinthe frappé (fra-PAY) is no longer real absinthe (that being outlawed because the ingredient wormwood causes brain damage), but the anise flavor is the same. It is served poured over crushed ice and is a good morning drink, but very potent.

New Orleans social drinking habits are typical of most other American cities. One nonalcoholic favorite is the Barq's soft drink, a cross between a root beer and a cola. Dixie is a tasty local beer, best drunk from "long neck" bottles. Bourbon is the majority's choice. Bloody marys are a bit hotter for adding Tabasco with freer hands. An amazing amount of champagne is consumed, probably because of all the Mardi Gras balls. Liquor laws are lenient, and you can even walk on the street with a drink in a cup, and you can drink on Sundays. The only rule to remember is not to bring an open metal or glass container on the street. That's a municipal offense.

CREOLE COOKING AT HOME

If you want to try some Creole recipes yourself, there are several good cookbooks available. Two are published by Doubleday: *The New Orleans Restaurant Cookbook* by Deirdre Stanforth and *The Plantation Cookbook* by the Junior League of New Orleans.

One old standard is *The Picayune Original Creole Cookbook*, published by the *Times-Picayune*. This book has remained practically unchanged since 1901; even the oven directions are for wood stoves. However, the ingredients are authentic, and, although the directions are rather sketchy, if you are a competent cook, you will have a lot of fun with this one.

Recipe collections from local Junior Leagues are popular: *Jambalaya* by the Junior League of New Orleans, *River Road Recipes* and *River Road II* by the Junior League of Baton Rouge, and *Talk About Good* by the Junior League of Lafayette are all usable books.

Howard Mitcham's *Creole Gumbo and All That Jazz* combines recipes with stories and jazz lyrics and makes a good souvenir. *La Bouche Creole* by Leon E. Soniat, Jr., is probably closest in feeling to the *Times-Picayune* cookbook but with better directions. *Chef Paul Prudhomme's Louisiana Kitchen* promises to be the definitive book on his Cajun-Creole style ("totally hot" is a good description!). *The Frank Davis Seafood Notebook* by the WWL radio weekend star should also be good.

Two microwave cookbooks use that appliance for Creole cooking: *Tout de Suite à la Microwave* by Jean Durkee and *Sauté* by Jeanne H. Landry. *Tout de Suite* has a second volume, too.

There are several restaurant cookbooks. One, *Creole Feast* by Nathaniel Burton with Rudy Lombard, features black chefs.

The New Orleans Cooking School, 835 Conti Street (525-3034), has a class at 10 A.M. Monday through Saturday. You can learn to make gumbo, jambalaya, bread pudding, and pralines, and have lunch, all for $15.

Lee Barnes Cooking School, 8400 Oak Street (866-0246), has classes in a variety of cuisines, including Creole, and is popular with local cooks.

Most New Orleans foodstuffs and seafood are available at gourmet shops. If you wish to buy here and send things home, try **Langenstein**'s, uptown, corner Arabella and Pitt streets. They are likely to have anything you are looking for and are well practiced in packing for shipping. **Creole Country** has marvelous sausage, hog's head cheese, and hams at 512 David Street, off North Carrollton Avenue near Orleans Street, and also at Lakeside Shopping Center.

If you want to shop the way nearly half New Orleans shops, go to a **Schwegmann's Supermarket.** The closest to the French Quarter is on St. Claude Avenue at Elysian Fields Avenue, the best one is on Airline Highway near Causeway Boulevard. Whatever you're cooking, Schwegmann's has the ingredients: they even keep the turkey necks in the seafood section because many people think that's the best flavoring for gumbo. You'll hear the New Orleans accent in its finest form, and, if you ask around at the meat or seafood counter or by the vegetables, you'll probably get several recipes from your fellow customers.

New Orleanians love their food: talk about cooking is right up there with real estate prices as a favorite topic for uptown cocktail-party chat. When two New Orleans couples go out to dinner, at least half of the conversation will be devoted to food. After you have eaten in New Orleans, you will understand this preoccupation, and, if you are willing, you can transport the taste to your own kitchen.

Nothing can compare with sitting around an oilcloth-covered table on your own screen porch cracking boiled crabs and sipping a cold Dixie while a ceiling fan whirrs overhead.

That, my friend, is what Creole cooking is all about.

MARDI GRAS

Mardi Gras in New Orleans is more a state of mind than just another legal holiday.

The mystique of Mardi Gras is an anthropologist's delight, teeming with folk customs and rituals. But in practice, Mardi Gras is a giant party with all the world invited.

"Mardi Gras" means, literally, "Fat Tuesday." This is the day before Ash Wednesday, the last feast day before the fasting of Lent begins.

Ever since 1699, when Iberville camped 30 miles from the mouth of the Mississippi River with a band of French colonists on Mardi Gras Day and named the spot Point du Mardi Gras, New Orleans has had some sort of pre-Lenten celebration.

Organized Mardi Gras began around 1857 when the Mistick Krewe of Comus appeared in a street parade Mardi Gras night. In 1870 the Twelfth Night Revelers appeared; in 1872 Rex and Momus came along; and in 1882 Proteus appeared. Except for intervals during wars, Mardi Gras has been celebrated every year since. Even when a police strike canceled New Orleans celebrations in 1979, the Jefferson Parish parades went on.

CARNIVAL SEASON

From the sixth of January to Ash Wednesday is Carnival Season. On Epiphany, or King's Day (celebrating the visitation of the Magi), the ball of the Twelfth Night Revelers opens the season.

Mardi Gras is strictly a private operation. Organizations,

called krewes, put on balls for their members and guests and parades for the public.

The older and better-known krewes (such as Rex, Comus, Momus, Twelfth Night, and Proteus) are representative of New Orleans society. There are other krewes for children, women, dancing teachers, and just about everyone else.

One new krewe, the Krewe of Clones, was begun by the Contemporary Arts Center. They parade on a Saturday night about three weeks before Mardi Gras. Clones is witty, irreverent, and fun—also you can buy a ticket and go to the after-parade party.

New Orleans' gay community has several exceptionally elaborate balls. If you can manage to get an invitation to one, go! The Krewe of Celestial Knights is the glitziest.

CARNIVAL BALLS

The larger balls are given at the Municipal Auditorium and are by invitation only. An exception is Bacchus, which puts on an excellent parade the Sunday before Mardi Gras and has an immense ball in the Rivergate Exhibition Hall at the foot of Canal Street.

If you really want to attend a ball, you might put an ad in the classified section of the *Times-Picayune.* Some krewes are very kind about inviting visitors. You can also ask at your hotel, or call the **New Orleans Tourist Commission** at 566-5011.

Mardi Gras balls follow a general pattern:

The krewe rides the floats of the parade in costume and attends the ball in that dress.

The ball begins when the court from the past year enters in evening dress. Then the krewe enters in costume. This will usually take place on the dance floor in front of the stage while the audience watches from their seats.

The Captain, head officer of the krewe, welcomes the guests in pantomime and the curtains part to reveal the tableau on the stage.

Then the dukes enter and the maids (usually debutantes) are

escorted to the stage. The King enters, masked, and then the Queen (also a debutante) is escorted by the Captain to the stage. The ladies of the court wear white ball gowns.

An entertainment following the theme of the ball is next. Most krewes are named for mythological characters and the ball themes can be very fanciful, such as "Alice in Wonderland" or "Camelot."

After the tableau the court has a grand march around the dance floor with all the officers of the krewe. Then important guests are presented to the King and Queen and then the krewe members themselves parade around.

After the pageantry the "call out dances" begin.

In the older krewes, members are carefully selected, often through family connections. Each member pays dues, which cover the ball and parade, and receives a certain number of invitations to the ball.

Old-line krewes give "carnival honors"—invitations to be Queen or a maid—to debutantes. One exception is Mystic, in which the Queen and the ladies in her court are married. Mystic also has its court in costumes, rather than the usual white dresses.

Committeemen in evening dress are asked to help with the ball, and it is their function to "call out" the ladies that each krewe member is to dance with in the first series of dances.

These ladies, wives, mothers, friends, and debutantes sit in the call-out section, near the dance floor.

As they are called out they dance with their partners and receive, in turn, a small gift, a call-out favor, from a little silken bag that each krewe member carries.

After the call-out dances there is general dancing, usually of the krewe and their ladies only, and the royal court will retire to the Queen's supper, where she entertains the court and her friends until the wee hours.

Each krewe varies a little from this format: the Queen and maids in newer krewes wear elaborately decorated headdresses and gowns; in Rex the court maids' escorts are not masked; in women's organizations the ladies call out the gentlemen; in Bacchus there is no court tableau, but the parade floats are drawn into the hall and serve as a backdrop for the dancing.

There are many krewes and many balls and parades, but there are schedules available everywhere throughout the Carnival Season. *The New Orleans Mardi Gras Guide* is published annually and is sold at bookstores, drugstores, and supermarkets. It contains parade routes, schedules, history, and anecdotes plus a souvenir doubloon!

MARDI GRAS DAY

The culmination of the Carnival Season is Mardi Gras Day itself.

Mardi Gras Day is a legal holiday—restaurants and bars may be open but banks and businesses are not.

The major New Orleans parades are best seen on St. Charles Avenue, between Napoleon Avenue and Canal Street. All parade routes are in the newspaper that day, along with photos of Rex and his Queen.

Plan to spend Mardi Gras on your feet. You might want to walk, look at costumes, move to a better parade-watching spot. Traffic near the parade routes is impossible; streetcars and buses will not be running consistently. Suffice it to say that you will need comfortable shoes.

Some families will picnic all day on the St. Charles Avenue neutral ground, the grassy traffic island in the center of the roadway. Some restaurants, such as **Kolb's** on St. Charles near Canal Street, may have a "package deal"—for a set price per person you can have lunch, watch parades, and wander in and out. Even with numerous portable johns on the parade routes, finding a bathroom is a major concern on Mardi Gras—especially with kids. Plan ahead! You can buy tickets for the stands at **Lee Circle** and along lower St. Charles by calling **Ticketmaster,** 587-3072. This may apply to day and night parades at other times, too.

Be sure you keep the kids behind the barricades. The floats and tractors pulling them are immense. Obey the police and keep safely away.

If you are energetic, you can affix a seat on a stepladder for the children. Every hardware store has supplies and you will see thousands of these contraptions. Bear in mind that ladders can tip over—this is not the safest way to see a parade.

Especially for children: bring bags to hold your "throws": beads, coasters, cups, doubloons, toys thrown by the maskers on the floats to the crowd—you will get enough clutter to last a year. (Economy-minded folks sell their beads after Carnival— watch the want ads!)

Suburbs also have Mardi Gras Day festivities; Jefferson Parish, St. Bernard Parish, and the West Bank have their own parades. They even have walking clubs.

In New Orleans the walking clubs set out early. If you like, you can start out at 7 A.M.

The walking clubs are really neighborhood krewes without floats. Most are in the Irish Channel area, and what they lack in social connections they make up in enthusiasm.

Clubs such as the Jefferson City Buzzards, the Lyons Carnival Organization, the Garden District Marching Club, and the Delachaise Marching Club begin at their clubhouse or a central meeting spot early Mardi Gras morning.

The members are costumed according to the theme of the year but do not wear full masks. Each carries a walking cane decorated with paper flowers to give to pretty girls along the route. They also carry doubloons, if the club has issued one, and other "throws" such as necklaces.

Every walking club has its own route, generally proceeding from one neighborhood bar to another where the proprietor provides free drinks to all members. Some clubs even have a "rehearsal parade" complete with bar stops a few weeks before Mardi Gras.

Then, accompanied by a marching jazz band, each club winds its way to St. Charles Avenue, usually via Washington Avenue.

The walking clubs proceed down St. Charles to Canal Street ahead of Zulu.

Zulu is the black Mardi Gras organization that specializes in throwing gilded coconuts (or rather, tossing them gently). The King, the Big Shot of Africa (sort of the assistant king), and the Queen all ride separate floats.

Zulu used to meander around all day but now he follows a route, preceding Rex down St. Charles from Jackson Avenue.

After Zulu comes Rex. Rex is the King of Carnival. He is unmasked and is usually a businessman with enough social connections to be a member of the Rex krewe.

The Rex floats always include a Boeuf Gras ("fatted ox") with members costumed as butchers riding the float. Rex also has bandwagons with jazz bands, and, like all the other parades, he has countless high school bands, majorettes, drill teams, and police escorts.

Rex issues doubloons, as do many other krewes. Since the 1960s the doubloon craze has swept New Orleanians into a frenzy of collecting. A doubloon is about the size of a fifty-cent piece, usually made of aluminum and engraved with a design, the krewe name, and parade theme. Doubloons are also traded and sold throughout the year, but they are best when caught from a float.

The universal cry of "Throw me something, mister" is heard through the crowd as the masked krewe members toss out trinkets.

Rex and Bacchus have animated floats, but all Mardi Gras floats are high, mountainous creations with precarious perches for maskers (some krewes require harnesses). Endymion, which parades Saturday night before Mardi Gras, is the largest krewe and is known for its immense floats.

After Rex, who will pause to toast dignitaries at the old city hall, Gallier Hall on St. Charles Avenue, and his Queen at the Boston Club on Canal Street, come the truck floats, the Elks Krewe of Orleanians, and the Krewe of Crescent City.

There are literally hundreds of truck floats. Any group of

families or club or fraternity can decorate a flatbed truck, install a portable john, and mask and parade all day behind Rex.

The truck floats are often elaborate and the maskers are most generous with "throws" (something to remember if you missed everything in Rex). If you haven't had enough Mardi Gras yet, you might try to see the Indians.

Indians are the black counterpart of the white marching clubs. They are garbed in fantastic sequined Indian dress, complete with war bonnets. They have their own songs to sing (calypso-sounding) and their own tribes: the Golden Blades, the Red, White and Blue, the Wild Magnolias.

The Indians used to be much more warlike than they are now and they spent Mardi Gras Day with their "scouts" and "chiefs" prowling around looking for another tribe to fight.

You can usually see Indians on North Claiborne Avenue. Regular feathered headdresses are for uptown tribesmen, "mummy crowns"—the frames of which touch the shoulders—are for downtown tribes. Even kids and females can be Indians, and there was once a white Indian, a Scandinavian scholar.

THE FRENCH QUARTER AT MARDI GRAS

Filled to the brim with college kids and other party-minded people, the French Quarter really swings at Mardi Gras.

One of the most unusual sights is the costume contest held Mardi Gras afternoon around 3 P.M. at Bourbon and St. Ann streets.

For reasons of their own, many "hes" who like to dress up as "shes" arrive in New Orleans for Mardi Gras. The costumes are amazing, as are some of the contestants.

If you miss the judging, you will still see some of the entries parading through the streets and posing for pictures in evening gowns and wigs or dressed as spacemen or snails.

Masking for Mardi Gras is not as widespread as it used to be, but you will still see a large percentage of the crowd in costume, some elaborate, but most homemade. Naturally, if you mask for

Mardi Gras, you'll feel more a part of the celebration. So bring along your Halloween outfit when you come.

On Mardi Gras night the Krewe of Comus parades. Like many other night parades, Comus uses flambeaux (flam-boh).

These are kerosene torches or flares wielded by skilled black flambeaux carriers who dance as they march and pick up tips from the crowds. Actually flambeaux carriers make good money for their work, but it is definitely hard work. You won't see any old flambeaux carriers.

Comus always wields a goblet instead of a scepter. His parade goes directly to the Municipal Auditorium.

That evening both Rex and Comus have balls, on opposite sides of the auditorium.

Just before midnight a messenger from Comus will invite Rex to join him. Rex and his Queen rise and walk to meet the Krewe of Comus.

This "meeting of the courts," with Rex going to Comus, is the finale of Mardi Gras.

Whether it is because Comus is older or more "in" or what, Rex goes to the Comus ball rather than vice versa.

Everyone in New Orleans—whether at the ball or watching on television—gets a bit sentimental during the grand march of Rex and Comus when the Mardi Gras song is played: "If Ever I Cease to Love."

This romantic little number was played for the Russian Grand Duke Alexis when he visited Mardi Gras in the 1870s. He was enamored of a music hall singer at the time and that was her favorite song. The verses are nonsensical: "When fish have legs and cows lay eggs," etc., but the charm is there.

Just like the official Mardi Gras colors of purple, green, and gold (Justice, Faith, Power respectively), Mardi Gras is a fantastic combination, but once you get used to it, you can't do without it.

MUSIC AT MARDI GRAS

Music at Mardi Gras is everywhere—at balls, from marching bands, from bands on trucks, blaring from loudspeakers at parades, from bars, and over the radio.

At the older balls, René Louapre is the orchestra leader of choice. He has a Lester Lanin or Meyer Davis sound, but you'll recognize some New Orleans jazz tunes on his program. The "Grand March" from *Aïda* usually accompanies the grand march of the court, and for the Rex and Comus meeting of the courts "If Ever I Cease to Love" is played in a slow and stately fashion.

The walking clubs and Zulu will have marching jazz bands, and Rex will have a jazz band on the Royal Bandwagon float. Jazz bands may appear at other parades, either walking or on floats or trucks. The Indian tribes will be singing their traditional songs and may have some rhythm accompaniment—this music will remind you of calypso or reggae.

Probably the most pervasive music will be rhythm and blues (or you could term it rock and roll). The New Orleans' sound of hard-driving, danceable rock music has influenced countless pop performers. New tunes for Mardi Gras come out annually, but there are many classics (some from the early 1950s). One of these is "Mardi Gras in New Orleans" by Professor Longhair. (There's a line about seeing the Zulu King "down on St. Claude and Dumaine": the corner doesn't exist, the New Caledonia Club where Zulu did appear was there but was torn down. However, a statue of Louis Armstrong, once King of Zulu, stands just about on that spot in Armstrong Park.) Other classics include: "Jock-A-Mo" by Sugar Boy and "Iko-Iko" by the Dixie Cups (two Indian songs—there are other rock versions also), "Mardi Gras Mambo" by the Hawkettes, "Carnival Time" by Al Johnson, and (surprisingly) "Let Me Take You to the Mardi Gras" by Paul Simon.

Not a Mardi Gras song but heard everywhere is "They All

Ask'd About You" by the Meters. In this song it is pronounced "aksed"—which is typically New Orleans. Even René Louapre plays that one.

"Dr. John"—a rock musician named Mac Rebennack—usually puts on a music show at Mardi Gras. The Dr. John name has voodoo connections. He will be costumed, present an extravaganza, and have some Indians on the program. The Wild Magnolias are an Indian recording and performing group. Irma Thomas, a singer, and the Neville Brothers, both band and singers, are New Orleans rock stars who shine at Carnival time also.

If you get up early enough, you can hear Pete Fountain—for free. He will be playing with the Half Fast Walking Club when they precede Zulu and Rex down St. Charles Avenue and along Canal Street on Mardi Gras Day.

MARDI GRAS FOOD

Mardi Gras in New Orleans even has a special dish: the King Cake. A brioche or coffee cake decorated with purple-, green-, and gold-colored sugar, King Cakes are first eaten on January sixth, Twelfth Night. Inside the cake is a doll. Whoever gets the doll is King of the party, or has to furnish the next cake. Thousands of King Cakes are baked and sold until Mardi Gras Day.

The Twelfth Night Revelers designate their Queen and maids by giving one gold bean and a few silver beans in cake slices served to unmarried ladies in the first call-out dance.

NEW ORLEANS JAZZ

Jazz has been called the only true indigenous American art form. Yards of books have been written on the subject and countless scholarly theories have been expounded on its intellectual subtleties.

But jazz never was, and never will be, anything you can define with words. You have to hear it, feel it, tap your toes, and wiggle with it. Jazz just is.

When you talk about jazz in New Orleans you are talking about traditional jazz. This is the basic form from which everything else named jazz (modern, cool, West Coast, etc.) developed.

Traditional jazz has several basic elements. It is not a particular tune or set of tunes. It is a way of playing.

It has a strong beat and a recognizable melody.

The musicians improvise around this melody.

As often as not, the musicians can't read music.

Solos are usually short. The band collectively improvises.

A typical jazz band will have rhythm instruments: a drum, a piano, perhaps a banjo. The band also has horns: a cornet or trumpet, a trombone, a clarinet (think of them as a bass, tenor, and soprano). Other instruments can be included: alto horns, saxophones, clappers, guitars, sousaphones, etc.

Traditional jazz is extremely personal. Each musician is telling you something with his instrument, in his own way. Jazz musicians use their instruments like voices: they talk together, occasionally someone will make a statement, but the conversation (or music) keeps roughly on the same topic (or theme).

Jazz was not suddenly invented in the back room of a brothel (although Jelly Roll Morton once claimed it was). Jazz grew out of many things, and it grew up in New Orleans.

When African slaves came to New Orleans, they found that the French Catholic climate was ideal for keeping vestiges of their own culture, while some other parts of America were not so lenient.

Through the nineteenth century slaves and free men of color were allowed to gather every Sunday in Congo Square (now part of Armstrong Park in front of the Municipal Auditorium on Rampart Street). At the Congo Square gatherings African music and dancing held on until late in the 1800s. Drums, rhythm instruments, and African songs and dances could be heard there every week.

Of course, at the same time, black people were picking up ideas from European music. New Orleans loved parades, military bands, and music for any occasion. Funerals with bands date back nearly to the eighteenth century.

The 1884 Cotton Exposition brought the Mexican Army band to town for almost a year. The instruments, arrangements, and tunes impressed local musicians. New Orleans bands still play "Sobre las Olas" but they call it "Over the Waves."

From African traditions came rhythm (intricate and syncopated) and ideas on improvising. Some African cultures make no distinction between playing music and dancing and talking. They were all ways of communicating.

From European music came melodies (Italian opera, French folk songs, concert music) and instruments.

Black people in New Orleans included not only farm laborers but also free tradesmen. Plantation workers in their music were cruder, had less formal training, and were closer to African traditions. The free men of color ("F.M.C." in old documents) sometimes called themselves "Creoles." In New Orleans they had their own society, supported a symphony, had access to good European music teachers, and had their own dances and balls. After the Civil War the "Creole" society mostly disappeared. But the men and their musical training remained.

No one knows when the first jazz band began. We do know that it was probably in the last quarter of the nineteenth century. This band probably had some trained musicians and some self-taught men who did not read music. All the men were black, but some were fairer than others, perhaps with blue eyes.

A band could get plenty of jobs in New Orleans then: dances and picnics and church socials and funerals and parades. Naturally they played what the folks wanted to hear: maybe some minstrel tunes, popular waltzes, or the syncopated piano music coming down the river from St. Louis called ragtime.

Pretty soon the New Orleans style of playing all those tunes became jazz.

"Jazz" is a word that can have several meanings. It can have sexual connotations or it can mean a trifle, something worthless as in "all that jazz."

The white musicians soon played jazz, too. One street band of white urchins called themselves the Razzy Dazzy Spasm Band, and a rival group began calling themselves the Jazzy Band. That may be where the name came from, too.

Jazz always was a folk music. For any ceremony of life music was the accompaniment. In New Orleans it was jazz music.

STORYVILLE

Some people think that jazz originated in the prostitution district of Storyville. While there were many bands that played dates there in clubs or dance halls, most of Storyville's music came from pianos.

The piano-playing "Professor" (a male pianist in a bordello) would entertain in the parlor of the house while the guests chose their partners. Or perhaps the "Professor" accompanied performances (the "naked dances" that Jelly Roll Morton mentions).

Jelly Roll played in a house in New Orleans. Most New Orleans musicians played in clubs on the fringes of the district, but wandering bands of youngsters were regular street performers.

When Storyville closed in 1917 many musicians went north to Chicago and on to New York.

THE FIRST JAZZ RECORD

In February of 1917 a white jazz band from New Orleans, the Original Dixieland Jazz Band (or Jass Band), recorded two sides for Victor in a studio out of New York. They had recorded once before for Victor and once for another company, but the carpenters in the next studio ruined the session by beating their hammers and laughing at all the racket.

In spite of what the company officials might have thought, the record of "Original Dixieland One Step" and "Livery Stable Blues" sold a million copies and jazz was off and running, setting toes to tapping around the world.

MARCHING BANDS

Louis Armstrong left New Orleans before 1920, but he was truly a New Orleans musician. He had his start in a marching band.

These groups wore fanciful outfits and paraded for Mardi Gras, volunteer firemen's outings, and anything else that called for street activity.

Marching bands still function in New Orleans. One distinctive New Orleans parade is the jazz funeral.

THE JAZZ FUNERAL

When blacks had difficulty getting insured, they joined burial societies—something that many other peoples have joined, too. This nineteenth-century practice still exists in New Orleans today.

Besides paying for the funeral, these societies would hire a band. Sometimes today the family will hire a band. Jazz funerals are almost always for black people, but occasionally a white jazz fan or musician will have one.

The band will gather at the lodge hall and play marches on the way to the funeral home to join the hearse. On the way to the church they will play hymns. The band usually does not go into the church.

From the church to the cemetery the band plays dirges, very slowly and solemnly, such as "Nearer My God to Thee."

The procession with the lodge members in front—followed by the band, then the casket and hearse, then other mourners— proceeds to the cemetery.

Then the band parts and lets the hearse go through first. This is called "turning him loose."

At the grave site the band may play a hymn. Mourning is general and loud.

After the burial the crowd gathers behind the band for the march back to the lodge hall or starting point.

Then the band breaks out with a hot number such as "I'll Be Glad When You're Dead, You Rascal You" or "When the Saints Go Marching In." The dancing crowd behind the band is called the "Second Line" and they prance and cavort all over the street and sidewalk, picking up new performers as they go along.

Many people will bring umbrellas to the funeral. They hold them furled until leaving the cemetery. Then they open them and dance around them. Often the umbrellas are decorated with feathers and ribbons.

Every band and every parade has its Grand Marshal. He struts in front, displaying his huge sash with the band's name or his title and perhaps waving a cane or his hat.

A jazz funeral is something to experience. Much can be said about the healthy religious atmosphere of celebrating after a body is dead and a soul goes to its rest. Another fact to remember is that a band, once hired, has to go back to its starting point and might as well entertain the crowd while it does.

JAZZ TODAY

Although many musicians left New Orleans, some remained behind. These men kept on playing their own kind of music for their own audience.

In the 1940s there was a revival of interest in traditional jazz. Out of this revival grew the **New Orleans Jazz Club** and the **Archive of New Orleans Jazz** at Tulane University.

The New Orleans Jazz Club started the New Orleans Jazz Museum. With state support, the museum is now located in the Old U.S. Mint building at Esplanade Avenue and the river. In the museum collection are souvenirs of countless jazzmen: Louis Armstrong's first horn, Bix Beiderbecke's cuff links, instruments from the Original Dixieland Jazz Band, priceless photographs and recordings.

The New Orleans Jazz Club also has a weekly radio program and a magazine, *The Second Line.*

The archive at Tulane was begun by William Russell and Richard Allen on a Ford Foundation grant to do an oral history of jazz through the Tulane University Department of History. Today the **William Ransom Hogan Archive of New Orleans Jazz** holds thousands of reels of taped interviews with jazzmen plus an immense collection of records, sheet music, band arrangements, programs, and posters. You must make an appointment to see the collection by calling 504-865-5688. The archive is located in the library at the corner of Freret Street and Newcomb Boulevard. The archive holds a Hot Jazz Classic each spring with seminars and concerts. The personnel always have information on local musical happenings.

There are many places to hear jazz in New Orleans. Best of all are the streets. Both the museum and the archive will be glad to tell you of upcoming parades and funerals, or, in the case of famous musicians, you will see the funeral in the news columns of the paper. Mardi Gras is the best time for hearing street bands, but parades for St. Patrick's Day and the Spring Fiesta have bands, too.

There is a "kitty hall" in the French Quarter. **Preservation Hall** features a traditional jazz band every night and for a minimum admission fee ($1.00) you are welcome to go in and sit all evening on benches or chairs. No liquor is served but soft drinks are available. Preservation Hall, 726 St. Peter Street, is open evenings until 12:30 A.M.

This hall gives regular work at fair wages to New Orleans musicians who might not be performing anywhere else.

Nightclubs in the French Quarter occasionally feature New Orleans jazz bands, and neighborhood bars scattered over the city will hire bands on weekends. The **Blue Angel** nightclub at 225 Bourbon Street has two alternating jazz bands and always has a good show.

Piano players, blues singers, and street musicians appear throughout the French Quarter from time to time. Blues, after all, grew up in the outlying districts of the South, so there are not many blues singers practicing in New Orleans.

The New Orleans Jazz and Heritage Festival held each spring provides a chance to see all kinds of musicians at work, from name concert artists to Cajun bands from southwestern Louisiana. The festival's Heritage Fair takes place over two weekends at the Fair Grounds Race Track. Foods, crafts, and several stages with continuous performances make this New Orleans' major music event.

The outdoor performances begin in late morning and end at dark. Evening concerts are also scheduled. The Jazz Festival issues a poster each year and these are collectors' items. This remarkable event has accomplished the impossible: it's about as much fun as Mardi Gras. Write for tickets to: New Orleans Jazz and Heritage Festival, 1205 North Rampart Street, New Orleans, Louisiana 70116.

Another local phenomenon is *One Mo' Time,* a musical about a black vaudeville show in New Orleans in 1926. The band is always good; the music is authentic; and the singing, dancing cast may change but is always enthusiastic. If you are the least interested in New Orleans music, go see this long-running show at the **Toulouse Theater,** 615 Toulouse Street; call 522-7852 for tickets.

If you want more information on New Orleans music, a good book for reference is *New Orleans Jazz: A Family Album* by Edmond Souchon and Al Rose. This includes biographical data and countless photographs of nearly every musician who ever played in New Orleans. Al Rose also has written *Storyville, New Orleans: Being an Authentic Illustrated Account of the Notorious Redlight District,* with many photographs by Ernest Bellocq. The movie *Pretty Baby* was partially based on this book, although the romantic plot was fictitious.

Books and records are fine for souvenirs, but if you really want to understand jazz, just get out in the street behind a band and do what comes naturally.

"If you ain't gonna shake it, what'd you bring it for?" as they say.

RHYTHM AND BLUES

Another sort of music, besides jazz, had New Orleans beginnings and shares African and New Orleans roots. Rhythm and blues existed before rock and roll. It is a sort of soul music with blues and boogie-woogie thrown in. The rhythm is very distinct and driving. Piano players like Professor Longhair and the great Fats Domino are important in this music. Bands always had drums, guitar, and piano. Bass, saxophone and other horns can be added.

Rhythm and blues began as a popular black form of music but, as rock and roll moved into wide distribution, the audience grew to include whites. Musicians who play rhythm and blues sometimes play traditional jazz, too. There have never been any fine lines drawn between the two musical types.

Chronologically, rhythm and blues hits were charted from 1946 to 1964. Rock and roll began around 1955. From 1964 on, New Orleans rock hits would be in the soul music category.

Although most musicians who play this music are black, there have always been local white fans and some white players. Mac Rebennack, known as Dr. John, has done much in recent years to promote the New Orleans sound, as a headline performer, studio musician, and arranger.

Dave Bartholomew, Tommy Ridgley, and Sugar Boy had well-known bands. Dave Bartholomew was closely associated with Fats Domino and continues to play today.

Fats (Antoine) Domino was the biggest star to come out of New Orleans, but Huey "Piano" Smith, Smiley Lewis, Shirley and Lee, and Earl King all had a following.

Much recording has been done in New Orleans and New Orleans studio musicians have been heard on many hits. (Even

Little Richard's "Tutti Frutti" was cut in New Orleans.) Paul McCartney and also the Rolling Stones have been influenced by the New Orleans sound.

To listen to New Orleans rhythm and blues today, check the entertainment calendars in *Gambit* and the Lagniappe tabloid in Friday's *Times-Picayune*. There is a very good New Orleans music magazine, *Wavelength*, $1.50 an issue (Box 15667, New Orleans, LA 70175 for subscriptions). The magazine has reviews of performers, books, records, and a schedule of performances.

The Contemporary Arts Center also keeps a schedule of who's appearing where.

You will find modern jazz as well as modern pop (New Wave, Punk, etc.) music in New Orleans performed by locally and nationally known musicians.

Some other New Orleans performers to look for: Irma Thomas, Ernie K-Doe, Aaron Neville, Allen Toussaint, and Lee Dorsey. Tipitina's (named after a Professor Longhair tune) is a club at the corner of Tchoupitoulas Street and Napoleon Avenue and is a good place to begin learning about New Orleans rhythm and blues.

As Shirley and Lee used to sing, "Come on baby, let the good times roll." You can't visit New Orleans without at least one live music session!

HOW TO SPEND YOUR TIME IN NEW ORLEANS

Trying to design a perfect New Orleans vacation is like being let loose in some grand candy shop: everything looks so good you just don't know where to start.

To begin with, read this book. Decide what sort of things interest you and what you will have time for. If you would rather do your touring in groups, there are several organized tours offered. If you didn't bring your car, you can still use public transportation for everything in town.

This week of New Orleans adventures is not in any particular order, but it will give you an idea of how to organize your time to see the best sights, eat the best meals, and hear the best music. If you have only one day in New Orleans, follow the pattern given on the First Day.

FIRST DAY

Get to the Café du Monde for coffee and beignets by 8:30 A.M., then see the river from the Moon Walk and stroll around Jackson Square. At 9 A.M. take a walking tour, either with guides from the Friends of the Cabildo or from Jean Lafitte National Historical Park. This will orient you to the French Quarter and brush up your history. Get in line for lunch at Galatoire's before 11:30 A.M. Have a light lunch. Afterward check out the Louisiana State Museum buildings around Jackson Square, the Historic New Orleans Collection, or Gallier House. Have a cocktail either at the Napoleon House (in the patio), the Chart House (on the balcony), or the Embers (also on the balcony). Have an early dinner at Antoine's—you may have to stand in line again. Then see *One Mo' Time* and then catch the last set at Preservation Hall.

SECOND DAY

If this is a Sunday, have a jazz brunch at Commander's Palace and walk through the Garden District. Ride the streetcar. Sunday is a good day to visit the zoo, and weekends are when the most street music can be heard in the French Quarter. If this is a weekday, get in line for an early dinner at K-Paul's Louisiana Kitchen. Have a full evening at Preservation Hall and a late-night coffee and pastry in the Esplanade Lounge piano bar of the Royal Orleans Hotel, or a drink at the Bayou Bar at the Pontchartrain.

THIRD DAY

Get out in the country. Go up River Road and see some plantation homes, or drive down to St. Bernard Parish for the Chalmette Battlefield and the Isleños Museum. Pick up some muffaletta sandwiches (round italian bread with meats, cheeses, and olive salad) to go from the Central Grocery Company or get a po' boy in Chalmette or some andouille gumbo in Laplace. For dinner, have seafood, maybe at Bruning's Restaurant at West End. Then go to Tipitina's for some music.

FOURTH DAY

Get some exercise: play tennis, go to the Jean Lafitte Park hiking trails on the West Bank or visit the Louisiana Nature Center. Have a very light lunch. See Longue Vue Gardens. Write in advance for reservations and have dinner at LeRuths.

FIFTH DAY

Have breakfast at Camellia Grill or get some biscuits from Popeye's Fried Chicken. Make your own picnic: pâtés from Langenstein's or Christian's foods, hog's head cheese from Creole Country, a loaf of french bread and some Dixie beer from Schwegmann's, cannolis from Brocato's. Go to City Park. See the New Orleans Museum of Art. Then rent a paddle boat and ride the train. Have a picnic under the oaks. Take a drive through New Orleans neighborhoods with your car radio on WWOZ-FM or, on weekends, WWL-AM. Make reservations and have dinner at a chef-owned restaurant: Crozier's, Maurice's Bistro. Or take the family out to Berdou's.

SIXTH DAY

Do your souvenir shopping in the French Quarter museum shops. Eat some raw oysters at the Acme. Be sure and ride the ferry. Walk around in the business district. Catch the museums you missed. Have a drink at Pat O'Brien's and then hear some music: Preservation Hall, the Blue Angel, the Maple Leaf, Tipitina's. Eat a Lucky Dog on Bourbon Street for dinner.

SEVENTH DAY

Have breakfast at Brennan's (this will occupy you into the afternoon). Stroll around the French Quarter. Buy some records. Have a drink at the Napoleon House. Go uptown for dinner at the Caribbean Room, and have a final drink at the Bayou Bar. Make reservations for your return trip.

You will find details on the restaurants mentioned in the "Restaurants" chapter, and bars and entertainment ideas in the "Nightlife" and "Entertainment" chapters. If you pace yourself —and it will take some effort—you will be able to eat your way through this week. With luck, you will find some festivals, side trips, or other diversions to keep you busy for however long a time you can stay here. Don't worry if you miss something. You will be back.

THE FRENCH QUARTER

The Vieux Carré (vyuh cah-RAY; Old Square), the French Quarter, is the first area you should visit in New Orleans. It lies downriver (or downtown) from Canal Street and is thirteen blocks deep (Canal Street to Esplanade Avenue) and about seven blocks wide (from the Mississippi River to Rampart Street). It covers the area of the original settlement, and the greater part of the city's ancient buildings and historic sites lie within the French Quarter boundaries.

If you have only an afternoon in New Orleans, spend it in the French Quarter. If you have longer, begin your explorations with the beginning.

The French Quarter is made for strolling. Whether you are inclined to meander along Bourbon Street, where the barkers open the doors of the striptease clubs for a quick glimpse of the acts, or you prefer to window-shop for antiques on Royal Street, walking in the French Quarter gives you the best free show in New Orleans. Royal Street is a daytime pedestrian mall for part of its length, and Bourbon Street is closed to cars at night. Jackson Square has also been blocked to traffic on three sides.

Although the French Quarter contains the area that was the first site of New Orleans, not everything in the French Quarter boundaries dates from the 1700s. The French Quarter is still part of a city, and it is still changing. Its buildings date from various times in New Orleans' past and present.

Because there were two big fires in the French Quarter's early years—1788 and 1794—little is left of eighteenth-century architecture, and styles and fashions in buildings have changed over the centuries.

FRENCH QUARTER

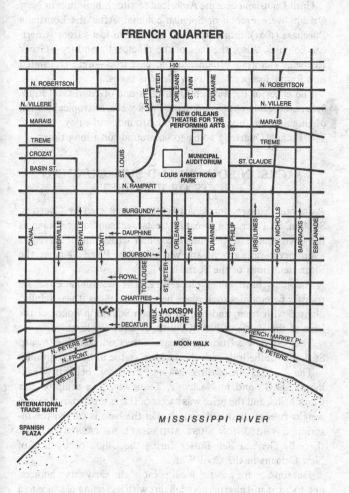

Until Louisiana became American territory, buildings in New Orleans were French or Spanish colonial. After the Louisiana Purchase (1803), more architects brought in ideas from American colonies. Also, the fads of the nineteenth century—Greek Revival, Victorian ornamentation, cast iron—were translated into forms acceptable to New Orleans tastes.

The effect of the French Quarter is one of charm, of atmosphere, of shady patios and damp brick walls, of tropical colors, of languid humidity. So relax, walk around, and enjoy yourself. The French Quarter's going to be around for a long time.

JACKSON SQUARE AND SURROUNDING POINTS OF INTEREST

Jackson Square, 700 Chartres Street, bordered by Chartres, St. Ann, St. Peter, and Decatur streets. Jackson Square began as the town square of the French colonial settlement. It served as a military parade ground and was called the Place d'Armes, the Plaza de Armas of the Spanish.

Hangings have taken place here. The Louisiana Purchase transfer ceremonies took place here. In the 1850s it was rebuilt, planted with trees, and named Jackson Square in honor of the hero of the Battle of New Orleans, Andrew Jackson.

The best view is from the Decatur Street side, looking toward St. Louis Cathedral, with the Jackson statue in the foreground.

The statue is one of three castings, the others being in Washington, D.C., and in Nashville, Tennessee. The sculptor was Clark Mills, and the price was $30,000. It was erected in 1856 and weighs twenty thousand pounds. On the base is carved the inscription THE UNION MUST AND SHALL BE PRESERVED, put there by General Ben Butler during the Union occupation of New Orleans in the Civil War.

Jackson Square was the focal point of the early city planners, and today it still charms and delights with its feeling of space and greenery in the urban area.

On the iron fences around the square sidewalk artists hang

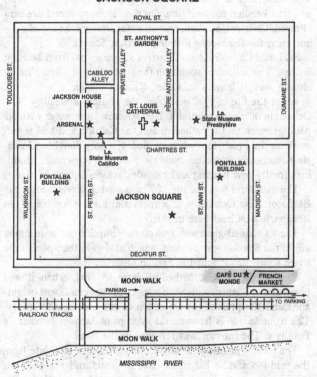

JACKSON SQUARE

ROYAL ST.

TOULOUSE ST.

ST. ANTHONY'S GARDEN

CABILDO ALLEY

PIRATE'S ALLEY

PÈRE ANTOINE ALLEY

DUMAINE ST.

JACKSON HOUSE ★

ST. LOUIS CATHEDRAL ✠ ★

La. State Museum Presbytère ★

ARSENAL ★

La. State Museum Cabildo

CHARTRES ST.

WILKINSON ST.

PONTALBA BUILDING ★

ST. PETER ST.

JACKSON SQUARE ★

ST. ANN ST.

PONTALBA BUILDING ★

MADISON ST.

DECATUR ST.

MOON WALK

PARKING

CAFÉ DU MONDE ★

FRENCH MARKET

TO PARKING

RAILROAD TRACKS

MOON WALK

MISSISSIPPI RIVER

their work, and on the Decatur Street side is a watering trough for the horses that pull the tour carriages.

Ceremonies still take place in the square: at Christmas there is carol singing, at Spring Fiesta there are festivities, and on weekends there is music. There are lots of pigeons, a fountain, and iron benches for lounging. Only on Decatur Street are cars allowed. Chartres, St. Ann, and St. Peter streets are for pedestrians only, for the blocks forming Jackson Square.

St. Louis Cathedral, 700 Chartres Street, across from Jackson Square. The cathedral stands on the spot where the first French church was. It honors St. Louis, King of France.

When the fire of 1788 destroyed the church, a wealthy New Orleanian offered to rebuild it. Don Andrés Almonester y Roxas paid for work on the cathedral and the Cabildo and had begun work on the Presbytère when he died. His only daughter, Micaela Almonester Pontalba, built the Pontalba Apartment Buildings (really row houses) and remade Jackson Square in 1856.

The cathedral was the site of Thanksgiving services after the Battle of New Orleans, and a memorial service for Napoleon Bonaparte was held here in 1821.

The six stained-glass windows on the church front were a 1962 gift of the Spanish government, which also gave the Spanish tile street signs throughout the French Quarter.

Part of the present cathedral dates to 1794, when it was planned in a Spanish style with round, low towers. It was heightened and the present towers added in the nineteenth century. The front facade is from an 1849 design of Jacques Nicolas de Pouilly's. The interior was repaired in the 1890s.

The ceiling paintings are by Dominic Canova and date from the mid-1800s. The balconies have no seats and are used for standing room. Ceiling paintings under and above the balconies on your right, facing the altar, are of former bishops and their coats of arms. There are markers for those men buried in the sanctuary, in French, Spanish, Latin, and English. Don Andrés Almonester is buried there.

The altar was made in the 1850s in Belgium. In the altar area is a representation of a pelican feeding her young, the Louisiana State seal as well as a religious symbol.

The Roman Catholic archbishops of New Orleans are commemorated by slabs in the walls near the altar.

Volunteer tour guides are available in the cathedral. As is the case with most older churches left in the city center when the original parishioners move away, contributions for the upkeep of the cathedral are appreciated.

The **Cabildo,** corner Chartres and St. Peter streets. The Cabildo began as a French police station and guardhouse. Some of the original arches still exist. Under the Spanish it was used as government offices and courts, and it later served as the city hall and the state supreme court. Now it is owned by the Louisiana State Museum. There is an admission fee.

The wide arches of the Cabildo show the Spanish influence. The mansard roof was added in 1847. The American emblems near the roof were done in 1821.

The actual signing of the Louisiana Purchase took place in the Cabildo, in the Casa Curial. When Lafayette visited in 1825 he was welcomed here and lodged in what was once the mayor's office. Notice how tiny the chairs are, built for slight nineteenth-century people.

Exhibits in the Cabildo focus on each period in its history: early French, Spanish, and American. There is a wealth of material. One of four death masks of Napoleon Bonaparte—a great hero to New Orleans—is displayed here. Traveling exhibits, such as a French government display on Louis XIV, also appear here.

The Cabildo is the starting point for the daily walking tours guided by volunteer members of the Friends of the Cabildo. There is a $5.00 fee, but the money goes toward museum upkeep, and the tours are very well done. The Louisiana State Museum buildings are open from 9 A.M. to 5 P.M. Tuesday through Sunday.

Between the Cabildo and the cathedral is **Pirate's Alley,** named that way for no traceable reason but a pleasant place to view outdoor art shows. William Faulkner lived at 624 Pirate's Alley while writing *Soldiers' Pay.*

Behind the cathedral on Pirate's Alley is **St. Anthony's Garden,** rumored to have been a popular dueling spot. Today it provides a pleasant view of the rear of the cathedral.

Jackson House and the **Arsenal,** 619 St. Peter Street. Jackson House dates from 1842 but was rebuilt by the Works Progress Administration in the 1930s. (The WPA did much to save New Orleans' heritage, both buildings and documents.) The Louisiana State Museum's collection of Louisiana folk art is here: primitive paintings, sculpture, crafts. In a connecting building, the Arsenal, are changing exhibits on New Orleans and a collection of fire-fighting equipment. The Arsenal dates from 1839. Behind it is the 1842 Creole House, which is the Friends of the Cabildo headquarters. At ground level are some remains of the old Spanish prison. There is an admission fee for Jackson House and the Arsenal.

The **Presbytère,** corner Chartres and St. Ann streets. The companion of the Cabildo, the Presbytère stands on the other side of the cathedral. It was supposed to be a priests' house, but actually it served as a courthouse until its present use by the Louisiana State Museum.

Between the cathedral and the Presbytère is **Père Antoine Alley.** This priest was first known as Fra Antonio Sedella.

He was Spanish and served as curate of the cathedral from 1783 to 1790. During this time he was the local representative of the Spanish Inquisition. There were no local inquisition arrests, but some Louisiana residents were tried in Mexico and jailed there. The Inquisition was against revolutionary politics as well as heresy. In Louisiana it seems to have been mostly ignored. Fra Antonio had a falling-out with authorities and went back to Spain.

However, he returned in 1795, was called Père Antoine, and was the beloved rector of the cathedral until his death in 1827.

The Presbytère holds historical displays of costumes and children's toys—plus changing displays from the museum's portrait, document, and memorabilia collections.

Admission procedures are the same as for the Cabildo. Ask at the desk.

The **Pontalba Apartment Buildings,** St. Ann and St. Peter streets on Jackson Square. Micaela Almonester Pontalba was the daughter of Don Andrés Almonester. Don Andrés was responsible for the cathedral, Cabildo, and most of the Presbytère. Micaela took care of the rest of Jackson Square.

Micaela was headstrong, red-haired, and impetuous. She married Celestin Pontalba, a distant cousin, and, although brought up in New Orleans, she moved to France. She and her husband's family did not get on well. Her father-in-law, the Baron Pontalba, engaged her in an argument at the family château. Micaela emerged with a missing finger and bullet wounds. The father-in-law then shot himself. Micaela became the Baroness Pontalba.

It was on a visit to New Orleans in the late 1840s that she decided to tear down the property she owned bordering Jackson Square and build her buildings—row houses with an arcade similar to one in Paris.

Micaela was a hard bargainer. She went through two architects and one builder: James Gallier, Henry Howard, and Samuel Stewart. She argued with the man who was making her wrought-iron balconies and switched to cast iron, thus setting a vogue from which New Orleans has never recovered. She would clamber over the construction site in an outfit of pantaloons she designed herself. When the buildings were finished, she saw to it that the popular singer Jenny Lind resided in one, in an attempt to make the buildings more acceptable.

The Pontalba Buildings were completed about 1851. Then Micaela began working on Jackson Square, changing the gardens and seeing that plans were laid for a statue of Andrew Jackson, and the change of name from the Place d'Armes.

Her work finished, Micaela returned to Paris and died at the age of seventy-eight. Her buildings are a proper memorial, imposing and long-lasting, sturdy yet delicate.

The initials *A* and *P* entwined in the cast-iron balconies stand for "Almonester" and "Pontalba."

The St. Peter Street building belongs to the city of New Orleans (the upper Pontalba) and the St. Ann Street one belongs to the state (the lower Pontalba). Both rent ground-floor shops and upper-floor apartments, on the square as well as on the side streets, Chartres and Decatur. Neither one advertises but both have long waiting lists.

1850 House, 525 St. Ann Street, is the property of the Louisiana State Museum and is furnished as one of the original units might have been. Ground floors were used for shops and kitchens; the second floor served as living quarters, with a usable balcony; the third floor was where the family slept; the fourth floor was for servants' quarters.

The furnishings, including utensils and toys, are all of the 1850 period, a sort of Louisiana French Victorian, with an immense tester (usually TEES-ter) canopied bed by the local cabinetmaker Prudent Mallard.

At 527 St. Ann Street is the **information center of Jean Lafitte National Historical Park.** Free walking tours begin here, and there is an audiovisual display on area history.

Also in the "lower," or St. Ann Street, Pontalba Building is the office of the **Spring Fiesta,** 529 St. Ann Street. This group sponsors three weeks of home and garden tours beginning the Friday after Easter. They also own an 1844 town house at 826 St. Ann, which is open for tours.

Brocato's, 537 St. Ann Street, has delicious Italian ices and pastries.

Now that the Pontalbas are well kept up, it is hard to realize that they were almost tenements around the turn of the century. Immigrants were keeping chickens on the first floors.

In the 1920s the plumbing wasn't much better, but the conversation was. William Faulkner and Sherwood Anderson, who lived at 540 St. Peter Street, were only two of the literary contingent that gathered in the Pontalba Buildings, not to mention the legendary cats—supposedly half bobcat, half ghost—that roamed the balconies.

In the "upper" Pontalba Building is **Swenson's Ice Cream,** 528 St. Peter, where you can buy little bags of corn for the pigeons.

There is a **Puppetorium** at 514 St. Peter Street with a puppet show, for a fee, about New Orleans history.

At the corner of St. Peter and Chartres streets is the **Café Pontalba,** which has a jazz band for Sunday brunch.

The **Moon Walk,** across Decatur Street at Jackson Square. The Mississippi River was there first. After that came New Orleans and Jackson Square. So take a look at the river when you leave Jackson Square. Just walk up the steps behind the fountain.

The Moon Walk gets its name from New Orleans Mayor Moon Landrieu. (He changed it from "Maurice.") There are rest rooms, a fountain, and a walkway over railroad tracks to the river.

If you drive on Decatur Street, you can enter the city parking lot by the Moon Walk. The lot stretches from here to Esplanade along the river. Tour boats dock here, the *Natchez* (with a calliope) and the *Bayou Jean Lafitte*. There's a kiosk near the Café du Monde with tour information.

The old **Jackson Brewery** building at Decatur and St. Peter streets is to become a shopping and amusement complex, with a restaurant.

St. Peter Street slants upward as it crosses the levee. If you walk this way, you will see a wall that was once part of the **Washington Artillery** building on St. Charles Avenue, blocks away. The Washington Artillery was as well known for its gala balls as its fighting. It has since been absorbed by the National Guard.

There is a wooden walkway over the railroad tracks to some wide steps on the riverbank. You can sit and contemplate the fact that the river is probably several feet higher than Jackson Square—a good example of New Orleans' peculiar drainage problems.

From this vantage point you can get a glimpse of New Orleans' main industry, the port. The New Orleans port is second only to New York's in annual tonnage handled.

To your right you can see the **Greater New Orleans Bridge—**

under which the river is flowing north—and the **International Trade Mart Building**—with a round top, a revolving bar, and a good place to sightsee.

Look to your left, and you will see why New Orleans is called the Crescent City. The river forms a distinct curve.

The Mississippi River is very deep and swift at New Orleans, and oceangoing ships can come all the way to the city, berthing sideways along the wharves.

The Mississippi is brown, but New Orleans is still getting city water from it, after much purification, of course.

For a good close look at the river you might take the free ferry from Canal Street (to your right from here) and ride back and forth.

The **French Market,** beginning at the Café du Monde, St. Ann and Decatur streets, extending down Decatur Street. The **Café du Monde** serves marvelous coffee and doughnuts, just the thing to get you in the mood for the French Market.

Indians already had a market on this site before the French arrived, and the colonists continued to trade there, setting up market sheds for meat, fish, and vegetables.

The Indians of Louisiana contributed filé to gumbo and street names to the map. There's not a great deal else in the city of Indian heritage, except the black maskers at Mardi Gras. Few Indian words, other than names, have passed into local language.

There's an expression: "Mardi Gras, chick a la paw." You may hear it yelled to a masker on Mardi Gras Day. One scholar thinks it may be part Choctaw, and "chick a la paw" is "chaka abaiya," meaning "bum" or "vagrant." However, it also may be French, or "choque a la paille," meaning "chew on straw." You can take your pick.

The French Market buildings have recently been totally renovated and now have shops selling candles and T-shirts.

You can watch pralines being made at **Aunt Sally's Praline Shop** or at **Evans Creole Candy Factory.**

Jazz bands play regularly on weekends in the market and musicians and performers can always be found.

The coffee stand is in the oldest building, the **Meat Market,** dating from 1813. The building between St. Phillip and Ursuline streets is from 1822. The **Red Stores,** St. Phillip Street near the river, was built in 1833, torn down a century later, and reconstructed in 1975.

Major market building renovation took place in the 1930s, 1960s, and 1970s. The only remaining actual market area is down toward Esplanade Avenue: the **Farmers' Market,** where you can get Louisiana strawberries, oranges, and sugarcane in season and fresh vegetables year round. On Fridays and weekends there's a **Flea Market** here, an immense garage sale of collectibles and assorted "junque."

Having seen the market, amble back to Jackson Square and do some people-watching. Listen to the Lucky Dog vendor's plaintive sales pitch, "Don't be a meanie, buy a wienie." Get some corn and feed the pigeons. Have your portrait done by a sidewalk artist, and rest your feet.

If this is the only sightseeing you had time for, come back another day.

FRENCH QUARTER STREETS

Rather than lead you on a rambling walking tour, this section will discuss all the French Quarter streets and what you might find on them. Each one has its own personality.

Because it is such a well-traveled and attractive thoroughfare, and because it is typical of many things about the French Quarter, the first street covered will be Royal Street, which runs from Canal Street to Esplanade Avenue. The next streets will be those parallel to Royal, beginning near the Mississippi River with Decatur Street and ending just outside the other edge of the French Quarter with Basin Street. After Basin Street the cross streets will be listed: those that run parallel with Canal Street.

As you walk around, look at the street signs and the house numbers, and you can easily find a description of what you are looking at. The lower numbers begin at Canal Street, or toward the Mississippi, depending on the way the street runs. Since French Quarter streets form an almost perfect grid, it is easy to use the map.

So be sure you have on comfortable shoes . . . and enjoy yourself!

ROYAL STREET

In New Orleans the French Quarter streets change names when they cross Canal Street (the Creoles of the French Quarter and the uptown Americans could never agree on anything). Royal Street becomes St. Charles Avenue.

Royal Street is best known for its antique shops, especially for its expensive antique shops. But in the 1800s Royal was known for its banks: there were three important ones right around one corner.

As with other French Quarter streets, Royal changes character as it moves away from Canal Street. By Esplanade Avenue —the end of the French Quarter—Royal is quiet and residential.

Royal used to be where the Streetcar Named Desire ran (in 1875 all but two streets in the French Quarter had streetcars). Today Royal is on the minibus route in peak hours: from 6 A.M. to 9 A.M. and from 4 P.M. to 6 P.M. During the day and until 12:30 A.M., the minibus runs on Dauphine and Chartres streets. The route is posted on bus stop signs, and the fare is sixty cents.

100 Block

This block now boasts a motel and some small shops and bars. The sazerac cocktail (for which New Orleans is justly famous) was invented in a bar at the rear of **116 Royal Street**. At **121 Royal Street** there was once a building that was the office of **Dr. Francesco Antommarchi**, Napoleon's physician, and here Napoleon's death mask was exhibited. If you want to see the death mask, there's a bronze copy in the Cabildo. At **127 Royal Street** the first carnival krewe, the Mistick Krewe of Comus, was organized in 1857, and the Gem Bar, which stood there, was the first place in the country to offer a free lunch to drinkers.

Where the Walgreen's Drugstore is located on the corner of Royal and Iberville streets was the site of the Citizen's Bank from 1854 to 1881. This is the same bank that issued ten-dollar bills with *dix* ("ten" in French) on the back. These "dixies" gave a nickname that came to mean the Southern states.

200 Block

The **Monteleone Hotel,** built in 1909 and costing $600,000 at that time, dominates this block.

300 Block

301–7 Royal Street. This was where the cabinetmaker Prudent Mallard had his shop in the nineteenth century. Mallard furniture is ornate, immense, and Victorian. Sometimes Mallard beds are fifteen feet high, including the canopy, or tester (TEES-ter). He often used rosewood and especially liked carving. If you want to buy Mallard furniture, you had better have high ceilings and big rooms.

343 Royal Street. This antique shop was once the Bank of the United States, built in 1800 probably by architect Barthélemy Lafon. The wrought-iron balconies are especially handsome.

Buildings in the French Quarter are identified by their architects: "Lafon" is a name you will come across often. Wrought iron, such as you see here, is usually earlier and more delicate than cast iron. Wrought iron is made by twisting iron rods; cast iron is poured into a mold. The wide balconies with the frilly cast-iron lace are later and were often added to an older building, replacing narrow wrought-iron-trimmed balconies.

344 Royal Street. This building was built in 1826 for the Bank of Louisiana. Today it is a tourist information center with both Louisiana and New Orleans tourism departments inside. Be sure to visit them. The Royal Street entrance and the fence were added in the 1840s by architect James Gallier. The gate is copied from a Robert Adam design.

400 Block

400 Royal Street. To build this courthouse in 1907 they tore down a block of typical French Quarter houses. The courthouse is in what could be called the City Beautiful style, common to courthouses and post offices all over.

401 Royal Street. This antique shop was once the Louisiana State Bank and was the last work, in 1820, of architect Benjamin Latrobe, who died of yellow fever before it was finished. Inside is a very attractive domed ceiling.

413 Royal Street. This was the birthplace (1813) of one of New Orleans' most uncommon people: Father Adrien Rouquette. Father Rouquette ministered to the Indians on the other side of Lake Pontchartrain. He also wrote poetry. At a time when no one else was particularly interested in Indians, Father Rouquette lived with them and even dressed like them, long hair and all.

417 Royal Street. This building was built circa 1796 for the great-grandfather of the painter Edgar Degas. Later it became the Louisiana Bank. Paul Morphy, the child prodigy chess champion of the nineteenth century, lived here. He died here, too, in a bathroom on the second floor. Now you will find Brennan's Restaurant here, complete with a lovely patio and an imaginative bar. The long lines of people are probably trying to get in for breakfast.

437 Royal Street. It was on this spot that an invention took place in the early 1800s that changed the social habits of Americans for all time: an apothecary named Peychoud concocted a drink of bitters and brandy and served it in an eggcup. The Americans, who could not pronounce *coquetier* ("eggcup"), called the drink a cocktail.

500 Block

The side of the Royal Orleans Hotel fronts this block. Actually there was a hotel here called the St. Louis Hotel from about 1836 to 1915, and the Royal Orleans was built in the spirit of the old hotel.

520 Royal Street. This building, now **WDSU-TV**, was built in 1816 for François Seignouret, another New Orleans cabinetmaker. Seignouret's furniture could also be classed as New Orleans Victorian. He specialized in S curves in his carvings, whether for his initial or just for the design is not known.

Visitors are welcome in the courtyard, and it is worth a look. It is often called the Brulatour Court, for an owner after Seignouret. Notice the bars in the transoms over the doors: these were the windows of the entresol, or mezzanine, and they were common in houses built around 1815.

533 Royal Street. The **Historic New Orleans Collection,** of the Kemper and Leila Williams Foundation, is housed here. This building dates from 1792 and was one of the few to escape the 1794 fire. The granite facade was added later, around 1830, when it became a fad. The collection is beautifully displayed in ten galleries and included are documents and art from Louisiana's past. There are well-informed guides to help you. Although there is a small admission, one gallery is always open for free. The gift shop is one of the best—books, crafts, even records.

Besides the galleries, you can tour the **Merieult House** (from 1792) and the home in the rear of the patio that the Williams family renovated and beautifully furnished and decorated in the 1940s. (Part of the complex was once a boarding house, and Tennessee Williams lived there when he moved to New Orleans in 1938.)

The Historic New Orleans Collection also has a fine research library. Collection hours are 10 A.M. to 3:15 P.M., Tuesday through Saturday.

As you look up at the Royal Street balconies, you will notice occasional fan-shaped devices on the ends of the balconies. These were called *gardes de frise,* and besides their structural functions they probably kept people you didn't want off your balcony.

600 Block

The 600 block of Royal Street was the fashionable place for nineteenth-century Creoles to live. The house at **611 Royal Street** was the home of Governor André Roman. John Grymes, the attorney who defended the pirate-smuggler Lafitte brothers, lived at **612 Royal Street.** Grymes married the widow of the first Louisiana governor, William C. C. Claiborne. Dr. Isidore Labatut lived at **616 Royal Street,** and in his law offices downstairs the jurist Edward Douglass White got his training.

621 Royal Street. U.S. President Zachary Taylor's daughter lived at 621 Royal Street, and he often visited her. President Taylor was not a Louisiana native, but he lived in Baton Rouge for many years. It has been said that the letter telling him he was nominated for President sat at the Baton Rouge Post Office for weeks because Taylor would not pay the postage due.

631 Royal Street. Here the opera singer Adelina Patti lived. Her first appearance in New Orleans was in 1860, when she sang in *Lucia di Lammermoor* and made a financial success of the opera season. The courtyard here is very attractive.

640 Royal Street. This building is often called the first skyscraper, because it is supposed to have been the first four-story building in the Vieux Carré. It was begun around 1795 and finished around 1810. Architects were Barthélemy Lafon, and the firm of Latour and Laclotte. The author George Washington Cable used it as the setting for his story "Sieur George." The iron railings still bear the initials of an early owner, Dr. Yves Le Monnier.

700 Block

700 Royal Street. This building has some of the most attractive cast-iron work in the French Quarter. The design is of oak leaves and acorns. The first owner was Jean Baptiste Labranche. Sometimes people in New Orleans named Labranche were Germans who had originally been named Zweig and had translated the word "branch," or "twig," into French.

At the corner of Royal and Orleans streets you get a wonderful view of the rear of St. Louis Cathedral, with St. Anthony's Garden (an ex-dueling spot) in the foreground. Pirate's Alley and Père Antoine Alley are on either side of the garden.

In the 700 and 800 blocks of Royal Street you can see many examples, if you look carefully, of row houses. These were series of houses built exactly alike, one right next to the other. Usually they were for investment and rental. Now they often have different owners, so the color of the walls or the style of the balconies may be different. Everybody invested in row houses, even the wardens of the cathedral, who owned the ones in the 700 block across the street from the garden. These were built around 1830, when row houses were really in vogue.

800 Block

823 Royal Street. This house, built after 1813, was once the home of Daniel Clark, the American consul in New Orleans in Spanish days. Daniel Clark is best known because of his daughter, Myra Clark Gaines, who had a bit of a legitimacy problem and spent most of her life in court trying to inherit his estate. At one time the Myra Clark Gaines case was the longest-running legal case in the country. She finally won a partial settlement, but paying the attorneys took most of the sweetness out of winning. She is buried in St. Louis Cemetery No. 1.

900 Block

908–12 Royal Street. These three row houses, built in 1838, belonged to the widow of Dr. Louis Miltenberger and her three sons. One of the sons went into the cast-iron business (the firm was Wood and Miltenberger) and replaced all the wrought-iron balconies with the present cast-iron ones. His firm was one of the most popular ironworks in the city, and his Philadelphia partner profited greatly by this Southern exposure.

It is said that in one of these houses, **910 Royal Street,** Alice Heine was born. There are counterstories that she was born on Dumaine Street. But, at any rate, she was a Miltenberger granddaughter, and related to the German poet Heinrich Heine.

Alice was born on February 10, 1858. When she was sixteen, she went to Paris with her father, and at seventeen she married the Duc du Richelieu, who died five years later. But in October 1889 she made history, of sorts, by marrying Prince Albert of Monaco, thus becoming the first American Princess of Monaco.

Alice separated from Albert in 1902 and lived in London, where she specialized in literary salons, until her death in 1925. She was said to be a great beauty, a blonde with brown eyes. She was also, through her father's family, Jewish, which made another first for Alice and Monaco.

919 Royal Street. This was the site of a courthouse where Andrew Jackson was fined $1,000 for contempt of court after the Battle of New Orleans. This was only one of many skirmishes between Creoles and Americans.

1000 Block

Just because there are no addresses listed for some blocks doesn't mean there is nothing to see there. Knowing what to look for makes walking enjoyable.

On Royal Street, or any French Quarter street, you might notice the following things. The idea of having shops on the ground floor and apartments above is nothing new: most French Quarter residences were built that way. Some houses may look askew: that is because they are. The water table in New Orleans has always made stable foundations a problem. The one-story wooden houses that look Victorian probably are: there was much construction in the late 1800s. As in many other New Orleans neighborhoods, the double house is common. In a one-story house the split is right down the middle. The extension on the rear of large French Quarter houses probably was for the kitchen and servants' quarters. A small building on the rear of the patio served the same purpose. Before the Civil War these were slave quarters. Now, like everything else in the French Quarter, they have been made into apartments.

One other thing: if a shoeshine boy offers to bet you that he can tell you where you got your shoes, he is going to win by saying that you got your shoes on your feet on the sidewalk in New Orleans. But you should give him something anyway, because you'd probably have lost the bet if you didn't already know the joke.

1100 Block

1101–41 Royal Street. These fifteen row houses date from 1830. The architect was Alexander Wood.

1132 Royal Street. This is the house that architect James Gallier, Jr., built for himself in 1857. The house is fronted by cement-covered brick, made to look like stone blocks, with slender columns supporting the balcony. The house has been beautifully restored, and it is now **Gallier House Museum,** furnished in period pieces, with historical exhibits. There is an admission (but you get dessert at the end of the tour). Hours are 10 A.M. to 4:30 P.M., Monday through Saturday.

Gallier House is a good example of the best way to run a "house museum." It completely reflects its period—even the rugs change in summer, as in a well-run nineteenth-century household. They've done an archaeological dig (at the privy site, as usual) for tips on the right kind of dishes to use. Even the painting inside, the *faux bois* (foe bwah, "false wood") and the *faux marbre* (foe marb, "false marble") work are authentic—using this way of painting makes cypress wood look like oak or marble. The docents, or guides, are filled with facts—if they don't answer all your questions, it's only because you didn't ask.

Gallier House deserves a visit—even if you really don't like touring houses.

1140 Royal Street. This is known as the Haunted House, the ghost being a little slave girl who jumped off the roof running from her mistress, Madame Delphine LaLaurie. Madame LaLaurie was attacked by a mob after a fire in her house disclosed that she was torturing servants. The mob wrecked the house, but she escaped. The house was rebuilt after the riot, in 1834.

1200 Block

The houses at **1215** and **1217 Royal Street** date from the 1830s. Cast-iron balconies were added to **1217 Royal Street** later.

1300 Block

The side of the house at **704 Esplanade Avenue** fronts this block, and you can get a nice view of this 1856 mansion and the high fence that guards its patio.

DECATUR STREET

Decatur Street used to be right near the wharves, but as levees were built and the river shifted away from the French Quarter, Decatur Street got farther from the water. For most of its length between Canal Street and Esplanade Avenue, Decatur Street runs two ways, but going away from Canal Street you have to veer right on North Peters Street to reach Esplanade Avenue.

100 Block

Dominating this block is the **U.S. Custom House, 423 Canal Street.** Construction began on the Custom House (the fourth one on this site) in 1848. It was not completed until 1880. The design is by architect Alexander Wood. The foundation rests on heavy cypress logs and concrete. The Marble Hall, the immense room on the second floor, is constructed of marble and iron and is fifty-eight feet tall. There are life-sized panels of Bienville and Jackson.

On the Decatur Street side you will see niches in the walls. These were for statues that were never added.

The Decatur Street blocks near Canal Street have several bars that cater to Spanish and Greek seamen. You will find Greek dancing in some of these bars, when the crowd is in the mood.

The renovation boom has come later to Decatur Street than to the rest of the French Quarter, but today you'll find many restored buildings, shops, and restaurants.

300 Block

300–6 Decatur Street. This building was once the Blue Stores, a kind of nineteenth-century shopping center. The Red Stores were at the other end of the French Market, and that building was reconstructed in 1975.

The owners of the Blue Stores, like many Creoles in the nineteenth century, traveled to Europe often and sometimes married and moved back to France. Even today it is surprising how many Orleanians keep in touch with their French relatives.

Decatur Street will take you past Jackson Square, and from St. Ann Street to Barracks Street you will find the French Market buildings, some dating from 1813 but some reconstructed by the WPA in the 1930s, or by the city in the 1960s and 1970s.

1000 Block

In about the 1000 block of Decatur Street you will find the Streetcar Named Desire, immobile now. The streetcar is located near the end of the stalls of the French Market, and it makes a good backdrop for photos.

There are some interesting row houses at **1101–41 Decatur Street** that were built for the Ursuline nuns in 1830. The rear of the **Old Ursuline Convent** faces these houses.

French Market Place, just off Decatur here, once was known as Gallatin Street, a headquarters for vice of all sorts.

CHARTRES STREET

Chartres Street, named for a noble French family and pronounced "Charters," was the shopping center for nineteenth-century New Orleans. Near Canal Street it was lined with shops and businesses, but absentee French landlords set the rents so high that the businessmen moved to Canal Street and the American sector.

400 Chartres Street. François Marie Perrilliat, whose monogram appears on the balcony, rebuilt this 1811 house in 1825.

416 Chartres Street. Stand in line at **K-Paul's Louisiana Kitchen** for weekday dinners you won't forget. Cajun food hits New Orleans and goes gourmet!

500 Chartres Street. The **Napoleon House**—now one of the nicest bars you can imagine—is so named because there is a persistent rumor that New Orleans Mayor Nicholas Girod planned to rescue Napoleon from exile and lodge him here. The house was built for Girod in 1814. It is attached to a wing on St. Louis Street that dates from about 1795. Right across the street, at the end of the 400 block of Chartres Street, stands the building that was Joseph Le Carpentier's auction house—one of the many places where Andrew Jackson was supposed to have planned the Battle of New Orleans.

Another nice rumor about Napoleon is that he is buried in Louisiana. That's right. In a cemetery on Bayou Barataria, right next to Jean Lafitte and John Paul Jones.

514 Chartres Street. This 1837 building was built for a druggist, Louis Dufilho, who had his shop on the ground floor. It is now a pharmacy museum (with a small admission) and has a lovely courtyard and exhibits of voodoo potions and medical curiosities. This is an interesting stop for the children—just reading the labels of old patent medicines will give them the giggles.

617 Chartres Street. This house was built in 1795 for Bartolomé Bosque and is known for its fine courtyard and wrought-iron balconies.

The great fire of 1788 probably began here when candles on an altar set up for Good Friday observances ignited the curtains in the home of Don José Vincente Nuñez.

Chartres Street runs in front of **St. Louis Cathedral, Jackson Square,** the **Presbytère,** and the **Cabildo.** For information on this section see the previous chapter on Jackson Square.

Between Chartres and Decatur streets, just above and below the Jackson Square area, run two one-block streets, Wilkinson and Madison. Madison (as in U.S. President James Madison) comes after St. Ann Street and before Dumaine Street. Wilkinson (General James Wilkinson, who first helped, then testified against, Aaron Burr) comes after Toulouse Street and before St. Peter Street. Burr's plan—to conquer Mexico and add it to Western states, forming a new nation—was quite popular in New Orleans. It is said that local officials felt duty-bound to name a street after General Wilkinson, but they disliked him, so they picked the shortest street in town. There's no explanation for President Madison, whose street is the same length.

In the 800 block of Chartres is a handsome row of six three-story row houses, built in 1828.

835 Chartres Street. The **Fortier Gallery,** with work by local college art teachers and students, is here, and the 1803 town house can be toured. The short-lived television series "Longstreet" used this as the detective's office. Open Tuesday through Saturday from 11 A.M. to 5 P.M.

1113 Chartres Street. This house was erected in 1826 and was most recently the home of the late author Frances Parkinson Keyes. Paul Morphy, the chess champion, probably was born here in 1837, and Civil War General P. G. T. Beauregard (sometimes known as "Old Alphabet," from those initials) lived here. The most exciting thing that happened here was in 1909 when four people were murdered in a Mafia battle. There were so many killings around here then that a little alleyway in the 1000 block of Chartres was called Vendetta Alley.

The house and garden are open (for admission) Monday through Saturday from 10 A.M. to 4 P.M.

1114 Chartres Street. The **Old Ursuline Convent,** now the **Archbishop Antoine Blanc Memorial,** holds the archdiocesan archives. The first floor of the convent and the church have been restored, but a rear building, containing part of an old chapel, is deteriorating. There are no plans to save it.

The Old Ursuline Convent was designed in 1745 and completed in 1750 on the site of an earlier convent. It is presumed by most people to be the oldest building in the French Quarter and is the only one that was definitely built during French domination.

The Ursulines used it until 1824, when they moved downriver to where the Industrial Canal meets the Mississippi. A century later they had to move again, to where they are now, on State Street at Claiborne Avenue, uptown.

This building held the state legislature in 1831 and was the office of the archbishop of New Orleans for many years.

The church next to the convent dates from 1846. Some of the windows are of painted glass, and one is said to have been donated by Andrew Jackson.

During the Battle of New Orleans the nuns prayed very hard for the Americans. Because their prayers were answered, the nuns pledged a Mass every anniversary of the battle. One of the nuns in the order had brought a statue of the Virgin from France. This statue, known as *Our Lady of Prompt Succor,* was credited with saving the convent from a fire in 1812 and helping the Americans defeat the British. The **National Shrine of Our Lady of Prompt Succor** is now at the Ursulines' State Street location, where the Mass is still celebrated every January 8.

The Ursulines' French Quarter property at one time included four square blocks. The military hospital (Governor Nicholls Street used to be Hospital Street) was within the compound, and the barracks (on Barracks Street) were nearby.

The convent church is now called Our Lady of Victory. For

many years it was a parish church known as St. Mary's and served the Italian community in the French Quarter.

The complex may be toured (for admission) on Wednesday at 1:30 P.M. and 3 P.M.

BOURBON STREET

Bourbon Street was named for the French royal family and not for bourbon whiskey. However, it might be said that the street has more in common with its latter, liquid namesake.

Bourbon Street glows with neon and pulsates with music. It is the street of the stripteasers, the barkers, the honky-tonks. It got that way in the years after World War II, when the favorite entertainers were Kalantan and Cup Cake.

Bourbon Street has a fine restaurant (Galatoire's, in the 200 block), and you can sometimes hear good jazz in the clubs. It has motels and guesthouses, noisy bars, quiet bars, and even gay bars. Bourbon Street is open twenty-four hours a day, and it is not an uncommon thing to walk down Bourbon at ten in the morning and see the strippers performing inside the nightclubs.

The fact that you can see the strippers from outside the clubs (this is because the barkers open the door to give you a peek) makes Bourbon Street popular with all sorts of people, particularly children. All you can do is speed up the car, jerk their arms, or hope that no one thinks they belong to you when they start talking about the ladies in the funny bathing suits.

But, day or night, Bourbon Street has a certain something about it that is typical of the French Quarter, and no visit to New Orleans is complete without a few minutes, at least, on Bourbon Street.

200 Block

240 Bourbon Street. This is the **Absinthe House.** The building dates from around 1806, and although it began as a residence with a first-floor shop, it has been a bar for longer than anyone can remember. It is a custom here to put a calling card or business card on the wall. When the original bar fixtures were sold some years ago, the old walls with the calling cards were moved to another spot down the street. This other bar is also called the Absinthe. Both got their name from the drink, a potent liqueur with a lethal ingredient, wormwood. Wormwood has long since been outlawed, but there are several safe absinthe-type liqueurs available, all with the same licorice flavor. The Absinthe House is another place where Andrew Jackson and Jean Lafitte (supposedly) planned the Battle of New Orleans.

500 Block

516 Bourbon Street. This 1831 house once held the rented rooms of the author Lafcadio Hearn, who climaxed his writing career by moving to Japan. One of the best descriptions ever written of a hurricane is in Hearn's book *Chita.* Hearn lived in this house after he came to New Orleans in 1877.

Hearn's taste in local companions was considered exotic. He was rumored to have had an *affaire* with Marie Laveau. After he left town, local gossips lost interest. He did write a nice cookbook with Creole recipes.

At the corner of Bourbon and Toulouse streets once stood the French Opera House. It was built in 1859, and besides being the place where Adelina Patti performed, it was the site of many Mardi Gras balls until it burned in 1919. Now its location is covered by a motel.

700 Block

At the corner of Bourbon and St. Peter streets, where the **Embers** restaurant is now, was once the Bourbon House. This bar and restaurant was the headquarters for the bohemians of the 1940s and 1950s. Tennessee Williams (who spent a lot of time in New Orleans) hung out here occasionally. When the Bourbon House closed in the 1960s, it had a brass-band funeral. There used to be murals on the walls of the bar depicting the Battle of New Orleans being fought on the wrong side of the river.

If you have a drink in the second-floor lounge here, you can listen to some great jazz from the balcony.

711 Bourbon Street. This house dates from the 1830s and is typical of that period. When it was restored in 1925, it was one of the first to be touched in the present rebuilding of the French Quarter. Although these houses stand for centuries, they do need a face-lifting every few hundred years.

900 Block

941 Bourbon Street. This little bar, **Lafitte's Blacksmith Shop,** is typical of the early French colonial period. The building is constructed in what is called "brick between posts." Because the local bricks were soft, they were used only as fillers in a wood frame, like the medieval half-timbered houses of Europe. When better brick was being made, this building method was soon outdated. It is possible that the pirate Jean Lafitte really had his blacksmith shop here. Obviously he had one somewhere, because he spent a lot of time away from his domain down on Bayou Barataria—and he had to be around to plan the Battle of New Orleans.

Once they made a movie about the Battle of New Orleans. The story persists that a New Orleans resident sued the movie company for defaming one of his ancestors and won. The ancestor was not Jean Lafitte.

DAUPHINE STREET

Dauphine (daw-FEEN) Street was probably named after the French Dauphiné brothers, who were active in French finances around the time of the founding of New Orleans, or it could have been named for the Dauphin, French heir apparent.

Dauphine Street increases in attractiveness as it moves away from Canal Street. Along its banquettes (BANK-ets) are houses typical of the French Quarter in all its ups and downs. A banquette, by the way, is a sidewalk. The word means, roughly, "little bench," and no one really can say why New Orleans has sidewalks called that. But you will still hear the word used by older natives.

505 Dauphine Street. John James Audubon, the artist who specialized in birds and other wildlife, supposedly lived and worked in this cottage from 1821 to 1822. Audubon did 167 of the 435 plates in his *The Birds of America* series in Louisiana, most of them up the Mississippi River near St. Francisville. But he did spend time in New Orleans, and on his last trip to Louisiana, in 1837, he came here first. Besides being a nice man who drew pictures of birds, Audubon was a competent scientist, an ornithologist. His records for species sighted in Louisiana are still standing, and he was one of the very first people to realize that birds, even tiny ones, migrate across the Gulf of Mexico.

At **716 Dauphine Street** there is a house, built in 1836, about which there is an interesting legend. It seems that in the middle of the nineteenth century a strange man who called himself a Turk lived there with a large "family" of young girls and servants. One night there were shrieks from the house. When the neighbors came to investigate, they found everyone murdered. It was said that the man was a brother of a sultan who had fled with his harem, only to be found and murdered later by his enemies at court, or by the crew of his ship, who robbed him of his jewelry, as you choose to believe. Whether the Turk existed or not is something else you might wonder about.

BURGUNDY STREET

Burgundy (bur-GUND-ee) Street was named for the Duke of Burgundy, another royal French relative. This is the street that the song "Burgundy Street Blues" is about, and the late, great clarinetist George Lewis's rendition of it will tell you everything you need to know about Burgundy Street, music, genius, and a few other things besides.

As you will notice in wandering around, the French Quarter is a mixed neighborhood. Rich people with town houses, young professionals with apartments, unkempt street people, and just plain people, black, white, and in-between—all of them call the French Quarter home.

1218 Burgundy Street. This is the **Cabrini Children's Museum,** with a collection of over five hundred dolls. It is open Monday through Friday from noon to 6 P.M. and Saturday from 9 A.M. to 5 P.M. The museum is part of the New Orleans Recreation Department, which also operates the adjoining playground.

The Children's Museum building dates from 1810 and is a house that is typical of many other houses in the French Quarter. This is what is called a Creole cottage. There were originally four rooms, split symmetrically. The two rooms facing the street each had one door and one window. Shutters, attic, dormer windows that made the attic into a second floor, and outbuildings were all possible additions. But the four-room cottage is a basic French Quarter design.

On the other side of Esplanade Avenue, Burgundy Street used to have another name. Since that part of the street ran through the subdivision of Bernard de Marigny, he named lower Burgundy after his favorite game. And Craps Street it was, for many years. Some churches with that address pressured the city for the name change to "Burgundy."

RAMPART STREET

Rampart Street is called that because the mud ramparts that protected early New Orleans were along here.

411 North Rampart Street. On the corner of Rampart and Conti streets is **Our Lady of Guadaloupe** Catholic church. This church was built in 1826 as a mortuary chapel. It was thought that burying bodies from the cathedral would spread disease, so the chapel was built convenient to the cemetery on the edge of town.

Our Lady of Guadaloupe has been renovated, and the steeple has been enlarged. It now serves as the Police and Firemen's Chapel and is the **National Shrine of St. Jude.**

Besides devotees of St. Jude (who specializes in impossible causes) there are also local devotees of St. Expedite. His statue is to the left of the main altar. He has the word *hodie* ("today") on his sword and, on a scroll under his foot, the word *cras* ("tomorrow"). St. Expedite (Expeditus in Latin) is the saint to invoke against procrastination, the saint for speedy process. St. Expedite (according to the *Acta Sanctorum,* 1866, Vol. April II, pages 616–17) was a Roman soldier who was martyred with others in Armenia, date unknown. His feast day was April 19. He was revered in Sicily and Germany in the eighteenth century.

There is an old New Orleans story that the statue arrived with EXPEDITE stamped on the box, and that's how the saint was named. That story is so old the early version has a box of bones from the catacombs being sent to a French convent in the seventeenth century with the stamp reading SPEDITE.

St. Expedite has been a voodoo saint for a long time, as voodoo and Catholicism have been intertwined in some people's minds. He still gets thanks in the classifieds of the *Times-Picayune,* along with St. Jude.

There never was any St. Fragile.

700 Block

This square, in front of the Municipal Auditorium, is now called **Beauregard Square,** after Civil War General P. G. T. Beauregard. Formerly it was Congo Square.

During the nineteenth century this was where the black people of New Orleans, slave or free, congregated on Sunday afternoons to dance and play music. Much of what they performed was African in origin. "The Bamboula" and "Danse Calinda" were two of the songs. Both have a mixture of French and African language, a combination called Gombo. The early jazz musicians of New Orleans drew much inspiration, not to speak of rhythms, from what they heard in Congo Square.

Near Congo Square was once a house that was the birthplace of the pianist and composer Louis Moreau Gottschalk. He was born here in 1829 and went to France to study. There his technique was praised by people like Frédéric Chopin. He was one of the first to use folk songs in his compositions, and his piece "The Bamboula" probably borrows much from what he heard in Congo Square.

Gottschalk was extremely popular and traveled all over the world giving concerts, sometimes commanding whole legions of pianists performing in stadiums before vast audiences. Some of his music, and certainly his showmanship, is reminiscent of Liberace. He died in South America shortly after collapsing onstage while playing his own composition "Morte!!" (Death).

Armstrong Park. As a memorial to musician Louis Armstrong, the park at the Rampart Street edge of the French Quarter provides a welcome green space and a cheerful collection of sprightly arched gateways, lagoons, fountains, winding paths, and restored buildings plus the Municipal Auditorium, Theatre of the Performing Arts, and the land that was Congo Square.

Buildings in the park include the 1826 **Perseverance Hall,** originally a Masonic lodge (its kitchen dates from 1830); the **Rabassa–De Pouilly House,** a raised Creole cottage dating from 1825 in which early New Orleans architect J. N. B. De Pouilly resided at his death in 1875; the frame **Reimann House;** and a yellow-brick fire station. The buildings can be rented for parties. The park is not recommended for nighttime strolls.

Community radio station **WWOZ-FM**, which plays lots of New Orleans music, has its studios in Armstrong Park.

BASIN STREET

Basin Street (that's right, the "Basin Street Blues" one) is called that because the turning basin for a canal used to be here. The canal is filled in and now Basin Street is only five blocks long.

At the corner of Basin Street and Bienville Avenue is a little green building, part of the Krauss Department Store garage. Actually, this is about all that is left of Storyville, the prostitution district that flourished here from 1897 to 1917.

This building was the saloon that madam Lulu White kept next to her house, Mahogany Hall (since destroyed). The New Orleans Jazz Museum has Lulu's curbstone, with her name on it. Louis Armstrong made a great recording of a song called "Mahogany Hall Stomp," after Lulu's establishment.

Actually the little saloon building is missing an upper story. If you are interested in what the saloon and Mahogany Hall looked like, go to the **Southeastern Architectural Archives** in the **Howard Tilton Library of Tulane University** (corner of Freret Street and Audubon Place). The archive has a scale model, down to the last brick, of the two buildings. You might find a reproduction of the *Blue Book,* the city directory of Storyville, listing all the girls and madams, at a gift shop.

The housing project bordered by Canal and Basin streets covers what was once Storyville. Except for another scattered building or two, there is nothing else to see of it. This is not a good place to park your car or walk at night.

St. Louis Cemetery No. 1, 400 Basin Street. St. Louis Cemetery No. 1 is bounded by Basin, Conti, Tremé (tra-MAY), and St. Louis streets. It dates from the 1740s. There was an earlier cemetery at Burgundy and St. Peter streets.

There is a free cemetery tour from the Jean Lafitte Park office in the 500 block of St. Ann Street. Do not go into this cemetery alone!

New Orleans cemeteries look like little cities. That is because the aboveground tombs were often designed by architects and took on some of the style of the day. The aboveground burial was necessary because of the marshy ground (it is difficult to dig dry holes) and the Latin burial customs of New Orleans' early settlers.

The overcrowding problem has been solved this way. Some tombs are rented, and some belong to families. After two years have passed, if another family member dies or someone else rents the tomb, the casket occupying it is opened and the remaining bones are removed and put far back in the vault.

It might be a little grim, but that's how it works and that's why one tomb can have so many names on the outside.

Because of the soggy ground some of the tombs themselves are sinking.

Cemeteries in New Orleans are at their best on November 1. This is All Saints' Day, and everyone whitewashes the tombs and cuts the grass and puts out flowers. Some people even come and sit on the little cast-iron chairs—called cemetery furniture—to receive friends. You can always tell All Saints' Day because that is when the buses and streetcars are full of little old ladies with armloads of chrysanthemums. Still, this is better seen at other, safer, cemeteries than St. Louis No. 1 and No. 2.

Some of the famous people buried in St. Louis No. 1 are: Étienne Boré, first mayor of New Orleans and the first commercial granulator of sugar from cane syrup, who died in 1820; his grandson, Charles Gayarré, a Louisiana historian, who died in 1895; Daniel Clark, wealthy merchant, who died in 1813; his daughter, Myra Clark Gaines, who died in 1885 after spending sixty-five years in court trying to prove she was legitimate; Bernard de Marigny, Creole entrepreneur and sometime craps player, who died in 1868; and Paul Morphy, the chess player, who died in 1884.

There is also a tomb that is supposed to belong to Marie Laveau, the Voodoo Queen of the nineteenth century. The tour guide will show you how to make a wish there, a process that involves marking x's on the tomb with brick dust. Marie may or may not be in there. But there are always offerings: coins, shells, beads. Even if people don't believe, they seem to still follow the rituals "just in case."

The walls of this cemetery are filled with "ovens"—rented burial vaults. Inscriptions in all manner of languages can make interesting reading.

St. Louis Cemetery No. 2 dates from 1823 but in most respects is similar to St. Louis No. 1. It extends along Claiborne Avenue from Iberville Street to St. Louis Street.

Municipal Auditorium. The Municipal Auditorium is actually in the 700 block of Rampart Street, but it covers a tremendous amount of area and you can reach it by walking along the extension of Basin Street to Orleans Street.

The building, constructed in a sort of WPA Renaissance style, dates from 1930. It can seat upward of twelve thousand people. Concerts, the circus, and most Mardi Gras balls are held here.

In the area of the auditorium was once the canal that linked the city and Lake Pontchartrain in 1796. Also near here was an early charity hospital and the old prison, where the suspected Mafia murderers of the police chief were lynched in 1891.

Armstrong Park, the **Theatre of the Performing Arts** (a smaller auditorium useful for plays and dance performances), and extensive parking lots are within the Municipal Auditorium complex.

IBERVILLE STREET

Iberville Street (EYE-bur-vill or IB-ur-vill) runs parallel with Canal Street, from the river to Rampart Street. It used to be called New Custom House Street but was renamed for the French-Canadian explorer Iberville, who claimed the Louisiana territory for the French King. If you like raw oysters, there are two great places to eat them in the 700 block: the **Acme Oyster House** and **Felix's Restaurant.** Both have oyster bars, and Felix has a sign that always says OYSTERS R IN SEASON, no matter whether the month has an *R* in it or not.

BIENVILLE STREET

Bienville (bee-EN-vill) Street was named for the founder of the city of New Orleans, Iberville's brother. Aside from a place for raw oysters, **Messina's Restaurant,** at the corner of Chartres Street, and **Arnaud's Restaurant,** one of the better-known ones, in the 800 block, there is not much beauty on Bienville.

CONTI STREET

Conti (CON-tye) Street was named for another noble French family.

600 Block

In the 600 block of Conti Street there is an alley that runs from Conti to Canal Street, with a cutoff at Iberville Street. This is Exchange Alley, and it was planned in the 1830s as a road that led straight to the old St. Louis Hotel (where the Royal Orleans Hotel is now). When they built the courthouse, they cut out a block of Exchange Alley.

The houses at the corner of Conti and Exchange were known as the Houses of the Fencing Masters. In the nineteenth century there were many duels in New Orleans, and the fencing masters specialized in teaching their pupils to win. Sad to say, many fencing masters themselves fell on the field of honor. One enterprising fencing master ended up owning a cemetery.

The houses along Exchange Alley near Conti Street are pleasant to look at, and there are several restaurants (including **Castillo's Mexican Restaurant** on Conti) bordering the alley, plus some intriguing shops.

ST. LOUIS STREET

St. Louis Street was named for the patron saint of France—
the same one the cathedral is named after.

600 Block

The **Royal Orleans Hotel** stands here now, right on the spot
where the old St. Louis Hotel once stood. In the former hotel,
torn down in 1915, Henry Clay made his only Louisiana speech
and was honored at a $20,000 supper. The St. Louis Hotel was
the state capitol during Reconstruction shenanigans between
1874 and 1882.

The old hotel fell into such bad repair that the English author
John Galsworthy found a horse wandering around in it and
wrote a story, "That Old-Time Place," about it. It was finally
torn down in a campaign to rid the French Quarter of rats during
a bubonic plague scare.

The old hotel had stores and business offices on the first floor
and an auction block in a central rotunda. Occasionally slaves
were auctioned there.

Part of the wall on the Chartres Street side of the hotel remains from the older building.

700 Block

713 St. Louis Street. Here is where **Antoine's Restaurant** has
been for over a century, and if you want to taste Oysters Rockefeller where the dish was invented, you can.

720 St. Louis Street. This house was built around 1830 by the
architectural firm of Gurlie and Guillot. Soon after it was built
it was sold to Pierre Soulé, a New Orleans attorney who was,
before his death in 1870, one of the primary exponents of the
States' Rights cause, and who is chiefly revered by those who
agree with him.

800 Block

820 St. Louis Street. The building and patio are among the loveliest in the French Quarter. The **Hermann-Grima House** was built in 1831 by an American architect, William Brand. It is more typical of the Georgian houses of the Philadelphia area than it is of New Orleans.

The house belongs to the Christian Women's Exchange, which has restored it and gives imaginative fund-raising events: nine-teenth-century evenings with appropriate entertainment.

The Hermann-Grima House has an authentic kitchen, and cooking demonstrations are regularly scheduled. This is another scholarly restoration project, and you'll enjoy the guided tours. There is also a nice gift shop. Open (for admission) Monday through Saturday (closed Wednesday) from 10 A.M. to 3:30 P.M. and Sunday from 1 P.M. to 4:30 P.M.

900 Block

In the 900 block of St. Louis Street are two attractive buildings, the house at **908 St. Louis Street,** which dates from the 1830s, and the house at **920 St. Louis Street,** which was built with the aid of the architect James Gallier, Jr.

TOULOUSE STREET

Toulouse (too-LOOSE) Street was named after the Count of Toulouse, a bastard child of Louis XIV's. There is an old New Orleans joke about Toulouse Street: "What corner in New Orleans reminds you of my gym suit? Toulouse and Broad."

Just because a joke is old doesn't mean it's good.

708 Toulouse Street. This is an early-nineteenth-century house with a pleasant courtyard with two stone lions. This "Court of the Two Lions" figured in a novel, *The Crossing* by Winston Churchill, as the home of the heroine. This Winston

Churchill, by the way, was an American who was a very popular writer around 1910.

723 Toulouse Street. This is the **Casa Hové,** an eighteenth-century town house. Nearby, at **727 Toulouse Street,** is the **Maison de Ville,** a tiny but choice hotel with a lovely patio.

ST. PETER STREET

St. Peter Street begins along Jackson Square, so see the chapter on "Jackson Square" for a description of the 500 block.

616 St. Peter Street. This is the little theater, Le Petit Théâtre du Vieux Carré. The organization began in 1916 and is one of the oldest community theaters in the country. Their productions include both musicals and dramas, with an occasional avant-garde work. Tickets are available by calling 522-2081. The building and courtyard are a reconstruction of an earlier house, but the wrought iron on the balconies is the original and was done by the man who did the wrought iron on the Cabildo, across the street.

620 St. Peter Street. This house was built in 1838 and is now Le Petit Salon, a women's club. The balconies are especially nice, and each of the three has its own ironwork design. The building diagonally across the street, the Arsenal, dates from 1839 and is part of the Louisiana State Museum complex.

700 Block

In the 700 block of St. Peter Street you will find an **A&P, Pat O'Brien's,** and **Preservation Hall.** Pat O'Brien's dispenses cheer continuously, in the form of sing-alongs in the lounge and hurricanes in the bar and patio. A hurricane is made of passion-fruit punch and rum and comes in a glass shaped like a hurricane lamp. You will see people carrying them throughout the French Quarter in cardboard containers. Preservation Hall offers traditional jazz every evening, and for a small admission charge you are welcome to sit on the wooden benches inside. No drinks are served, but, if you like, you can bring your own.

The A&P has a sign on the door saying DRUNKS, DERELICTS AND DIRTY PEOPLE NOT ADMITTED. So don't go in if you are.

The first theater in New Orleans was supposed to have been in the 700 block of St. Peter Street. Whether it was here or not, there were actors and plays around as far back as 1791 (for French plays) and 1809 (English).

ORLEANS STREET

Orleans (or-LEENS) Street was named for the Duke of Orléans. It is difficult to know exactly how to pronounce "Orleans," but as a general rule the town New Orleans (noo OR-luns or noo OR-lyuns or just NOR-luns) is always pronounced differently from the street (or-LEENS). There is even a women's club on St. Charles Avenue called the Orleans Club, which pronounces its name the French way (or-lay-AWNH).

Orlèans Street begins at St. Anthony's Garden, behind St. Louis Cathedral on Royal Street. The garden was supposedly the site of many duels fought over the ladies who danced at the Orleans Ballroom, in the 700 block of Orleans Street, now enclosed in a hotel.

The Orleans Ballroom did exist, and the stairs and the ballroom are inside the hotel. One of the chandeliers is at the **Sun Oak** house, 2020 Burgundy Street.

What went on at the ballroom is a matter of conjecture. The story goes that young girls who had some black ancestry, or were "quadroons," were introduced at dances here to the white men, who would set them up as mistresses in little cottages near the French Quarter. These "Quadroon Balls" were supposed to have been wonderful affairs with lovely ladies of creamy skin and dark, shining eyes.

One fact is certain: in New Orleans newspaper reports of dances and theaters in the 1800s there was usually a marked distinction over whether the clientele could be black, white, or free men of color (usually lighter than black). The likeliest story is that the "Quadroon Balls" were probably a facade for prostitution, with some racial discrimination thrown in. The entire story is confusing and not a nice part of New Orleans history. But facts are facts. Many "free women of color" were given or left cottages by local white men, as real estate records show. Some of these *plaçage* (plah-sahj) arrangements were very happy and long-lasting.

The Orleans Ballroom once was used by the state legislature. In 1881 the property was purchased by a black philanthropist, Thomy Lafon, and became a convent for black nuns, the Sisters of the Holy Family.

The Sisters used to have a sign over the ballroom door: I HAVE CHOSEN RATHER TO BE AN ABJECT IN THE HOUSE OF THE LORD THAN TO DWELL IN THE TEMPLE WITH SINNERS.

A peculiar entertainment venture was located next to the convent in the late nineteenth century: Signor Faranta's Iron Theater. This metal building was, for all practical purposes, windowless, and must have attracted only ardent fans to its vaudeville spectacles. Somehow it caught fire. The nuns prayed frantically and the convent was untouched, but the iron theater was burned. Perhaps two prayers were answered.

The Sisters of the Holy Family moved far downtown when the building was sold to a hotel. They now operate a school and care for children and the elderly.

ST. ANN STREET

St. Ann, St. Peter, St. Louis, and St. Philip streets were all, of course, named for saints. "Ann," "Peter," "Louis," and "Philip" were also common names in French royal families. Most of the French Quarter streets were named for public relations reasons when John Law, the Scotch financier, had control of the French economy and was pushing Louisiana as the Promised Land and selling worthless stocks. This maneuver of his was called the "Mississippi Bubble" and happened in the early 1700s.

636 St. Ann Street. The Voodoo Museum and Gift Shop is located here, and for a fee you can tour this museum with such displays as "the amazing BLEEDING TOMB," according to the information sheet. They also have tours—the "Voodoo Ritual Tour" warns that "Blindfolds may be issued to and from the ritual site." They also do "voodoo type entertainment for conventions." Call 524-5906.

826 St. Ann Street. The New Orleans Spring Fiesta owns this town house, which dates from the 1840s. It has been remodeled with modern kitchen and baths. There are some nice antiques, and you'll get an idea of what a comfortable home in the French Quarter today looks like. Open (for admission) Monday and Thursday from 11 A.M. to 3 P.M. and also available for party rental.

1022 St. Ann Street. This is the site of the house where the Voodoo Queen Marie Laveau was supposed to have lived. The house was torn down in 1903. Marie (or there might have even been two Maries, mother and daughter) commanded a great following in the nineteenth century.

Voodoo came to New Orleans after 1790 with refugees from slave uprisings in Santo Domingo. Some of the refugees were slaves, some white, some free men of color.

Voodoo was a hodgepodge of ritual and religion, borrowing heavily from the hierarchy of Catholic saints and African gods. By using voodoo as a sort of black magic, errant lovers would become attentive and enemies would sicken and die. Of course, voodoo has its greatest effect when the victim believes in it, too.

Little charms, or gris-gris (gree-gree), were used, as were various colored candles (blue for love, black for death). Powders and potions and ceremonies (on the shores of Lake Pontchartrain or Bayou St. John) added to the cult. Today it is almost nonexistent and lives on in superstitions and patent medicines. In Marie's time it worked well enough to give her a comfortable living and a formidable reputation. Because she developed voodoo into a folk religion for Catholics, she was never thought a witch.

For whatever reasons, hardly anyone would have the nerve to say anything bad about Marie Laveau.

DUMAINE STREET

Dumaine (du-MANE) Street was named for another bastard child of Louis XIV's, the Duke of Maine.

632 Dumaine Street. Madame John's Legacy, as this house is known, was built about 1788 and now belongs to the Louisiana State Museum.

The house is one of the oldest surviving buildings in New Orleans. It was built by Robert Jones, an American builder, for Don Manuel de Lanzos after the original house on the site was burned in the 1788 fire. Don Manuel wanted a house just like his old one, and Jones provided it. The aboveground basement is brick (because of possible floods) and the upper story is brick between posts covered with horizontal boards. The roof has a double pitch to cover the gallery. This house is typical of the Louisiana colonial style.

The name "Madame John's Legacy" comes from a story, " 'tite Poulette," by George Washington Cable.

There are many stories written about the French Quarter. George Washington Cable, Lafcadio Hearn, and, later, Frances Parkinson Keyes have glorified New Orleans over the years with romantic legends and tales. Other things have been written in the French Quarter, too: the novel *The Bad Seed* by W. E. M. Campbell and the saccharine poem "Just Before Christmas" by Eugene Field were both composed in the Vieux Carré. The movie and stage production *Green Pastures* came from a book of stories by Roark Bradford. William Faulkner, Sherwood Anderson, and Tennessee Williams have all written in the French Quarter. In spite of the lazy atmosphere, a lot of creative work gets done there, even today.

700 Block

707 Dumaine Street. This little cottage is different because it has a flat roof. After the 1794 fire a law was passed saying that houses in the French Quarter had to have flat tile roofs. This house never covered its flat roof with a conventional one, as many French Quarter houses have. When the roofs were flat, people used them like patios, or gardens. You could even walk down the street on the roofs of houses.

ST. PHILIP STREET

521 St. Philip Street. The **Religious Order of Witchcraft** is headquartered here. There are various herbs for sale and lots of occult pamphlets. Next door the **Witches Closet** sells second-hand clothes.

606 St. Philip Street. This is a pleasant little restored cottage that dates back to the eighteenth century. In those years there were cafés on or near St. Philip Street that were frequented by people who came to New Orleans to flee social upheavals at home. The Café des Réfugiés was supposedly for those fleeing the French Revolution, and the Café des Émigrées was for those who fled slave uprisings on Santo Domingo. Both groups could forget their troubles at the theater that once stood where the school is now, between Royal and Bourbon streets. All of them, the cafés and theater, are gone now.

URSULINES STREET

Ursulines Street runs by the side of the Old Ursuline Convent and was named for the long-suffering nuns, who have been with Louisiana since it was nothing but an inhospitable marsh.

829–33 Ursulines Street. This is supposed to be the place where, in 1835, Stephen F. Austin met with some fellow Freemasons and planned the Texas War for Independence.

GOVERNOR NICHOLLS STREET

Governor Nicholls Street used to be Hospital Street but was renamed after a Louisiana governor who was in office around the time of the Civil War.

721 Governor Nicholls Street. This 1814 house was built by architects Arsène Latour and Henry Latrobe and is one of the earliest examples of the Greek Revival style in the French Quarter. The house was restored in 1940.

The restoration business is a booming one in New Orleans. The main problem seems to be whether the house should be made exactly as it was or whether it should be remodeled to suit the new owner's purposes. The most visible problems are solved by the Vieux Carré Commission, which was set up by state law to police construction and renovation in the French Quarter. Although they have never actually put anybody in jail, the commission can make offenders feel uncomfortable.

724 Governor Nicholls Street. Though this apartment building began life as a livery stable and still looks rather stableish, it is charming. It dates from 1834.

BARRACKS STREET

Barracks Street got its name from the army barracks that were located there. At **706 Barracks Street** the artist John James Audubon is supposed to have had a studio during his stay here in 1821.

1000 Block

1001–5 Barracks Street. This building is sometimes known as the "Morro Castle," after the Cuban fortress-prison. No one knows why. Actually it was built in 1832 by Paul Pandelly. It was the first all-granite house in New Orleans, and the stone was brought here from Quincy, Massachusetts. Mr. Pandelly immediately ran into financial troubles and had to sell his house before it was completed.

ESPLANADE AVENUE

Esplanade (es-pluh-NADE) Avenue was the parade ground for

the soldiers in the barracks on Barracks Street and for the fort that was located at Esplanade Avenue and Decatur Street. Today it is still a lovely promenade, and the "neutral ground" —that's a New Orleans word for "traffic island"—blooms in season with all manner of flowers. Esplanade Avenue was the place for the grand town houses that were built in the boom periods before and after the Civil War. When the French Quarter began to fill up with Italian immigrants—after 1870—the Creoles began moving to Esplanade and beyond, either farther downriver or out toward the lake. Today Esplanade has the apartments, small bars, and restaurants that the French Quarter abounds in, and only a handful of the town houses are one-family mansions.

400 Esplanade Avenue. The **Old U.S. Mint** now belongs to the Louisiana State Museum. In its time the building has been the site of a ball and a hanging, and served as a prison as well.

It was built in 1835 in Greek Revival style. It rests on the spot where Fort St. Charles was erected in 1792 to guard the city. Andrew Jackson reviewed his troops here before the Battle of New Orleans.

It is constructed of bricks stuccoed and trimmed with granite. The walls are three feet thick on the ground floor. The ball was held in 1850 when the director of the mint gave a party for his daughter.

The hanging took place after the city was occupied by Federal troops in the Civil War. William Mumford took down the American flag that flew over the mint, and as an example to the people, U.S. General Benjamin Butler hanged Mumford from the middle of the mint's front porch.

No coins were issued here after 1909 (the ones issued had an O under the eagle as a mint mark). For a time it was a Veterans Administration center and federal prison.

The Old U.S. Mint today holds the **Louisiana Historical Center,** a research facility with archives, manuscripts, and the oral history tape collection done by the Friends of the Cabildo.

Also here is the **New Orleans Jazz Museum** with records, memorabilia, and such instruments as Louis Armstrong's first horn. An extensive Mardi Gras collection, with costumes and other souvenirs and documents, can be seen here also.

The **Amistad Research Center,** an archive of black history, is also in the mint building.

Esplanade Avenue, like all the streets in the French Quarter, has its unusual houses, its architectural gems, its stories. But the best thing about Esplanade is the view, the total perspective of the houses and the trees, the bright blue sky of New Orleans that turns purple and green in the sunset, the clouds and the birds, the pigeons, and the people out walking their dogs. Everything seems to take on a pastel glow, a sort of sheen that blinds your eyes to a dirty gutter or an unwashed window or just plain poverty that's passing as charming decadence.

You can wander around for a whole lifetime, but there's always some new way to look at the "Quarter."

THE GARDEN DISTRICT

Former rulers of Mardi Gras—ex-Rexes and their queens—have the privilege of flying the official purple, green, and gold Rex flag in front of their homes during Carnival season.

The Garden District always has the most flags flying.

From its beginning the Garden District was the address to have. The rich Americans who built their homes there after 1840 liked the Garden District for its greenery, its accessibility to town on the railroad that ran along Nayades Street (now St. Charles Avenue), and mostly because it was far away from those French-speaking Creoles who lived in the Vieux Carré.

The Garden District was one of New Orleans' first suburbs.

The land above Canal Street (upriver) was divided into farm holdings (later to be faubourgs, or suburbs) and was sparsely settled in the early 1800s. When the Americans and Creoles balked at living in the same place, two promoters named James H. Caldwell and Samuel J. Peters decided to develop an American section. In 1822 they decided to try for the land below the French Quarter, the Faubourg Marigny, owned by one Bernard de Marigny.

Marigny was rich; he was Creole; and he was known as the man who brought the game of craps to America. He also hated Americans. The land sale to Caldwell and Peters did not go through (one reason being that Madame de Marigny would not agree to it).

So they looked to the other side of the French Quarter, to Canal Street and beyond. And they made some deals and began developing the first area, the Faubourg Ste. Marie. As the development continued, more businesses moved in and the wealthy

Americans moved farther uptown. Today the Faubourg Ste. Marie is in the business district, and the remaining town houses are mostly commercial buildings.

About two miles from Canal was the little city of Lafayette. Due to the American-Creole problems, New Orleans was separated into three municipalities during the mid-nineteenth century. In addition, little residential areas would set up their own governments. Lafayette was one of these. It existed from 1833 to 1852, and the Garden District was located in its boundaries.

Going up St. Charles Avenue, you will cross Felicity Street. This was the lower end of the city of Lafayette. A little farther on you will come to Jackson Avenue, where the Garden District begins. It ends at Louisiana Avenue, a distance of less than fifteen blocks. From St. Charles the Garden District extends to Magazine Street, toward the Mississippi River. Anything closer to the river or nearer downtown is usually called the Irish Channel, from the Irish immigrants who settled there in the 1800s, or the Lower Garden District.

There are some lovely homes in the Irish Channel, and there are some hovels in the Garden District. So the boundaries meander more than you might suppose.

One Irish Channel politician (the channel always produced a good crop of those) explained the problem this way: "If ya make the society page they say ya live in the Garden District. But in the police reports they call it the Irish Channel."

The Garden District was once part of the Livaudais plantation. In the 1820s there was a terrible flood, and the Livaudaises were left with ruined crops and acres of river silt. The silt made the land higher, and so it was decided to develop it for residences.

The Americans began moving in. They spared no expense on their homes; they planted gardens and left space for wide lawns. Today the area is a monument to their foresight. Shaded streets, live oaks, magnolias, camellias, palm trees, and all manner of greenery make the Garden District live up to its name.

The era of the Garden District began around 1840. With the booming pre–Civil War economy more houses went up until

1860. After the war there was another spate of construction. Since then most of the construction work has been renovation.

The style of Garden District homes falls somewhere between Newport robber baron and Southern planter, the Victorian Age and the Louisiana style combined.

Victorian architecture you know about: turrets and cupolas and gingerbread, vast rooms and dark woodwork.

The Louisiana style was dictated by the weather. Because of the possibility of floods, the raised cottage was popular. This put the living area on the second floor, the first floor being brick or plaster supports, suitable for storage but not enclosed into rooms.

Because of the heat, the houses had covered porches or galleries, offering a shady place to sit and keeping direct sunlight off the windows.

Also for coolness the houses had high ceilings, center halls (for a nice breeze), and shutters on tall windows. The thicker the walls, the cooler the house, so an eighteen-inch wall was not uncommon.

Louisiana architecture borrowed much from West Indian. Both had French influence. The style that evolved mixed well with Victorian. The cast iron on the balconies was really gourmet gingerbread.

SEEING THE GARDEN DISTRICT

Since the Garden District is a private residential area, most homes are not open daily for tours. An exception is the **Women's Opera Guild** house at 2504 Prytania Street, which is open weekdays from 1 P.M. to 4 P.M.

The Spring Fiesta—three weeks long, beginning the first Friday after Easter—offers a Garden District homes tour. But there are other tours throughout the year, sponsored by schools, churches, and garden clubs. The dates of these tours vary. Check with the **Greater New Orleans Tourist and Convention Commission,** Royal and Conti streets, or read the "Calendar" section of the Lagniappe tabloid in the *Times-Picayune* on Fridays, and see if any tours are scheduled during your stay. If you have a group, call **Louise S. McGehee School,** 561-1224. The school does tours of private homes as a fund-raiser. Guides are well-trained volunteers.

There is still much to see in the Garden District if you can't get inside any houses. You can spend half a day strolling and looking, or you can drive around in your car.

A pleasant way to see the Garden District is via the St. Charles streetcar. Board at Canal Street, corner of Carondelet Street. The ride costs sixty cents—exact change only—and the streetcar runs all day and all night.

You might get off at Washington Avenue and begin walking. **Commander's Palace,** Washington and Coliseum Street, would be a nice place for lunch. Afterward you could take the streetcar uptown to Audubon Park and the universities.

POINTS OF INTEREST

The following description of things to see in the Garden District is arranged simply by streets. Lower street numbers are toward Canal Street or the river, depending on the direction the street runs.

You don't have to look at everything. If you have a special yen to see where Gentleman Jim Corbett trained or where Jefferson Davis died, just check the address and take a walk.

ST. CHARLES AVENUE
(runs from Canal Street uptown)

2265 St. Charles Avenue. Built in 1856–57 by architects James Gallier, Jr., and John Turpin. It once served as the Episcopal Diocesan House for the state of Louisiana.

The side wing was added after the house was built.

2336 St. Charles Avenue. This early cottage dates from the 1840s, when St. Charles was called Nayades and was a dirt road.

2427 St. Charles Avenue. Built around 1890 in a mostly Queen Anne style, this house has all its original millwork and is now the **Hedgewood Hotel,** a guesthouse.

2901 St. Charles Avenue. Christ Church Cathedral, built in 1887 in Victorian Gothic design. Every spring the ladies of the church sponsor a Creole cooking school, which should not be missed. It benefits their tutorial projects for children.

2926 St. Charles Avenue. This house dates from 1882. The number 710 in the glass above the front door is from a street numbering system that ended in 1895. The iron fence came from the Spanish Fort amusement park, when it was demolished in 1934.

PRYTANIA STREET
(runs parallel with St. Charles Avenue)

2127 Prytania Street. Erected in 1857–58. The center hall is sixty-seven by twelve feet. Restoration is complete, even to the pull-type doorbell.

2221 Prytania Street. Designed by Henry Howard in 1850. A Victorian "villa" with Greek Revival touches.

2340 Prytania Street. Probably the oldest surviving house in the Garden District. It was built in 1838 on the edge of the Livaudais plantation. Thomas Toby of Philadelphia intended for his overseer to live here, but he moved in himself. It was remodeled in 1855. The style is best described as typical Louisiana plantation. An outside stair to the second story has been removed. Mr. Toby suffered financial reverses by heavily backing the Texas Revolution.

2343 Prytania Street. Louise S. McGehee School (private, for girls) has been here since 1929. The house was built in 1872, probably by the architect James Freret, who had studied in Paris at the École des Beaux-Arts. The school sponsors tours of homes (call 561-1224) and has had published an excellent booklet on *The Great Days of the Garden District* by Martha Ann Brett Samuel and Ray Samuel.

2504 Prytania Street. This home was built in 1858 and later enlarged. It was left by the Seebold family to the Women's Guild of the New Orleans Opera. It is open (for admission) weekdays from 1 P.M. to 4 P.M. The house is Greek Revival and the additions are Italianate. There is some uncommon furniture and a display area on opera in New Orleans: souvenirs of singers and of the old French Opera House. Since this is the only Garden District home open on a regular basis, it is worth a visit.

2507 Prytania Street. This house dates from the 1850s. All the rooms are twenty-two feet square except the hall (eleven by forty-four feet) and the grand ballroom (twenty-two by forty-four feet). The ballroom was paneled and decorated in 1870 in a motif of Louisiana birds. Restoration was complicated by a 1954 fire.

2521 Prytania Street. Our Mother of Perpetual Help Chapel is located here. The congregation began farther downtown as a French Catholic church, at a time when there were three Catholic congregations in one area: German, Irish, and French. The German and Irish churches are still standing. The chapel is housed in this 1857 mansion that has a marble entrance.

2605 Prytania Street. This Gothic cottage dates from 1850.

2727 Prytania Street. The **Rink** shopping center began life in 1885 as the Crescent City Skating Rink. The owner had hoped to prosper from the crowds on their way to the Cotton Exposition then on in Audubon Park. Later it was an undertaker's and later a garage. There is a small restaurant here, **Indulgence,** and some nice shops and galleries.

2900 Prytania Street. Typical frame town house dating from the nineteenth century but notable as the place where F. Scott Fitzgerald rented a room while visiting here in January 1920.

COLISEUM STREET
(runs parallel with St. Charles Avenue)

2604 Coliseum Street. Built around 1880. The leaded-glass door is typical of New Orleans.

2627 Coliseum Street. This house manages to combine

wooden gingerbread and cast iron in a combination that might be called Swiss Chalet. Dates from around 1870.

2700–26 Coliseum Street. These houses were once exactly alike and were built as speculative housing by architect William Freret, brother of architect James Freret, in 1861. They are sometimes called "Freret's Folly," as the intervening Civil War made the venture unprofitable.

MAGAZINE STREET
(runs parallel with St. Charles Avenue)

Magazine Street is mostly commercial now and the best used-furniture and antique shops are on this street. Many of the dealers refer to their wares as "antiques and classy junque," but it is possible to find both bargains and fine period pieces here. You can catch the Magazine Street bus and return to Canal Street (fare is sixty cents, exact change).

There are also some art galleries on Magazine, such as the **Bienville Gallery,** at Hastings Place below Jackson Avenue. Note the nineteenth-century commercial building styles. Even the former orphanage in the 3000 block lends itself all too well to business use.

The Garden District always had some sort of commercial area. At first it was near the river. Livestock coming in from the West was kept there and there were slaughterhouses, as well as other business and trading establishments.

In Jefferson City, just up from the city of Lafayette, the slaughterhouses attracted so many buzzards that the Mardi Gras walking club, the Jefferson City Buzzards, was named for them.

2319 Magazine Street. This house was built by architect John Turpin in 1853–54 as his own home. Turpin was a native of London and became a partner in the Gallier-Turpin firm with James Gallier. This house is typical of their work. The architectural styles of New Orleans were always being added to by Englishmen such as Turpin, or men like James Freret, with French training.

JACKSON AVENUE
(crosses St. Charles Avenue)

1224 Jackson Avenue. This raised cottage was built at the time of the Civil War. To the right of the entrance is an unusual octagonal bay. The iron design in the railings is of lyres entwined with flowers. Inside is a spiral central staircase.

1329 Jackson Avenue. Trinity Episcopal Church, built in 1851 in Victorian Gothic design. Leonidas Polk, the "Fighting Bishop" of Civil War fame, was headquartered as bishop here. The church has fine stained-glass windows, including a memorial to Bishop Polk. Of late, Trinity has been active in social causes in its impoverished immediate neighborhood. Trinity School and other church buildings take up almost two full blocks.

1410 Jackson Avenue. This mid-nineteenth-century residence, complete with cast-iron railings, gardens, and Ionic columns, for many years was a secretarial school, Soulé College.

PHILIP STREET
(crosses St. Charles Avenue, parallel to Jackson Avenue)

1220 Philip Street. Constructed all of wood in the 1850s. At one time this was the residence of Isaac Delgado, whose art collection was the start of the New Orleans Museum of Art in City Park.

1238 Philip Street. This house was built in 1853–54 and is a good example of the typical Garden District house with a two-story gallery with columns. It was added to in 1869.

1433 Philip Street. This raised cottage with columns and iron-work was built in the late 1850s. It is rather typical of New Orleans to call these elegant houses cottages. But they do that at Newport, Rhode Island, too.

FIRST STREET
(crosses St. Charles Avenue, parallel to Jackson Avenue)

1134 First Street. Jefferson Davis, ex-president of the Confederacy, died in this house in 1889, when it was owned by the Fenner family. Davis died in a first-floor guest room, to the left rear. The house was built in 1850 and the exterior is stucco-covered brick. The gardens and summerhouse are exquisite.

1236 First Street. Erected in 1847, this house is typical of Greek Revival. Inside are elaborate plaster ceiling medallions from which hung chandeliers. The mantels are black marble. The later the period in the nineteenth century, the more elaborate the fireplaces. Often people would replace their wooden mantels with marble ones as time went on.

1239 First Street. In 1857 this house cost $13,000. It was designed in Greek Revival style by James Calrow, who worked in New Orleans only a few years but is well represented in the Garden District. The decorative fence was a patented design. Inside, the woodwork is especially elaborate. The hexagonal addition on the side was added in 1869.

1331 First Street. Architect Samuel Jamison built this house and the one at 1315 First Street in 1869. The 1331 First Street house has three cast-iron galleries, the smallest, on the north, being the nicest. During restoration a canvas ceiling mural was found.

SECOND STREET
(crosses St. Charles Avenue, parallel to Jackson Avenue)

1427 Second Street. Supposedly this was a plantation house moved here in the 1850s. The door moldings are the same pattern as those in the Pontalba Buildings in the French Quarter.

THIRD STREET
(crosses St. Charles Avenue, parallel to Jackson Avenue)

1331 Third Street. Built in 1850 for the Musson family, relatives of the painter Edgar Degas's (his portrait of Estelle Musson hangs in the New Orleans Museum of Art). James Gallier, Sr., designed this as an "Italian villa," but it acquired its cast iron and present appearance in 1884.

1415 Third Street. One of the most opulent of the Garden District mansions, and one of the largest. It was built in the late 1850s or early 1860s. The living and dining rooms have painted ceilings. The dining room also boasts an interesting chimneypiece containing a carved wooden eagle found in the river after a hurricane. The winding staircase in this house is superb and the furniture is all that can be expected.

1417 Third Street. This was once a carriage house, built in 1853. The walls are thirteen inches thick.

FOURTH STREET
(crosses St. Charles Avenue, parallel to Jackson Avenue)

1448 Fourth Street. Architect Henry Howard designed this house in 1859. The double parlors measure forty-three by twenty-six feet. Around the turn of the century the curved bay window (Prytania Street side) was added to the dining room. The cornstalk fence, with morning glories entwined, is similar to the fence in the 900 block of Royal Street.

WASHINGTON AVENUE
(crosses St. Charles Avenue, parallel to Jackson Avenue)

Washington Avenue and Prytania Street. This gymnasium was once the Southern Athletic Club and here is where Gentleman Jim Corbett trained for his bout with John L. Sullivan. The first turkish bath in New Orleans was here, too.

Washington Avenue from Prytania Street to Coliseum Street. Lafayette Cemetery No. 1. This was the cemetery for the city of Lafayette and was the first completely planned cemetery in town. The road through the middle is Magnolia Avenue. Lafayette No. 1 is a good place to see two examples of New Orleans burial practices: aboveground tombs and ovens. The tombs here are aboveground because that was the custom, whether because of the water table, which made digging graves almost impossible, or because Latin countries often have aboveground tombs. The ovens are the vaults in the walls along the outside of the cemetery. These are usually rented for a year or so, and any old residents are pushed to the back to make room for new ones. Lafayette has some unusual group tombs, as for volunteer fire companies, and a wealth of foreigners. This may have been because the cemetery was first activated when yellow fever was carrying off so many new immigrants.

SIXTH STREET
(crosses St. Charles Avenue, parallel to Jackson Avenue)

1240 Sixth Street. Built in the late 1860s, this was the Music School when Newcomb College was in the Garden District. The modern homes on Conery Street near here were built when the building that housed the school was torn down.

SEVENTH STREET
(crosses St. Charles Avenue, parallel to Jackson Avenue)

1506 Seventh Street. This house dates from the 1850s. Inside are the original cornices and chandeliers (now electric).

EIGHTH STREET
(crosses St. Charles Avenue, parallel to Jackson Avenue)

1313 Eighth Street. Built in 1874, this was the house of George Washington Cable, Louisiana author. During the 1884–85 Cotton Exposition the poet Joaquin Miller lived here.

HARMONY STREET
(crosses St. Charles Avenue, parallel to Jackson Avenue)

1328 Harmony Street. This typical raised cottage with wide central hall and front and back galleries dates from the 1860s.

LOUISIANA AVENUE
(crosses St. Charles Avenue, parallel to Jackson Avenue)

1424 Louisiana Avenue. Circa 1860 raised cottage. Note the double chimneys and brick gable ends.

1525 Louisiana Avenue. This 1850 mansion was erected by architect James P. Freret. Inside this luxurious renovation are frescoes on the second floor and several black marble mantels.

The houses detailed are just a few of the more interesting ones in the district. There are many more, but those listed will give you an idea of architectural styles and periods. Although some of these homes have been made into apartments, many of them are still maintained as private residences. Part of the charm of the Garden District is that it has kept its character as a residential neighborhood all these years.

UPTOWN

Uptown New Orleans is one of those vaguely defined areas that are more a state of mind than a geographic location. The silk-stocking wards, private schools, Audubon Park, Tulane and Loyola universities—all of these are found "uptown." But if you look carefully, you will also see some poorer housing and shabby back streets—in other words, everything you would find in any metropolitan residential area.

The St. Charles Avenue streetcar goes right through the uptown area and a sixty-cent ride on this streetcar is the best way to see it. If you look at a map, you will note that St. Charles Avenue roughly parallels the Mississippi River. As the streetcar moves away from Canal Street, you will first pass through the business district, then Lee Circle, then another commercial area, and when you cross Jackson Avenue—about the 2000 block—you enter the Garden District, which stops at Louisiana. The next areas were developed for residences after the Garden District. Development quickened with a street railroad of the mid-1800s, which was where the streetcar is running now.

The Garden District was, until 1850, the city of Lafayette. It began with Felicity Street (which, like the other streets mentioned, crosses St. Charles) and ended with Toledano Street. From Toledano to Joseph Street was the city of Jefferson. From Joseph to Eleonore Street was Hurstville, from Eleonore to Webster Street was Bloomingdale, from Webster Street to Audubon Park was Burtheville, and from Audubon Park to Lowerline Street was Greenville. Lowerline was the bottom boundary for the city of Carrollton, which extended to what is now the Jefferson Parish line.

Of all those subdivision names the only one that is still in use is "Carrollton." When St. Charles Avenue ends, the streetcar turns right on Carrollton Avenue and stops over a mile later at Claiborne Avenue. So if you want to ride back to Canal Street on the streetcar, just wait—and pay sixty cents again.

There is a Streetcar Store in the 100 block of St. Charles where you can buy a $4.50 all-day pass on the streetcar. For $5.95 you can get a book with maps, descriptions, and shop ads keyed to the numbers on the streetcar-stop signs.

If you drive your car, you can keep going straight at the corner of St. Charles and Carrollton. On your left you will see the levees of the Mississippi River. The road will begin to veer right, parallel to a railroad track. You will make a sharp left turn to cross the railroad track, and the road will begin curving along with the levee still on your left. This is River Road, and you can stay on it almost all the way to Baton Rouge and tour plantation homes (see the section on that area).

But for a short "country" afternoon in New Orleans, there is nothing nicer than a ride on the bouncing streetcar under the oak trees of St. Charles Avenue, with a picnic in Audubon Park for lunch.

ST. CHARLES AVENUE

Places of interest on lower St. Charles Avenue are covered in the "Business District" and "Garden District" chapters. One thing you will notice are the numerous high-rise apartment buildings and hotels along the avenue. Basically, the river side of the avenue (on your left, coming from Canal Street) is the better residential section until past Jefferson Avenue, where the areas on both sides of the avenue have high-income residents. But you will find mansions side by side with hovels almost anywhere you look "uptown."

The following interesting locations can be seen from the St. Charles streetcar, after passing the Garden District, which ends at Louisiana Avenue.

3900 St. Charles Avenue. Rayne Memorial Methodist Church dates from 1876 and is of red brick in Gothic design. It calls itself the Church with the Lighted Steeple and there is always a light burning up in the belfry.

4338 St. Charles Avenue. Touro Synagogue was built in 1909 and is named for Judah Touro, who died in 1854 and through his philanthropies left the city with Touro Synagogue, **Touro Infirmary** (on Prytania Street, one block off St. Charles Avenue just above Louisiana Avenue), and a home for the aged. He was born in Newport, Rhode Island, a son of the rabbi of the oldest synagogue in America. He never married and was injured in the Battle of New Orleans. The ark in Touro Synagogue was given by Touro to the congregation in 1840.

4521 St. Charles Avenue. "The Rosary"—the **Academy of the Sacred Heart**—buildings were completed in 1917, but the brick buildings, the shuttered windows, and the gardens can stand up to New Orleans' oldest architecture for sheer beauty and harmony. The school is private, for girls, and is operated by the nuns of the Order of the Sacred Heart. You will recognize the students of Sacred Heart on the streetcar by their green plaid skirts. (The McGehee's School girls' plaid skirts have blue in the pattern. Holy Name School is red and gray.)

5005 St. Charles Avenue. This gray mansion dates from 1868 and now houses a private women's club, the **Orleans** (or-lay-AWHN) **Club.** Besides luncheons and lectures, the Orleans Club is sometimes rented for debut teas and wedding receptions, at which the guests cannot throw rice because the floors and front steps are too slippery. The club building is typical of the larger mansions you will see all along the avenue. Some are still family residences, while others have been turned into apartments. Others have become homes for unwed mothers, hotels, private clubs, and nearly everything else.

5120 St. Charles Avenue. The **Milton H. Latter Memorial Library** was donated to the city by the parents of a military officer killed at Okinawa. The house was built in 1907 and was once owned by a silent film star, Marguerite Clark (there are some photos of her in the magazine reading room). The house still has some original interiors and some early painted ceilings.

5800 block St. Charles Avenue. Rosa Park, a horseshoe cul-de-sac, was laid out as a small subdivision in 1891 and named for Rosa Solomon Da Ponte. The big homes in this area date mostly from around the turn of the century.

2635 State Street. A few blocks off the streetcar line, near Claiborne Avenue, the **Ursuline Museum** is located at **Ursuline Academy** at this address. The Ursulines started out in the French Quarter in 1727 (you can tour the original convent, which is now the **Archbishop Blanc Memorial** at Chartres and Ursulines streets in the French Quarter). In 1824 the nuns moved downriver and in 1912, when the Industrial Canal was built through their land, they moved here, to State Street. In the Ursuline Museum here is a 1726 document with the seal of Louis XV that is the original agreement that brought the Ursulines here. In 1804 Thomas Jefferson wrote to assure them they could keep their land and keep up their work even if Louisiana had become a part of the United States—you can see that letter. The museum also displays handwork of the nuns, embroidered vestments, quill work, wax fruit. The chapel is the **National Shrine of Our Lady of Prompt Succor,** and the 1810 statue before which the nuns prayed during the Battle of New Orleans is there. Each January 8, the anniversary of the battle, a special celebration is held. If you wish to tour the museum and chapel, call 866-1472 for a weekday morning appointment. A small donation is requested.

6300 St. Charles Avenue. Loyola University is a Jesuit university established in 1911 from a preparatory school on the site that began in 1904. It has over four thousand students. Behind the brick-front buildings is a modern student union, the **Danna Center.** In the student union you can eat—at the cafeteria or snack bar—and get information on university activities. There is a university theater, a newspaper—the *Maroon*—the **Film Buffs' Institute,** for vintage movie viewings, and several programs that bring in lecturers and performers. **Loyola Field House** is the university's largest arena, located on Freret Street (parallel to St. Charles and only a few blocks away).

The church on the Loyola campus at St. Charles is **Holy Name of Jesus Church.** It dates from 1918 and is a sort of Tudor-Gothic combination. The steeple was damaged by Hurricane Betsy in 1965. One of the loveliest views in New Orleans is of the Holy Name spire as seen across the oak trees and lagoons of Audubon Park, from the park road that runs from Magazine Street to St. Charles. This church is the namesake of the Jesuits' first mission church in Louisiana, which was destroyed when they were expelled in 1763. (They did come back later and have thrived here since.)

6330 St. Charles Avenue. The **Round Table Club,** for men, has been here since 1917. While you are riding uptown keep an eye out for the **Roman Candy Wagon.** For twenty-five cents you can get chocolate, vanilla, or strawberry toffee in a long waxed-paper-wrapped roll. This candy will remove loose fillings, but the mule-drawn wagon and the sound of the handbell rung by the vendor are a cue for every kid in hearing range to run up with their quarters.

6400 St. Charles Avenue. Tulane University dates back to the Medical College of Louisiana (1834) and the University of Louisiana (1847). A bequest by Paul Tulane in 1883 persuaded the school to change its name. The buildings date from after 1894. Tulane is known for its medical school (located far downtown on Tulane Avenue near Charity Hospital) and its law school (specializing in the peculiarities of Louisiana-Napoleonic law, which differs from the other forty-nine states' laws). The **Tulane University Center** is located on the other side of Freret Street, and there you will find information on what's going on on campus (plays, lectures, performances, basketball games, movies) and a cafeteria and snack bar. There is even a bar, serving beer only. Tulane's football team, the Green Wave, plays at the Superdome.

Part of the Tulane campus is taken up by the buildings of

Harriott Sophie Newcomb Memorial College for Women, founded 1886. Newcomb College was located in the Garden District before its 1918 move to this area. Now it is an undergraduate college of Tulane University. The **Newcomb Art School**—on Newcomb Place one block from Willow Street—has exhibits of student work and traveling shows. The Newcomb chapel, on Broadway Street, has some fine Tiffany windows. Concerts at midday are held here on Wednesdays during the school year.

The **Howard Tilton Memorial Library of Tulane University** is on the corner of Freret Street and Newcomb Place (a continuation of Audubon Place, which crosses St. Charles). In the library is an extremely good collection of early New Orleans material, plus rare books and documents (**Special Collections** and the **Rare Book Room,** fourth floor). Also, this is where both the **Archive of New Orleans Jazz** (fourth floor) and the **Latin American Library** (fourth floor) are located. These collections are open weekdays from 9 A.M. to noon and from 1 P.M. to 4:45 P.M., and Saturday from 9 A.M. to noon. In the library basement is the **Southeastern Architectural Archive,** with building models and plans by local architects on display on weekday afternoons.

On the Tulane campus are two auditoriums, **McAlister Auditorium,** on McAlister Drive, and **Dixon Hall,** just off Newcomb Place on the Newcomb quadrangle. These auditoriums are often in use for concerts and other performances.

Middle American Research Institute. M.A.R.I. at Tulane University has a gallery of pre-Columbian art and other exhibits pertaining to Latin American early cultures. The collection is in **Dinwiddie Hall,** the building between Holy Name Church and the main Tulane building on St. Charles, Gibson Hall. You will see the side of Dinwiddie Hall from the streetcar. The M.A.R.I. collection is very good and is located on the top floor of Dinwiddie (no elevator). Hours are 10 A.M. to 4 P.M., Monday through Friday. It is best to call in advance to see if they are open (865-5110). M.A.R.I. operates its own digs in Mexico, so they will have up-to-date information. A guide to the collection is available for $1.00.

Audubon Park. You can't miss Audubon Park—it is right across St. Charles Avenue from Tulane and Loyola. The park runs from St. Charles to the Mississippi River. The other boundaries are Exposition Boulevard (lower) and Walnut Street (upper). Inside the park you will find picnic tables and shelters, an incredibly good zoo, a bandstand, a miniature train, horses for rent, a golf course, tennis courts, a large swimming pool and some wading pools for children, fountains and statues, trees and flowers, and bushes and meandering lagoons.

The other streets that run parallel with St. Charles and go through the park are Tchoupitoulas Street (along the river) and Magazine Street (right through the middle of the park). Both Tchoupitoulas and Magazine have bus lines that go right to Canal Street, so you can get off the streetcar and wander through the park and catch a bus back home.

The park was purchased by the city in 1871. Before that it was plantation land. It is said that Étienne Boré, first mayor of New Orleans, granulated sugar on his land, which is now part of the park. The alleys of oak trees may date back to the plantation period.

The first serious use of the park was in 1884–85 when the World's Industrial and Cotton Centennial Exposition was held here (that's where Exposition Boulevard got its name).

The Cotton Exposition had the largest building in the world for an exhibit hall but, sad to say, the enterprise was financially unsuccessful, and everything but a Horticultural Hall was sold in a sheriff's sale. The Horticultural Hall later was blown down by a hurricane. The exposition buildings were on what is now the golf course. (And the big red rock that's supposed to be a meteorite is actually a leftover exposition exhibit: a piece of iron ore from Alabama.)

After the buildings were taken down, the city began plans for a real park, but it was not until after 1900 that work began. The park was planned by John C. Olmsted of Brookline, Massachusetts.

Most park facilities are open daily from 9:30 A.M. to 4:30 P.M., and a little later in summer. There is a river-view pavilion on the Mississippi River that is worth a drive or a walk. The strangest thing in the park is Monkey Hill, in the zoo near the river. This hill was put up so the children of flat New Orleans would know what a hill looked like.

Audubon Zoo. The Audubon Zoo holds many endangered species in beautifully designed moated enclosures. There's a special area for children, the elephants put on performances (and sometimes carry riders), and the amphitheater often has plays or music for zoo patrons. You can eat at the restaurant, patronize the gift shop, or just relax on a bench and watch the free-ranging peacocks strut. There is an admission fee—and it's worth every penny. With or without kids, the Audubon Zoo is a guaranteed pleasant experience! (Even the members of a national zoo association found this one of the best small zoos in the country.)

If you like, you can reach the zoo from the river. The stern-wheeler *Cotton Blossom* leaves Canal Street at the river and visits the zoo daily. Call 586-8777 or 524-9787.

Live Oak Society. In the Audubon Zoo, by the rhinoceroses, is a huge oak tree. This is the Martha Washington Oak (George died). It is a member of the Live Oak Society, the world's only club for trees. The society was founded in 1934 by the then president of the University of Southwestern Louisiana in Lafayette, Dr. Edwin Louis Stephens. Dr. Stephens wanted to preserve the trees, so he began a club for live oaks over one hundred years old. Trees are measured four and a half feet from the ground. If their circumference is sixteen feet, they are eligible (over eight feet makes trees junior members). The rules include: "Members shall not be whitewashed" and "No members shall be desecrated with advertisements." The president, the largest tree, is the Seven Sisters Oak in Mandeville, Louisiana. If you have a live oak you want to propose for membership, write Mrs. Louis Pfister, 3112 West Metairie Avenue North, Metairie, Louisiana 70001. Owners and sponsors of trees are referred to as the tree's "attorneys." Membership is drawn from throughout the United States, and presently numbers over eight hundred.

Audubon Place. This street is just past Tulane University and begins on St. Charles. It was developed by a Fort Worth, Texas, man named George Blackwelder as a subdivision with large lots on a central park area. There is a gatehouse at the entrance that is older than all the other houses. Audubon Place is spacious, attractive, and lined with houses that truly deserve to be called mansions. Since the gate at the Freret Street entrance is always locked, Audubon Place is not a through street, but the watchman at the St. Charles Avenue end may let you walk through.

Broadway Street at St. Charles Avenue. On this corner is a dollhouse, a brick miniature of the main house. Many people think this is where Lillian Hellman spent the night when she ran away from home, heading for Jackson Square. Since she never lived above Valence Street while a child here, it's not likely. Read about it in her autobiography.

Broadway has a bus line that you can take toward the river to **Uptown Square**—an attractive shopping center built to look like a cluster of town houses. There may also be a free shuttle bus service between the streetcar stop, the shopping center, and Carrollton Avenue. The **Broadway Café** at Uptown Square has very good food.

7214 St. Charles Avenue. These buildings were constructed for St. Mary's Dominican College for women, dating back to the 1860s, when a group of Irish Dominican nuns came to New Orleans. The main building—the white wooden Victorian one—dates from 1872. The planetarium here has an especially nice Christmas show.

719 South Carrollton Avenue. Benjamin Franklin Senior High School, drawing its gifted student body from throughout the city, began holding classes here in the late 1950s, but this building was built in 1855 as the parish courthouse when Carrollton was part of Jefferson Parish. There used to be a jail here and also a gallows, last used in 1858. Carrollton was annexed to New Orleans in 1874 and then the courthouse became a school. This section of town is still called Carrollton.

Carrollton was probably named for General William Carroll,

who served in the Battle of New Orleans and was later governor of Tennessee. The railroad that began in the 1830s where the streetcar now runs was the reason for the settlement's growth from plantation land to urban neighborhood.

Some of Carrollton was swallowed by the river, and the Carrollton Hotel, a popular nineteenth-century resort visited by William Makepeace Thackeray, has long since disappeared.

1015 South Carrollton Avenue. This grand brick Gothic mansion was built for an Englishman named Wilkinson around 1849. The gardens owe much to Colonel George Derby, who bought the house in 1902.

Other interesting buildings can be found in this neighborhood. **7835 Maple Street** was built in the 1840s as a Presbyterian center —although it looks like a Greek Revival plantation house. Both 924–6 Joliet Street and 832–6 Fern Street were built as schools in 1854.

Restorations of the nineteenth-century houses in the area of Carrollton near the river make it pleasant for strolling—and the shops on Dublin and Dante streets (one and two blocks uptown) are worth a look. There is another shopping area on Oak Street, which crosses Carrollton about six blocks away. Remember, stroll in daylight only.

The end of the streetcar line is at Claiborne Avenue. **Palmer Park** here was named for the Reverend Benjamin Palmer, a Presbyterian minister of the nineteenth century.

If you want to go back to Canal Street, pay another sixty cents and enjoy watching the motorman switch the backs of the seats to face the other way—the streetcar doesn't turn around, it just switches to the track on the other side of the neutral ground.

THE BUSINESS DISTRICT

The business district of New Orleans begins with Canal Street, which is also the end of the French Quarter. The business district began as common land and plantations. Before 1800 it was subdivided, and streets were laid out. After the Louisiana Purchase in 1803 it became the first "American Sector," where the English-speaking residents of New Orleans went when they wanted to get away from the French-speaking Creoles in the Vieux Carré. The separation was so complete that even the streets that cross Canal Street change names in the business district.

For our purposes we will say that the business district is bounded by Canal Street, the Mississippi River, the elevated expressway that runs parallel with Canal ten blocks away, and Loyola Avenue, which lies eleven blocks from the river.

In this area are the high-rise office buildings and rush-hour traffic jams common to any commercial area. But here you will also find some pleasant squares and plazas and a blending of the old and the new that is particularly New Orleans'.

In recent years the face of the business district has been changed by a restoration boom and by much new construction.

Poydras Street from the Superdome to the river is marked by new skyscrapers.

The riverfront, from Canal Street to the bridge, was once mostly a barren warehouse area. With the Canal Place development, the International Trade Mart, convention halls, wharf entertainment areas, and the World's Fair site—the strip along the river has blossomed.

Preservation has brought many restored town houses used as offices, a mall area focused on Lafayette Square, and designation as historic districts for much of this area as a prohibition against widespread demolition.

When all American cities must be concerned with downtown blight, New Orleans has attacked the problem and even won a few rounds. Going "downtown" is still fun in New Orleans.

You must get one thing straight about New Orleans directions: even if Canal Street and the business district can be called "downtown," when you are pinpointing a location, everything below or downriver from Canal Street is "downtown" and everything upriver is "uptown." If you want to point out an address, you relate it to Canal Street, and also to the "lake" (Lake Pontchartrain, on the outer edge of the city) or the "river." Now if someone tells you to meet them on the downtown lake corner of Poydras and Tchoupitoulas streets, you'll know where to go: Mother's Restaurant.

Another distinction is made between "back of town," which means toward the lake, probably on the other side of Claiborne Avenue, and "front of town," which means near the river.

All of this proves you should use a map.

SEEING THE BUSINESS DISTRICT

Driving in New Orleans is difficult, not only because of the peculiarities of the local drivers but also because of the one-way streets. So if you want to go uptown from the French Quarter, the easiest way is to get on Royal Street and keep going when it becomes St. Charles Avenue, then go around Lee Circle halfway until you're on St. Charles again. If you want to get on the expressway to get out of town (away from the river), follow the same route and take the expressway entrance to your right, one block after you round Lee Circle.

One way of getting around the business district is by the shuttle bus. For thirty cents you can ride down Poydras Street to the river, and then to Canal Street and back.

Or ride the streetcar. Board at Carondelet Street and Canal

THE ST. LOUIS CATHEDRAL overlooks Jackson Square in New Orleans' French Quarter.

THE BOEUF GRAS float in the Rex Parade on Mardi Gras (Fat Tuesday) is a reminder that the fasting of Lent begins the next day.

Louisiana Office of Tourism

SIDEWALK ARTISTS in Jackson Square. The portals of the Cabildo are seen in the background.

Louisiana Office of Tourism

LAFITTE'S BLACKSMITH SHOP is supposedly the spot where the Barataria pirate had his New Orleans headquarters to merchandise smuggled goods.

GALLIER HOUSE was the home of architect James Gallier, Jr. Today it is a museum accurately depicting nineteenth-century New Orleans family life.

Gallier House

THE HISTORIC NEW ORLEANS COLLECTION has ten galleries of exhibits, a research library, the eighteenth-century Merieult House, and a "hidden house" behind the courtyard.

THE PIAZZA D'ITALIA with the St. Joseph Fountain in the shape of Italy is a witty architectural treasure of New Orleans' business district.

Louisiana Office of Tourism

GALLIER HALL, once New Orleans' city hall, overlooks Lafayette Square in the business district.

THE LOUISIANA SUPERDOME on Poydras Street is a massive indoor stadium and an integral part of New Orleans' skyline.

Louisiana Office of Tourism

Street and ride up St. Charles Avenue to the Garden District. You can see Lafayette Square, Gallier Hall, and Lee Circle from your window.

And don't let the skid-row types around Lafayette Square get you down. Even Thomas Alva Edison lived on Lafayette Square for a while, when he was working for the telegraph office. And Walt Whitman lived in this area, near Poydras on St. Charles, when he wrote for *The Daily Crescent* in 1848. Although the New Orleans illegitimate child he claimed was probably fictitious, Whitman truly enjoyed the city:

"New Orleans was a great place and *no* mistake," he wrote.

CANAL STREET

From building front to building front Canal Street is over 170 feet wide. The street is named for the very shallow canal—more like a ditch—that was dug in the early days of the city along the ramparts of the Vieux Carré. There was never a true navigational canal here, although it was considered.

Canal Street was once residential but now is completely commercial in the business district. This is where you will find the downtown department stores—Krauss and D. H. Holmes—and the larger women's clothing stores—Godchaux, Gus Mayer, Saks Fifth Avenue. There are also movie houses, drugstores, and everything else that can add neon and tinsel to downtown. However, Canal Street manages to look civilized, probably because it is so wide and well lit with picturesque lampposts ornamented with plaques of the different governments that have ruled New Orleans.

On Mardi Gras Day, Canal Street is wall to wall with people. The crowds are biggest and the "throws"—tossed to the crowds by maskers on the floats—are best in front of the Boston Club.

The Foot of Canal Street

Where Canal Street meets the Mississippi River is a good place to set off on a boat tour. You can take the free ferry here and ride back and forth to Algiers, in your car if you like.

Or you might take a bayou cruise on the *Voyageur*. Call 523-5555 for times and charges. This tour goes through the Harvey Canal to the bayou at Lafitte, Louisiana.

The *Cotton Blossom* is a small replica of a steamboat and leaves on a cruise up to the zoo. Call 586-8777 for details.

The big side-wheeler steamboat docked at Canal is the S.S. *President*. Every Friday and Saturday night the *President* makes a moonlight dancing cruise, complete with rhythm and blues or rock band on board. The hours are 8 P.M. to midnight; the fee is $5.00 per person, more for name bands; drinks and food available. There is probably no nicer way to spend a Saturday night in New Orleans than on the steamer *President*. Besides the trip up the river you get to hear some good dancing music. Call 586-8777.

Be sure you're on time if you're going on a cruise: the boat might just leave without you.

If you just want to look at the river, you might do it from the observation deck of the **International Trade Mart** building (the one with the round top). The thirty-first floor is open daily (for admission) from 9 A.M. to 5 P.M. There is also a media presentation on New Orleans at the **Viewpoint** on this floor. Or you might try the revolving bar two floors up (don't leave your purse on the windowsill, you'll be going around and it won't).

Near the I.T.M. building you will see the **Rivergate Exhibition Hall,** the **Spanish Plaza,** statues of Joan of Arc and Winston Churchill, and also the simple granite shaft that is the **Liberty Monument.**

The monument recalls an 1874 battle between the "White League" of local citizens and the last Reconstructionist state government, which was barricaded in the U.S. Custom House across Canal Street. Several people died in the street fighting. The "White League" won.

The Rivergate dates from 1968, and inside its vast halls there is room for about eighteen thousand people. Bacchus, one of the Mardi Gras krewes, has its ball here the Sunday night before Mardi Gras Day. All the floats and the entire parade come inside for decoration.

Also in this area are the wharf entertainment complexes (or their future locations).

423 Canal Street. The **U.S. Custom House** here was begun in 1848 with General P. G. T. Beauregard in charge of construction. Architects were Alexander Thompson Wood and James Harrison Dakin. Inside, on the second floor, is the "Marble Hall"—a vast Greek Revival room with columns and sculpture. The hall is open weekdays from 9 A.M. to 5 P.M.

622 Canal Street. The elaborate cast-iron front on the upper floors is painted in authentic colors on this 1859 building.

623 Canal Street. This was the address of the first movie theater in America. Vitascope Hall opened July 26, 1896, at the corner of Canal Street and Exchange Place.

The **Louisiana Maritime Museum.** At 130 Carondelet Street, just off Canal. Call first, 581-1874, to verify the address, as a move is planned. If you have any interest in ships or the Mississippi River, you won't want to miss this collection. There are ship models, a lighthouse beacon, ships' wheels, anchors, flags, documents—even a radio with current chat by the Harvey Canal bridge tender and tugboat captains. Open daily (for a small admission) from 9 A.M. to 5 P.M.

824 Canal Street. The **Boston Club** is a men's club and is named for a card game called Boston. It was founded in 1841. The clubhouse is the only remaining residence on Canal Street in this area. It was built in 1844 by James Gallier, Sr., and his plans quaintly called for "a residence and tenement." Today it is a quiet and exclusive men's club that every year puts up a viewing stand during the Mardi Gras season. The Queen of Rex greets her consort from in front of the Boston Club—and this is why this is such a good place to catch "throws" from the parade. Also you can wave at the television cameras, stationed during Mardi Gras on the neutral ground (traffic island) across from the Boston Club.

Saenger Theater. This theater, on Canal at North Rampart Street, now houses traveling Broadway shows and concerts in a unique and elaborate 1927 three-thousand-seat former movie house. Emile Weil was the architect. The Saenger has a huge organ and a ceiling that can resemble a starry sky.

Orpheum Theater. 129 University Place (across from the Fairmont, just off Canal) is the home of the **New Orleans Symphony.** Built between 1918 and 1921, it was designed as a showplace of the powerful Orpheum vaudeville circuit. Architect was Sam Stone. The theater seats two thousand. The Orpheum was saved from being leveled for a parking lot, and restored for the symphony's use.

MAGAZINE STREET

Magazine Street is a continuation of Decatur Street. Until the coffee companies became air-pollution-conscious, you could smell roasting coffee in the Magazine Street business district area every afternoon. It smells rather like burned fudge. The aroma is not so strong now, but you can still catch it every now and then.

The nicest thing on Magazine is the **Board of Trade Plaza** in the 300 block. This pleasant oasis was built in 1968. Until 1967 the Board of Trade Building (the rear of the plaza, creamy yellow and white) had no street view, but this little park with a Spanish fountain solved that. This is a nice place to sit and rest, or just listen to the fountain splash.

Magazine Street was named for the "magazines" (corruption of French *magasins,* "stores") in this area.

CAMP STREET

Camp Street was named for a slave camp. At Camp and Gravier streets (200 block) is the **International House,** a private men's organization. Inside International House is the office of the **Foreign Relations Association.** They can offer all manner of assistance to foreign travelers, including translators. Call them at 524-2168.

725 Camp Street. St. Patrick's Church, the second oldest parish in New Orleans, served the early Irish (or English-speaking) Catholics. The building was begun in 1838, and before it was finished architect James Gallier, Sr., was called in to help. He designed the inside, including the altar. The murals behind the altar were added in 1840 by artist Leon Pomarade. The church is supposed to have been patterned after York Minster in England, but somehow the painted ceiling seems more Art Nouveau than Gothic.

Camp Street is New Orleans' skid row after the 600 block. If you are really down on your luck, you can stand in line for a free meal at the **Ozanam Inn, 843 Camp Street,** men only.

900 Camp Street. The **Contemporary Arts Center** is irreverent, fun, and a good place to check in for information on entertainment. The galleries are open (for admission) Tuesday through Sunday from noon to 5 P.M. Plays, music, films, and videotapes also are scheduled here, and they keep a list of who's playing where for musical entertainment. The C.A.C. also sponsors the Krewe of Clones Mardi Gras parade and party.

929 Camp Street. This is the **Confederate Memorial Museum,** open (for a small admission) Monday through Saturday from 10 A.M. to 4 P.M. Such relics of the Confederate States of America as General Braxton Bragg's ivory toothpick are displayed in this 1891 hall, designed to blend with the adjoining red-brick building, corner of Camp Street and Howard Avenue. If you are a Civil War buff, you will find their displays informative.

The building at Camp and Howard is now used for offices, but

it was intended to be a library. It was built in 1888 from a design
from the Boston architecture firm of H. H. Richardson. Richardson died before the building was completed. He was a native of
Louisiana, and this is perhaps the best example in New Orleans
of his "Romanesque" style.

ST. CHARLES AVENUE

St. Charles Avenue is really St. Charles Street in the business
district. This was the main street of the American sector, and for
a while it seemed that it would outshine the French Quarter in
beauty. There were English theaters, English dance halls, and
English churches—but the area is now filled with strictly American office buildings.

545 St. Charles Avenue. This is known today as **Gallier Hall,**
because of its architect, James Gallier, Sr. It was built between
1845 and 1850 and is now restored to its Greek Revival best. The
pediment (above the front columns) is decorated with a relief of
Justice attended by Commerce and Manufacture. When the city
was split into three municipalities, it was the city hall of the
Second Municipality (American sector). After the city went back
together (1853) it was the city hall for the whole town.

Today Gallier Hall is open only to large groups by appointment. Luncheons and parties can be held in its vast parlors, and
the decor—tending toward red velvet and crystal chandeliers—
is conducive to gaiety.

Gallier Hall is also headquarters for the **New Orleans Recreation Department** drama division, which puts on plays and musicals in a theater in the basement. Call 586-5275 for information.

LAFAYETTE SQUARE

Lafayette Square is the second oldest square in New Orleans
(Jackson Square is the oldest). It encompasses a full square block
and is today surrounded by federal buildings. Directly across
from Gallier Hall is the statue of John McDonogh, a nineteenth-

century philanthropist who left his fortune to the schools of Baltimore and New Orleans.

The other statues in Lafayette Square are of Henry Clay—a great favorite with New Orleans—and Benjamin Franklin. There is also a latitude-longitude marker for the U.S. Coast and Geodetic Survey in the square.

Lafayette Square is always beautifully planted, but it loses something of its charm because the benches are often filled with sleeping winos from the neighborhood.

However, Lafayette Square is the center for revitalization of the area. The **Hale Boggs Federal Buildings,** with benches and outdoor sculpture, the vista of Gallier Hall, and the renovations on the square's neighboring streets will make it a nice place to rest from touring. At lunch free concerts are sometimes held.

LEE CIRCLE

Lee Circle has always been a circle. The Robert E. Lee statue was raised in 1884, and since that time the bronze Confederate general has faced north from his pedestal.

If someone wagers that you can't name which hand Robert E. Lee has his hat in, don't even guess. He has it on his head.

At Lee Circle and St. Charles Avenue stands the **Katz and Besthoff Building,** designed by the architectural firm of Skidmore, Owings and Merrill. **K & B Plaza** is the site of a remarkable sculpture garden.

The **Virlane Foundation** collection is one of the best in the country for modern sculpture. Pieces are outside on the plaza and inside the lobby, where brochures are available during business hours. There are works by Isamu Noguchi, Henry Moore, Lin Emery (an Orleanian), Umberto Boccioni, Leonard Baskin, Renoir, George Segal, and Arthur Silverman (another Orleanian). Even the streetcar stops here are sculpture, by Frank McGuire. The folding chairs and stools are painted steel. Do not miss this collection!

JULIA STREET

In the 600 block of Julia Street are the 1830 town houses that are Julia Row. Once elegant homes, more recently flophouses, these are being restored as offices and apartments.

The New Leviathan Oriental Foxtrot Orchestra (a remarkable large ensemble playing pre-1917 pop music with great showmanship) rehearses in a Julia Row building. Artist George Schmidt, known for his large, witty paintings on Mardi Gras and jazz, has a studio here.

604 Julia Street is the location of the **Preservation Resource Center.** You can tour their building (just ask), or they can schedule (for a fee) architectural tours for you in the business or warehouse districts and uptown residential areas. They are well informed and have numerous pamphlets on New Orleans' architectural treasures. Call 581-7032 weekdays from 8:30 A.M. to 5 P.M.

DRYADES STREET

1139 Dryades Street. This is the **Church of St. John the Baptist** with the gilded dome that you can see so clearly from the expressway. The church was built in 1871 for an Irish parish. Today it is notable for its nineteenth-century brickwork and for the Stations of the Cross inside, which were painted by Dom Gregory Dewit, O.S.B. Dewit also executed the sacristy murals, sometime before 1963. Dewit is a Belgian artist who worked in this area during and after World War II. His most important local work is a fresco of the Last Supper at **St. Joseph's Abbey** outside of Covington, across Lake Pontchartrain.

LOYOLA AVENUE

Loyola Avenue is called Elks Place when it crosses Canal Street. Loyola is the site of the **Civic Center,** and from Tulane Avenue to the expressway—about ten blocks—it is bordered by the **New Orleans Public Library** (corner Tulane—noontime films and art exhibits), the **Louisiana State Supreme Court** (with a statue of Edward Douglass White, Louisiana-born U.S. Supreme Court Justice and Chief Justice until his death in 1921), city hall, state and federal buildings, and the **Union Passenger Terminal** (with a statue of Bienville, a priest, and an Indian, by Angela Gregory). There are some noteworthy murals inside the terminal.

There are parks and benches in the area in front of city hall, and a fountain and sculpture memorial to the late New Orleans Mayor deLesseps S. Morrison. On the neutral ground of Loyola Avenue—which continues as the neutral ground of Basin Street —are statues of such Latin American heroes as Simón Bolívar, Benito Juárez, and Francisco Morazán.

POYDRAS STREET

The **Superdome.** This huge indoor stadium seats over seventy thousand people for football games (the New Orleans Saints pro team and the Tulane Green Wave) and up to ninety-five thousand for special events. Basketball, prizefights, rock stars, conventions, and trade shows all use the dome. There is ample parking. The dome has purple, green, and gold plastic seats. Somehow football games were more fun outside—but New Orleans climate being what it is, a covered stadium is a necessity. Tours are available daily. Call 587-3645.

Piazza d'Italia. This plaza at Tchoupitoulas and Poydras streets was done in 1978 by architect Charles Moore, and the architectural firm of August Perez and Associates. It's fun to look at (find Moore's own portrait in the sculptured frieze). The fountain is shaped like Italy. Bright colors are used. In October the **Festa d'Italia** has food and entertainment. There are plans for an Italian cultural center here, but as it is, the Piazza d'Italia is one of the best things to happen to New Orleans' business district.

BARONNE STREET

The **Church of the Immaculate Conception, 132 Baronne Street,** was rebuilt in 1929 with parts of the 1851 original.

The altar is of gilt bronze and won a prize at the Paris Exposition of 1867 for its designer, New Orleans architect James Freret.

This church is usually called the Jesuit Church on Baronne Street. It has Masses at noon and early in the morning. Before the new rules about Saturday Masses, this church used to have the earliest Sunday Masses in town, which everyone called the Fishermen's Mass. There is always a vegetable vendor near the Jesuit Church.

THE IRISH CHANNEL

That portion of New Orleans that lies above the business district, near the river, below the Garden District, includes what was originally called the Irish Channel. Adele Street, now covered by the St. Thomas Housing Project, ran to the river, and along this little street the early Irish immigrants settled. Why it was called the Irish Channel no one really knows, but the name stuck.

This part of town is now also called the Lower Garden District and most of it falls under historic-district designation. There has been a good bit of gentrification—with the white middle class moving in to restore old homes and have a convenient neighborhood near the city center. The Coliseum Square area and those streets running from Magazine Street to St. Charles Avenue between the expressway and Jackson Avenue have many examples of older houses brought back to their former glory. But this is still, as a whole, a poor area with much substandard housing and a large public housing project near the river. It is well worth touring, though, and the story of the people who have lived there in the past and who live there now is part of the story of New Orleans.

From its beginnings New Orleans welcomed many types of immigrants. There were blacks from Africa, there were French refugees from slave uprisings in the West Indies, and in the nineteenth century there were thousands of immigrants from Europe. There were even so many newly converted European Latter-Day Saints arriving that the Mormons set up a tourist office to guide new members up the Mississippi to Missouri and, later, Utah.

The Irish came to New Orleans partially because New Orleans

was connected with Liverpool through the cotton trade. Liverpool was the jumping-off point for many Irish immigrants.

When they came here they stayed. Many were afraid to move farther on and farm again. They knew the horrors of famine and farming.

German immigrants came to America in periods when they faced religious persecution of one kind or the other and when Germany was gripped by revolution. New Orleans and the river were gateways to the farmlands of the Midwest, where many Germans were headed. Some stayed and made their home here.

There were early German and Irish settlers. In 1721 two hundred Germans arrived in Biloxi. There were Irish soldiers in the Spanish Army when New Orleans was a Spanish colony.

But the main migrations were between 1820 and 1860. There were 152,000 German and 101,000 Irish immigrants to New Orleans then. Enough of them remained in New Orleans to change the composition of the town from predominantly black to predominantly white.

By 1850 one in five New Orleanians was Irish.

Had the Irish lived, New Orleans would have had more than Boston. But many of them did not survive. New Orleans needed cheap labor, for digging canals, for the construction boom just before the Civil War. The Irish were willing to work, and it was judged that they were more expendable than slaves for the hardest labor.

And the epidemics took their toll. Yellow fever and cholera carried them off almost before they were off the boats.

There was a ditty current then that tells the story:

> Ten Thousand Micks, they swung their picks
> To dig the New Canal,
> But the choleray was stronger 'n they
> And twice it killed them awl.

The Germans were somewhat more fortunate. They organized societies to help settle new immigrants and most of them moved on to farm. By the Civil War there were fifteen thousand Germans in New Orleans. Not all of them were sympathetic to the Confederacy, but by the twentieth century they were politically assimilated.

One fact you will learn about New Orleans as soon as you get here is that the Southern drawl is not a typical New Orleans way of talking. The harsh, twangy "Brooklynese" you hear is the New Orleans native accent.

Locals refer to people who speak this way as "yats." This is because "Where yat" ("where you at") is a New Orleans greeting. "Where yat, yuh muthah" is another form. Most native Orleanians do not have to try very hard to sound like yats.

There are many theories about this. One might be that the same immigrant groups that settled Brooklyn settled New Orleans in the nineteenth century. One could be that both are seaports. Still another would have it that people who speak certain other languages before English end up with this pronunciation.

But you will hear "dese" for "these" and "true" for "through." One example is that "Throw the ball through the hoop on three, sophomore" comes out "Troe de ball true de hoop on tree, southmore."

The place where you are most likely to hear this speech, in its best form, is still the Irish Channel.

Although the channel is now not strictly Irish or German, and the numbers of poor black people have increased, and a new wave of Hispanic immigrants are settling there, the channel retains something of its old flavor. In spite of its being in the inner city, it still has some characteristics of a neighborhood, a street friendliness that keeps it from the hard-edged despair of a true ghetto.

As the years pass and more and more of the old homes are restored, the character of the neighborhood may change. However, at least some of those adventuresome couples moving back can claim that their grandparents lived in "the Channel" before them.

Today it's still the best place in town to find neighborhood bars, to watch the St. Patrick's Day Parade, to dance behind a jazz band on Mardi Gras Day, or just to get a better idea of what New Orleans is really like.

PLACES TO SEE

There are buses that leave from the corner of Canal and Camp Streets and go up Magazine Street. Another bus route goes up Tchoupitoulas Street, leaving from the corner of Tchoupitoulas and Common streets, one block off Canal. Tchoupitoulas runs near the river, and Magazine Street is between Tchoupitoulas Street and St. Charles Avenue, which has its streetcar line. The Irish Channel is not the place for strolling, and the best way to see its sights is by car. Take Magazine up from Canal, follow Prytania Street or Tchoupitoulas down from Louisiana Avenue.

Margaret Haughery Statue, corner of Camp and Prytania streets. This monument to a daughter of Irish immigrants who devoted her life to caring for orphans and left her earnings from a bakery and dairy to charity was one of the earliest statues raised to a woman in this country. The statue was unveiled in 1884, cost $6,000, and is of Carrara marble. The inscription reads simply MARGARET. The **Louise Day Nursery,** begun in 1850, looks on the small park where the statue is located.

Coliseum Square, bounded by Camp, Coliseum, and Race streets, Melpomene Avenue. This began as a fashionable neighborhood. It was planned to have a university called the "Prytaneum" here on Prytania Street. The cross streets in this area are named after muses, but in the typical New Orleans way they have all been somewhat mispronounced. Melpomene (MEL-po-meen) and Calliope (CAL-ee-ope) and Clio (CLY-oh) might make a Greek scholar shudder, but everyone in New Orleans will understand you. (Actually it's not too far from a French pronunciation.)

There used to be a streetcar on Clio Street—you will drive

over abandoned streetcar tracks all over New Orleans—and on the front it had the single word: CLIO. So many people called it the C-L-ten streetcar.

Uncommon places on Coliseum Square include the **Coliseum Place Baptist Church, 1376 Camp Street,** built for the oldest Baptist congregation in the city, but now not in full use. The building was constructed in 1854 and the auditorium is on the second floor. The design might be called Gothic perpendicular.

The house at **1228 Race Street** is of stucco-covered brick and was built during the Civil War, when the Freedman's Bureau was set up by the occupying army in a house at **1420 Euterpe Street,** also on the square at that time.

At **1729 Coliseum Street** is the house that was the boyhood home of Sir Henry Morton Stanley, best known for his "Dr. Livingstone, I presume?" speech when he was a famous journalist looking for the missing doctor in Africa.

Stanley was originally named John Rowlands, but he was adopted by the Stanley family and took his foster father's name.

This house used to stand on Orange Street at Annunciation Square but was moved to this spot and restored.

Louisiana author Grace King once lived on Coliseum Square at **1749 Coliseum Street.**

Coliseum Square began building up shortly after 1830 and, with its many restorations, is once again becoming a fashionable neighborhood. The park itself is attractive, if not very safe for strolling.

St. Vincent's Infant Home, corner Magazine and Race streets. Designed and built by Thomas Milligan in 1864, St. Vincent's is typical of New Orleans orphanage construction. The city was dotted with these buildings during the nineteenth century when yellow fever and cholera created large numbers of orphans. Generally of brick with galleries and an enclosed garden, the orphanages of New Orleans, at least on their exteriors, were a pleasant form of institutional architecture. **St. Elizabeth's,** on Prytania Street at Napoleon Avenue, is another example. In the 900 block of Webster Street a stable of the German Protestant Orphanage has been made into an elegant home. **St. Anna's, 1823 Prytania Street,** has been altered but has the most elegant main floor remaining. St. Vincent's provides temporary care for babies. St. Elizabeth's is a home for girls, and St. Anna's for elderly ladies. The edifice in the 3000 block of Magazine Street holds offices now.

Annunciation Square, Annunciation, Race, Chippewa, and Orange streets. This square is now a rather drab playground, but it was once a fine residential section. After the Civil War it reverted to warehouses and Ku Klux Klan meetings.

The Stanley house once stood on the corner of Orange and Annunciation streets.

Kingsley House, 1600 Constance Street. Kingsley House began in 1902 and is New Orleans' answer to Hull House. There are activities here for children, adults, elderly people, and everyone else.

In its early years Kingsley House also sponsored weekly summer dances, with a band, on its pavilion.

In 1907 a Tulane University graduate student named Edward E. Pratt lived a few blocks from here and attempted to write a sociological study of the neighborhood. In an excerpt from his thesis, Mr. Pratt tells more about his own musical prejudices than he probably intended to:

> The Negro bands of the vicinity are almost beyond description, even those which "read their music," an accomplishment which is highly prized since most of them play by ear. On several occasions these bands have furnished music for the dancers, which has been entirely without harmony or time, a brassy cornet or a flaring trombone making the majority of the noise. Yet on another occasion when a good orchestra was obtained whose music was tuneful and harmonious, and whose time was excellent, indeed whose playing was really of a high order, the people were dissatisfied. They preferred the Negro bands with their terrible discords which are their accomplishments. One young fellow was voicing the sense of the community when he said of the good orchestra, "Why, you couldn't hear them a block away!"

It just goes to show you that graduate students aren't always the best jazz critics.

You get the best view of the Kingsley House buildings through the fence on the Market Street side.

Redemptorist churches and schools, Constance Street between Josephine and St. Andrew streets. The Congregation of the Most Holy Redeemer, a Roman Catholic religious order, ministered to several immigrant groups in the mid-nineteenth century. But the Redemptorists, as they are commonly called, had the same problem as everybody else in town: ethnic groups didn't mix well and each liked its own language best. So the Redemptorists had three churches: French, Irish, and German.

The French church is gone, but the congregation has become the **Chapel of Our Lady of Prompt Succor** on Prytania Street near Third Street in the Garden District.

The Irish and German churches are in the Redemptorists' ecclesiastical square and are both fine examples of nineteenth-century baroque brickwork.

St. Alphonsus Church, 2029 Constance Street, was the Irish church. The cornerstone was laid in 1855 and the architect was Louis Long of Baltimore. The baroque spires were never completed. The painted ceilings inside are attractive and the columns and gallery are slightly reminiscent of St. Louis Cathedral.

St. Mary's Assumption, Josephine and Constance streets, was the German church. It has been extensively restored since 1965, when it suffered severe damage from Hurricane Betsy. The cornerstone of this church was laid in 1858. The baroque brickwork tower is worth seeing.

Inside, the decoration is ornate and German. The altar came from Munich, and the bells—Mary-Joseph, Pius, and Gabriel— came from France, as did the stained-glass windows. The pulpit is special—huge, canopied, carved, and gilded.

Buried in St. Mary's is Father Francis Xavier Seelos, a Redemptorist in New Orleans from 1866 to 1867, when he died of yellow fever. Many miracles are credited to Father Seelos and there is an active effort to have him beatified, a stop on the way to sainthood.

Behind St. Mary's the Redemptorists have an attractive enclosed garden. While visitors are always welcome at St. Mary's, you must ask at the rectory to see the inside of St. Alphonsus, which is closed. The priests are agreeable, and if you leave a small donation toward the repair of the church they will be very appreciative. The decline of the neighborhood has affected their congregations and there is little money for old churches in the Irish Channel these days. (If you would like to see the original wooden church built as St. Mary's in 1845, it has been moved to the St. Joseph Cemetery at 2220 Washington Avenue.)

Jackson Avenue Ferry, Jackson Avenue at the Mississippi River. The free ferry at Jackson Avenue will take you and your car on a short boat ride across the Mississippi River. On the other side is the little town of Gretna, with a small town square. You can return to New Orleans via the Greater New Orleans Bridge.

DRIVING DIRECTIONS

If you use your car to see the Irish Channel, begin at Canal and Magazine streets. Take Magazine uptown—it is a one-way street here. Go about ten blocks, turn right on Calliope Street, and go one block.

At the corner of Calliope and Camp streets, turn left on Prytania Street. You do this by crossing Camp and veering to the left under the overpass.

At the corner of Prytania and Camp is the **Margaret Haughery statue.**

Go past the statue, turn left on Clio Street, go half a block to Coliseum Street, and turn right.

Continue on Coliseum to **Coliseum Square.**

Turn left on Race Street—the end of the park. At Magazine

Street is **St. Vincent's.** Cross Magazine, go two blocks, and turn right on Annunciation Street. This is **Annunciation Square.** Continue on Annunciation to Orange Street, turn left on Orange and then right again on Annunciation.

Continue on Annunciation two blocks. To your right you will see a brick building. This is **Kingsley House.** Turn right on Market Street, veer right on Felicity Street for half a block, and turn right on Constance Street. This takes you to the front of Kingsley House.

Turn left on Richard Street, go one block, and turn left again on Magazine. Keep in the left lane and when an arrow tells you to turn (about three blocks), turn left on St. Andrew Street. Go one block and turn right on Constance.

To your right in this block is **St. Alphonsus Church** and to your left at the next corner is **St. Mary's Assumption.** Continue one more block on Constance and turn left on Jackson Avenue. Continue on Jackson to the **Jackson Avenue Ferry.**

The drive should take from fifteen minutes up, depending on the traffic.

(If you continued four blocks on Constance past Jackson, you would reach **Parasol's Bar,** Constance and Third streets. Have a roast beef po' boy and a Barq's and get acquainted with the heart of the "Channel." No time estimate is possible!)

DOWNTOWN

As you know by now, everything "downriver" from Canal Street is downtown. The French Quarter ends at Esplanade Avenue. On the other side of Esplanade lies the Marigny tract, or the Faubourg Marigny.

Bernard de Marigny, the proud Creole who refused to let the Americans develop his land and forced them to move to the Garden District, decided to set up his own subdivision. He named the streets himself (making them change their names when they left the French Quarter), and besides a Craps Street he also had Piety and Desire streets. Most of the street names have been changed, for the sake of conformity.

All of that was, of course, far back in the 1800s. Today this part of town is old and a bit run-down. But it is worth some time, if only to say that you were in the area where the Streetcar Named Desire ran. You will also enjoy the parks and museums of St. Bernard Parish, New Orleans downriver neighbor, and you can get an idea of the vastness of the port industry of New Orleans.

From the French Quarter, take Decatur Street going downriver. Stay in the right lane and pass the side of the Old U.S. Mint. Continue past the corner of Esplanade Avenue. The street curves to your left, and you can veer left on to Elysian Fields Avenue.

The area near the river below the French Quarter can be termed the Creole Faubourgs. (Faubourgs are suburbs made of the original grants of farmland and they went in strips, starting from the river.) The Faubourg Marigny runs from Esplanade to Franklin Avenue. Many of these houses were first built by free people of color. Because of their proximity to the center of town, these areas have much restoration going on but still function as old-fashioned neighborhoods.

From Elysian Fields, turn left on Royal Street. You will see Washington Square on your right. This is the heart of the upper Faubourg Marigny residential section, known as the Marigny Triangle. In one block, on Frenchmen Street, turn right and go two blocks to Burgundy Street. Turn left.

2020 Burgundy Street. This Creole cottage, known as Sun Oak, was built in 1836 by a Mr. Nathan. The furnishings are very attractive and the restoration work is interesting. Even the privies have been excavated and the relics resulting are displayed. This house museum is available for touring (for admission). Call 945-0322 to make an appointment. This small house will give you an idea of nineteenth-century New Orleans life outside the French Quarter mansions.

Take Burgundy to Touro Street, turn left, and left again on Dauphine Street.

On Washington Square you can see the home of the son of the first governor of Louisiana, W. C. C. Claiborne II, **2111 Dauphine Street,** built in the 1850s. At **2105-7 Dauphine Street** you can see a typical Creole cottage: the roof line overhangs the front and is sharply pitched. Sometimes in Creole cottages there are dormer windows. The rooms on each side are "shotgun" style (one behind the other) and there is no center hall. Throughout this section you will see variations of the Creole cottage, the Victorian shotgun (either single or double), and the Creole or American town house (two-storied with balconies).

If you drive around Washington Square, continue on Elysian Fields (note **820 Elysian Fields Avenue,** on your left: it dates from the first decades of the nineteenth century) until Rampart Street. Turn right on North Rampart and go one block. Turn right again on Marigny Street. The 800 and 900 blocks of Marigny Street can give you a good idea of the massive restoration that is being done: you will see Victorian (all that wooden jigsaw work), Italianate (curvier over the door and window openings), and Edwardian (the elaborate house at **820 Marigny**

Street—the initials etched in the glass of the door are for the Dr. Faust who built it). Also, as you pass the corner of Burgundy Street you can see **St. Peter and Paul Church.**

Just as in the Irish Channel, the Catholics of the Creole Faubourgs (or the Third Municipality when the city split into three districts in the nineteenth century) wanted to worship in their own language.

St. Peter and Paul was an Irish Catholic church and dates from the 1860s. The two towers are of different height and design and the brickwork is worth noting. Inside, the church has not been renovated so much that the original details disappear.

Continue on Marigny Street to Chartres Street and turn left.

As you drive you will see many examples of nineteenth century housing, simple and elaborate. Also note corner stores, with their overhangs covering the banquette.

You may wish to make detours off Chartres. **Holy Trinity Church,** built for German Catholics in 1853, is at 721 St. Ferdinand Street, and **St. Maurice Church,** built for French Catholics in 1857, is at 605 St. Maurice Avenue.

At 3933 Chartres Street is the **Lombard plantation house,** which dates from 1826. Originally it had outbuildings and a garden around it, but you can see the typical raised cottage style: main floor off the ground, covered gallery, high ceilings, and thick walls. (Even if it seems to hide behind the next-door barroom.)

Continue on Chartres and turn left only when you reach the gray buildings of the Port of Embarkation. Above the levee you may see the tops of ships. Turn left on Poland Avenue and then turn right on St. Claude Avenue.

You will go over the Industrial Canal, one of New Orleans' most important shipping waterways.

If you ever look at New Orleans from the air, you will realize what a vast drainage problem the city has: it is crisscrossed and nearly surrounded by water.

The river is higher than the city. Draining New Orleans involves pumping water up as the city sits like a saucer between the river and lake. Heavy rains can cause street flooding. Storms in the Gulf can cause tides that back up through the Industrial Canal. The worst recent flood followed Hurricane Betsy in 1965, when most of the city below the Industrial Canal was underwater.

Steamboat Houses. Turn right on Reynes Avenue as soon as St. Claude crosses the bridge. Go toward the river, until you come to Chartres Street again. The buildings on your right are **Holy Cross High School,** run by the Christian Brothers.

Turn left on Chartres and then right on Egania Street. In one block you will come to the corner of Egania and Douglass streets, where two of the most original houses in New Orleans can be seen.

Captain Milton Doullot was a river pilot—as was his wife—and a shipbuilder. When he knew that the day of the steamboat was over, he decided to memorialize the floating gingerbread palaces in his own way: he built his house to look just like one. He built the house—the one nearest the river—in 1905, and in 1913 his son Paul built one like it across the street.

The houses are octagonal, with a first floor all of white tile brick. The second floor—or deck, you might say—has fantastic wooden trim on the porch roof. It looks like white beads strung from the tops of the columns. Inside, some walls are of embossed tin. On top of each house is a little pilothouse windowed all around and looking over the river. The ceilings of the porches are painted green or blue in the New Orleans way.

These houses look more like landlocked boats than residences. It is worth a trip just to take a look at them. Both are still family homes, so confine your looking to the street. Or go and walk around on the levee.

Jackson Barracks. Not far downriver from the Steamboat Houses are the buildings of Jackson Barracks, now the headquarters of the Louisiana National Guard. The barracks face Delery Street and the Mississippi River. The plantation-type buildings date from 1834. Jackson Barracks was a depot for the troops that were stationed at the river forts, but it was designed like a fort itself. It has been suggested that Andrew Jackson, who never got on well with the Creoles, wanted the barracks to be secure against an attack from New Orleans as well as from an enemy. The buildings are of brick with white trim and columns. Jackson Barracks has the Louisiana Military History and State Weapons Museum in its 1837 powder magazine building. Any weapon or military-vehicle buffs would enjoy this collection, which has uniforms and flags as well as guns. To see the collection call 271-6262 and make an appointment. There is no admission and hours are 7:30 A.M. to 3:30 P.M., Monday through Friday. Among officers serving at Jackson Barracks in the 1850s were both Robert E. Lee and Ulysses S. Grant.

When you leave Jackson Barracks get back on St. Claude Avenue and turn right. Chalmette Park is about a mile away.

CHALMETTE

The site of the Battle of New Orleans is now part of the National Park Service, as one of the divisions of Jean Lafitte National Historical Park. This spot, 6 miles downriver from New Orleans, is where Andrew Jackson and the Americans defeated the British on January 8, 1815.

(If you want to get to Chalmette National Historical Park by bus, take the St. Claude Refinery bus on Canal Street at North Rampart Street for sixty cents. In the 6900 block of St. Claude Avenue you will have to take a St. Bernard Avenue bus in front of the Rockery Inn for fifty cents. Tell the driver where you want to go.)

Chalmette Battlefield. During the War of 1812 the British had three major offensives against the United States. The first two— on Lake Champlain and on Chesapeake Bay—failed, so all British hopes were on capturing control of the Mississippi River and hampering American westward expansion.

In December 1814 seventy-five hundred British troops marched to attack New Orleans. By December 23 Andrew Jackson and a motley crowd of Creole dandies, Tennessee and Kentucky backwoodsmen, U.S. Army units, and pirates had gone down to meet the British and attacked them. Jackson fell back to Chalmette plantation and set up his earthworks and line.

The British, on January 14, formed ranks and marched toward the American line. But Jackson and his sharpshooters mowed them down. There were over two thousand British casualties and only thirteen American ones.

There were other British-American skirmishes across the Mississippi, but Jackson's victory was decisive. England did not get the American foothold it wanted. Anyway, by the time the battle was fought, a treaty had already been signed, although the armies did not know it.

At Chalmette Park there are markers showing all details of the battle. There is a monument—a 110-foot marble obelisk—and a plantation house, which dates from 1832 and was remodeled in 1856 by architect James Gallier, Jr.

In the plantation house are exhibits on the Battle of New Orleans, including displays and an audiovisual show. The park is open daily from 8 A.M. to 5 P.M. except Christmas Day, New Year's Day, and Mardi Gras Day.

If you want to picnic, there are tables at two locations in the park. Or you may wish to picnic on the levee behind the plantation house.

From the levee you get a view of the Mississippi River and—to your right facing the river—the Chalmette Slip, a deep-water shipping terminal.

You can even arrive at the Chalmette Battlefield by boat. The *Voyageur* tour boat has a cruise daily at 10 A.M. that goes all the way to Lafitte and Barataria via the river and bayou. There is a half-hour stop at Chalmette. Tickets are: adults $9.50, children $4.75, under six free. The *Voyageur* also has a harbor cruise in the afternoon from 3:30 to 5:30 that stops at Chalmette. Tickets are: adults $5.50, children $2.75, and under six free. Board at Canal Street and the river.

The best time to visit the Chalmette Battlefield is the weekend nearest January 8, and on January 8 itself. Then there are reenactments of the battle, displays, crafts, and performances of the period and a musketry display. This celebration in recent years has gotten better and better and is not to be missed.

Also in the park you will find a military cemetery, with two veterans of the War of 1812 buried there. There are many thousands of graves, including fourteen thousand Union soldiers.

St. Bernard. If you are driving and want a day in the country, continue on St. Bernard Highway. This Louisiana parish is where shrimpers, fishermen, and trappers live. It is crisscrossed with waterways and marshlands and has some worthwhile places to visit. (If you didn't picnic, eat at **Rocky and Carlo's** in Chalmette. This typical family restaurant has good seafood and is right on St. Bernard Highway.)

A few miles below the De La Ronde Oaks the highway comes to a fork. You can go either toward Braithewaite (Highway 39) or Delacroix Island (Highway 46).

De La Ronde Oaks. If you leave the park and turn right on St. Bernard Highway, you will see an alley of oak trees on your right in about a mile and a half and the ruins of the de la Ronde plantation in the middle of the road. The oaks were once the entrance to the plantation home of Pierre de la Ronde. The oaks were planted in 1762, and some people think that British General Edward Pakenham died under them after the Battle of New Orleans. He probably didn't.

Pakenham, by the way, was the brother-in-law of the Duke of Wellington, the hero of Waterloo. As was the custom, Pakenham's body was shipped home in a cask of rum.

There are picnic tables under the oaks, although the area is not in the most immaculate condition.

ISLENOS CENTER

Take Highway 46 for about 7 miles to this unit of Jean Lafitte National Historical Park. The Isleños were Canary Islanders who settled in St. Bernard (and some Spanish is still spoken here).

The **Isleños Center** is located in a nineteenth-century cottage and has displays and artifacts about the crafts and language of these Spanish settlers. They even had special songs, *decimas,* sort of rhyming satires on people and events. You can learn about St. Bernard industries such as fishing and trapping. The park ranger will be a native, so be sure and stop to chat.

Next door is the **Ducros Museum,** the St. Bernard Parish museum. In this cottage is the local library and displays about St. Bernard. There is a large collection of seashell fossils dredged up in canal construction, plus photographs, pottery, and other souvenirs of St. Bernard's people. Together the two little museums will tell you much about an area that even New Orleanians don't know well.

You can continue on Highway 46 to Delacroix Island, which is a fishing village. If you fish or hunt, St. Bernard is a good place to remember. If you are just driving through, notice the landscape about you.

This part of Louisiana is often hard hit by hurricanes. The great storms sometimes follow the path of the river, leaving the countryside a shambles behind them. Twisted trees, abandoned house foundations—the storms leave their mark, and you will see this in Plaquemines Parish (next downriver) as well. But there is always some hardy soul ready to rebuild and try again.

In St. Bernard you will also see groves of pecan trees (with a pretty alley of trees on Highway 46 at Docville) and orange trees. There are acres planted in tomatoes here, too, and many New Orleans vegetables come from the St. Bernard gardens. Be sure and check at roadside stands for whatever is in season. At Delacroix, if a boat is in, you might even be able to buy some shrimp.

After seeing the St. Bernard museums you may wish to go back and follow Highway 39 down the river. Head toward Chalmette and take Highway 39 to Braithewaite. You will soon see signs for the St. Bernard State Park.

ST. BERNARD STATE PARK

This 350-acre state facility has picnic areas, a place to launch boats, overnight camping for fifty-one tents or vehicles (all hook-ups and showers available, inexpensive rates), and plenty of bird-watching and hiking opportunities. There are canals in the park and lookout points for viewing the Mississippi. There is even a swimming pool. Call 504-682-2101 for camping reservations. This state park is fairly new and uncrowded.

ENGLISH TURN

Fourteen miles below Chalmette there is a marker pointing out ENGLISH TURN. In 1699 Bienville, the French explorer, was sailing down the river when he met some English ships. Knowing he could not defeat them if they chose to take over his country's Louisiana claims, he decided to bluff: he told them there was a French fleet just up the river behind him. The English turned around.

If you continue past English Turn, you will come to a ferry landing a few miles on. If you like, you can cross the river and return to New Orleans via Highway 23. Or you can go back the way you came.

The roads down the river from New Orleans are not super-highways, but if you want to get out and walk on the levee or stop and look at the solitary brick chimney of a ruined sugar mill —well, you won't feel the least bit rushed or guilty about it.

ESPLANADE, BAYOU ST. JOHN, CITY PARK, AND THE LAKEFRONT

Bayou St. John flows out of Lake Pontchartrain. Though placid today, it was long used for navigation and commerce.

The Indians had a portage route between the Mississippi River and Bayou St. John. This path today is followed by Bayou Road, an extension of Governor Nicholls Street in the French Quarter. Bayou Road began at a fort on Rampart Street. The road went to Bayou St. John and also met Gentilly Boulevard, as it does today. Gentilly Boulevard was then the Spanish Trail, which went around the lower end of Lake Pontchartrain and included a boat trip and led to the Florida parishes on the other side of the lake.

The spot where Bienville planted a French cross to claim New Orleans was probably at Bayou St. John somewhere near Esplanade Avenue. After the city was founded there were many plantations and farms along the bayou. Later there was a Spanish fort built on an earlier fortification along the bayou and this gave the name to an amusement park, Spanish Fort. Both are gone, although some ruins of the fort remain.

Bayou St. John was connected to the city proper by canals. Now it is not navigable and the canals are filled. The bridges are so low over the bayou that boats cannot pass. But the houses on either side have a good view of the water and, if you don't want to go far, it's a nice place to sail or row.

The area on the shores of Lake Pontchartrain early became a summer resort. Besides the voodoo believers who had ceremonies at secret spots on the lakefront, there were restaurants and dance places. Milneburg, named for a Scotsman, Alexander Milne, was the best-known resort area. Even Oscar Wilde stayed there. The Milneburg Lighthouse is now much farther inland, because in land reclamation projects after 1920 the shoreline was extended to where the lighthouse stood.

Another path in the early days was on the Metairie ridge. This became Metairie Road and begins near the cemeteries at the end of Canal Street. Metairie Road was a farm-to-market road. Today it leads into Jefferson Parish and the beginnings of the suburbs.

All of this area—Bayou St. John, City Park, the lakefront, and Metairie—was at first farm or resort land and then the city grew to include it. As a result, you will find many old homes, some surrounded by a housing development from the 1890s or the 1950s. The reclamation of land from Lake Pontchartrain enabled developers to bring contemporary suburbia right to New Orleans' Victorian doorstep. However, there are those who prefer the winding roads and spacious lawns of the lakefront section to the cheek-by-jowl construction nearer the center of town.

TOUR ROUTE

Begin on Esplanade Avenue heading away from the river. When you pass Rampart Street the area to your left (between Esplanade Avenue and St. Philip Street) is called Tremé (tra-MAY). Dotted with restorations, this area of many nineteenth-century buildings was an early home for many free men and women of color and still has a substantial black population. Tremé extends to Claiborne Avenue (where you can see the black Indian maskers on Mardi Gras Day and on St. Joseph's Day, March 19). Lots of jazzmen and early rhythm and blues artists played first in clubs and halls here.

Esplanade extends from the river to City Park. It is a pleasant wide thoroughfare with a spacious neutral ground for most of its length. Almost every type of nineteenth-century residential building style can be found on Esplanade. Fortunately, many of the houses are built at an angle to face traffic (and building watchers) more directly.

Esplanade is the route many Creoles took when they moved from the French Quarter. You will still find many French surnames along its route.

Some addresses on Esplanade Avenue to look for:

1240 Esplanade Avenue. Built in 1854, this town house has a handsome service wing behind it, best seen from the side street.

1338–40 Esplanade Avenue. A brick Creole cottage, right on the banquette and built as a double house in 1852.

1418 Esplanade Avenue. A center-hall cottage dating from the 1850s. The center-hall style was a perennial favorite with Orleanians.

1519 Esplanade Avenue. This once elegant home dates from 1846. The expressway and adjoining gas station are pure twentieth century.

1707 Esplanade Avenue. An Italianate mansion dating from 1859. Most of the big Esplanade Avenue houses are cut up into apartments, but often the fine mantels and ceiling medallions remain.

2200 Esplanade Avenue. Gayarré Place is a tiny triangular park honoring Louisiana historian Charles Gayarré. Esplanade has several little triangles, showing where various annexations of city land left eccentric street alignments.

2306 Esplanade Avenue. This 1854 house was closely associated with the Musson family, relatives of French Impressionist Edgar Degas, and it is here that Degas stayed when painting his sister-in-law Estelle Musson's portrait (which can be seen at the New Orleans Museum of Art). It is said that Estelle's marriage was unhappy, and she lost her sight. But in the painting she seems very happy arranging flowers. Degas's "The Cotton Market in New Orleans" painting is probably his best-known New Orleans work.

2453 Esplanade Avenue. This mansard-roofed house dates from the 1870s.

2936 Esplanade Avenue. This 1880 Gothic villa presently houses Hare Krishna sect members.

Sauvage Street. The Fair Grounds Race Track is down this street. Take Ponce de Leon to your right, briefly, then turn on Sauvage. There are 101 days of racing, starting each Thanksgiving Day. The main entrance is on Gentilly Boulevard. The Fair Grounds is also where the annual Jazz and Heritage Festival holds forth.

Mystery Street. Right here is the **Whole Food Company,** surely one of New Orleans' pleasantest grocery stores. Lots of organic this and that, plus excellent cheeses and gourmet supplies. Right around this point on Esplanade is also where Grand Route St. John angles off to your left, if you wish a shorter version of this tour.

1438 Leda Street. This large apartment house just off Esplanade was designed by James Gallier, Jr., for a German merchant named Luling in 1865. It has lost two wings (which contained a kitchen and a bowling alley). As the home of the Louisiana Jockey Club in the 1870s, this was the site of a grand party for Grand Duke Alexis of Russia.

Just past Leda Street, **St. Louis Cemetery No. 3** begins. The cemetery gates on Esplanade date from the 1850s, when the cemetery was first opened. People buried there include Valcour Aime (1798–1867), the fabulously rich planter from up the river; Father Adrien Rouquette (1813–87), poet and missionary to the Choctaw Indians; and Thomy Lafon (1811–93), black philanthropist. A monument to architect James Gallier, Sr., and his wife was placed there by his son, James junior. The elder Galliers died in a shipwreck in 1866.

Esplanade Avenue reaches Bayou St. John just past the cemetery.

BAYOU ROAD

If you want to follow the old Indian portage route, you can go back to the 2200 block of Esplanade Avenue and veer right from Esplanade on Bayou Road at Galvez Street (Gayarré Place). The house at **2257 Bayou Road** dates from 1859. It was the Greek Consulate under its first owner, Nicholas Benachi. The house was acquired by Peter Torre in 1886 and left to the Louisiana Landmarks Society by his heirs in 1978. A young family has purchased and is restoring it. The house at 2275 Bayou Road dates from around 1800, with remodeling done in 1836.

Keep on Bayou Road, going straight until you cross North Broad Street. Bayou Road veers right and becomes Gentilly Boulevard. In about half a block turn left on Grand Route St. John.

Although not the fanciest house on this street, **2863 Grand Route St. John** is said to have been the final home of Josie Arlington (who kept a true "fancy house" in Storyville). The house was moved from Esplanade.

Grand Route St. John recrosses Esplanade around Mystery Street. Then it reaches Bayou St. John. The road along the bayou is Moss Street.

MOSS STREET

1300 Moss Street. This house, to your right, on the corner of Grand Route St. John and Moss Street, is sometimes called the Old Spanish Custom House because people think that goods being shipped via the bayou were checked or stored here. The land was granted as a farm in 1708. The house dates from around 1784 and is typical of the West Indian style—raised living quarters, gallery, sloping roof.

1342 Moss Street. Turn right on Moss Street and continue. This is now the rectory of Holy Rosary Church. The house dates from around 1834 and shows the influence of the Greek Revival.

1440 Moss Street. The **Pitot House,** named after James Pitot, the second mayor of New Orleans, who moved there in 1810. The house dates from about 1799. It used to stand where the modern

Catholic school is nearby. It was moved in 1964 and has been renovated by the Louisiana Landmarks Society.

Admission is $2.00 and the house is open Thursdays from 11 A.M. to 4 P.M. Call 482-0312 for other days. This eighteenth-century house is a good example of early settlers' ideas for a suitable suburban home. Rooms open to the galleries on front and rear; shutters and thick walls shut out the heat. Paint colors and the picket fence are authentic reproductions. This is a well-run house museum worth visiting.

924 Moss Street. This house is located four blocks on the other side of Grand Route St. John and dates from before 1800. It is in West Indian style.

City Park. Located on the far side of the bayou at the corner of Esplanade. The entrance is behind a large statue of Civil War General P. G. T. Beauregard. To reach the park, continue on Moss Street from the Pitot House (bayou on your left) and cross the bayou at Esplanade. There is a good book, *Historic City Park* by Sally and William Reeves, that can tell you about the park's interesting past.

Inside City Park is the **New Orleans Museum of Art,** the oak trees near which are sometimes called the Dueling Oaks because of the duels fought there. City Park was once a dairy farm. Now there are pleasant lagoons for boating and fishing, golf courses, tennis courts, a miniature train, fountains, statues, carnival rides for children, horses, picnic tables, rose gardens, and a bandstand. Altogether it is a pleasant place to spend an afternoon.

The artwork dating from the 1930s Works Progress Administration is especially notable—there are statues in the rose gardens, fountains, metal plaques on the City Park Stadium gates, and countless federal eagles watching over Roosevelt Mall.

The New Orleans Museum of Art houses a variety of paintings, sculpture, photographs, and other artworks. There are often traveling exhibitions and a full program of lectures, films, and classes. The Rosemonde E. and Emile N. Kuntz rooms display Federal and early Louisiana furniture and decorative art. The Kress Collection has sixteenth- and seventeenth-century

Italian painting. There is also an extensive photography collection (with remarkable early work by an Ursuline nun, Mother St. Croix), a Japanese collection, and the Billups glass collection. There's even a nice restaurant for lunch!

The museum is open Tuesday through Sunday from 10 A.M. to 5 P.M. Admission: adults $2.00, children $1.00, free for all on Thursday.

A children's museum, with lots of "hands-on" exhibits, will be located in the park at Roosevelt Mall and Marconi.

If you turn left at the Esplanade Park entrance of Wisner Boulevard, you will soon reach City Park Avenue—about a block. Turn right on City Park Avenue. Pass Delgado Community College. You will soon reach the cemeteries, at the corner of City Park and Canal Boulevard.

There are many cemeteries in this area. The largest one is **Metairie Cemetery.** To reach it, continue on City Park Avenue under the expressway overpass. You are now traveling on Metairie Road.

Metairie Cemetery used to be a racetrack. The cemetery dates from the 1870s. Many Confederate generals are buried there, including John B. Hood, Richard Taylor, and Fred N. Ogden. The remains of first Louisiana governor William C. C. Claiborne now lie here.

There are several interesting tombs. One belongs to a Mrs. Moriarty. There are four tremendous female statues on top of it, supposedly Faith, Hope, and Charity, and Mrs. Moriarty. Also there is a tomb showing a young woman knocking on a door. It first belonged to a madam, Josie Arlington Duebler, and was supposed to represent her being turned away from her parents' door. At one time a red traffic light flashed attractively over this tomb.

Metairie Cemetery has trail markers for a drive through, and a very good book, *Metairie Cemetery, An Historical Memoire* by Henri Gandolfo, will tell you more about it. Enter from the I-10 service road and get a Heritage Trail folder from the information office.

In all the cemeteries in this area are large society tombs, for everyone from Greeks to the Chinese and including Odd Fellows, volunteer firemen, and veterans.

Some of the other cemeteries near Metairie Cemetery are Cypress Grove, Firemen's Cemetery, St. Patrick's, Holt Cemetery, Greenwood, and Congregation Gates of Prayer.

Bottinelli Place. This one-block street runs off Canal Street just before City Park Avenue in between cemeteries. Bottinelli Place's builder, Theodore Bottinelli, used cobblestones, bricks, and pieces of torn-down buildings in an eccentric but pleasing complex. The towers came from a synagogue that used to stand near Lee Circle.

Longue Vue Gardens, 7 Bamboo Road. Open Tuesday through Friday from 10 A.M. to 4:30 P.M. and weekends from 1 P.M. to 5 P.M. Admission is $5.00 and includes the house. Inside the gardens are beautifully planted walkways with fountains. There is even a wild garden with native iris. The view of the golf course of the New Orleans Country Club is spectacular. There are regular programs of interest to gardeners and also performances of dance and music on the lawns.

Longue Vue House was completed in the 1940s for the late Mr. and Mrs. Edgar B. Stern. The lavish home serves as a museum of decorative arts—besides the best in interior design of the 1930s and 1940s, the art, fine furniture, porcelain, and pottery are well worth a visit. There are changing exhibits as well, and the guides are factual and entertaining.

Lake Pontchartrain has a scenic route, Lakeshore Drive, along its shore. To reach it, return on Metairie Road to the Pontchartrain Expressway and get on the expressway going left. Keep going on Pontchartrain Boulevard.

West End is a parklike area on Lake Pontchartrain, with seafood restaurants, the New Orleans Marina, and the Southern and New Orleans yacht clubs. Turn left at Lake Avenue to reach West End. Orpheum Avenue—right next to Bruning's Restaurant—is now a footbridge leading to Bucktown, which has other seafood spots and fishing camps.

At West End you can take North Roadway left to Breakwater Drive. There is a boat launch, fishing pier, and if you follow the road curving right to "the point" you'll be at a favorite teenage "parking" spot. Some of the two-story boathouses have very elaborate interiors, and you will see several yachts. Then return to Pontchartrain Boulevard.

Lakeshore Drive will veer right from Pontchartrain Boulevard when you get to the shore of the lake.

There is a seawall, picnic tables, and benches all along the lakefront. The fishing is not good, but you can at least catch something.

The Mardi Gras Fountain will appear on your right in about a mile. The fountain shoots up water and is lit in the Mardi Gras colors, purple, green, and gold. Around the base are plaques for all the Mardi Gras krewes. This is a favorite spot during summer evenings. There are services here at Easter and a nativity scene at Christmas. The Orleans Parish Levee Board keeps up the lakefront and the fountains.

By continuing along Lakeshore Drive you will pass the modern campus of the **University of New Orleans.**

Lakeshore Drive will finally take you on a bridge over the Industrial Canal, and just past that is New Orleans Lakefront Airport, used for charter and private planes.

St. Roch Campo Santo is not easy to reach, but if you are interested, you will find it at St. Roch Avenue and North Roman Street. Take Franklin Avenue from Lakeshore Drive—Franklin reaches the lake between Pontchartrain Beach and the airport—and turn right, much later, on North Roman Street or Derbigny Street.

St. Roch is the work of one man, a priest, Father Thevis. He built a chapel to St. Roch after the saint helped save his congregation in an 1868 yellow fever epidemic. Today the chapel still stands, in the middle of the cemetery. On the right of the altar is the "ex-voto" room with plaster and plastic effigies of the various limbs St. Roch has helped to heal, along with little stone plaques reading THANKS or MERCI. Stations of the Cross are around the cemetery walls. There are various long local legends about how proper praying at St. Roch's will help unmarried maidens find husbands.

To return to the French Quarter take St. Roch Avenue—turn left, outside the cemetery—to St. Claude Avenue and turn right. St. Claude will become Rampart Street, which will cross Esplanade Avenue.

PLANTATION TOUR

Take a day, or a weekend, and get into plantation country.

Our tour suggests homes you can tour, and can be taken in stages. I-10 runs between New Orleans and Baton Rouge in less than two hours. Highway 61, Airline Highway, covers the same distance.

Best of all is a drive along River Road. It is possible to follow the levee to Baton Rouge from New Orleans on the East Bank. If you have time, it's well worth it. However, sections of this drive may be closed. If the river is high, the Bonnet Carré Spillway may be filled with water. Above the Sunshine Bridge the road may be gravel or it may be under construction. If you get lost, just take the next numbered highway away from the river and you'll reach Airline Highway or I-10.

If you take this East Bank route, allow a full day. You can spend the night in Baton Rouge or take the I-10 back to town. If you start early, you can tour East Bank homes, cross the river at White Castle, see Nottoway and Oak Alley, and get back after dark.

The highways that run nearest the Mississippi River on both sides are called River Road. The reason the houses are there is because once the river *was* the road. Transportation by water was the quickest way to get crops to market, and the plantation homes were built by farmers, people who depended on crops in a big way. The plantations along Bayou Lafourche shipped goods via the bayou to the river, for at that time the bayou was navigable and was not dammed at Donaldsonville. Bayous are usually sluggish streams and can be either salt or fresh. The word can be pronounced by-you or by-uh.

Thinking that everyone in Louisiana lived in a plantation home before the Civil War is like thinking that everyone in Texas has an oil well. Plantation homes are as elaborate as their owners could afford; some are rather simple. Almost all date from before 1865, because with the liberation of the slaves and the economic and political problems of the postwar period, the economy that produced these mansions crumbled.

The plantation owners all had personalities, but all were united in that they depended on large-scale farming before mechanization. This meant they had to have lots of workers— slaves at that time. It also meant that they were gamblers. An early freeze or a hurricane could ruin a sugarcane crop; and too many bad years could lead to bankruptcy.

Because they lived on their land, the plantation owners were far from town amusements. This made them ready to spend money on their houses and gardens and furnishings. There was not much else handy to spend it on. Also, it created a social structure that depended on long, long visits and houseguests. Families were larger in those days, and each plantation had to be self-sufficient. You could not run to the neighborhood store for supplies. You ordered in advance, or you made things yourself. All the workers had to be fed and housed and clothed. The larger plantations were like small factory towns. In fact, the sugar mills that processed the cane were very much like factories.

The main crop in the area around New Orleans was sugarcane. The earliest crop was indigo, but when sugar was granulated from sugarcane syrup around 1795, it became commercially feasible to plant cane. Cotton grew better in higher land than in land near the river. Rice became a major crop later and was suited to even wetter land than cane.

Today there are only a few plantation homes that still have working farms. Some houses fell into decay as crops failed and the land was sold to factories. Oil refineries, chemical plants, large sugar refineries, shipbuilding works, and other industries are now located on old plantation land on the river. Some houses burned, too far from city fire departments for aid, and some houses were swallowed by the river as it changed its path over the years. Some were torn down. Families that could not afford the upkeep let the house die from neglect.

None of the houses open for tours is still owned by the family that built it. All have been renovated, at least to the extent of electricity and plumbing. (Only a handful of Louisiana plantations had real bathrooms—only chamber pots and privies.)

People who buy and restore plantation homes love their houses and give them all the care they can afford. Some bring in family heirloom furnishings. All of them try to present the house in its best light, and some of the guided tours through the houses are entertaining, not only for the information but also because they bring you in contact with nice people you might otherwise not have met.

There were many things wrong with plantation life. But the houses and all that they stood for are part of the past, and we are fortunate to be able to step back in time and see them, and imagine what it was like to live there when the house was new, and the land was rich, and the plantation owners could live a little like kings.

The plantation tour will take you through country Louisiana. Some is industrial, some is tacky, some is just plain dirty. But you can always drive up on the levee and look at the river, and the breeze is pleasant even in summer. And around the bend in the road there might be a mansion.

A nice time to drive up River Road is just before Christmas. All along the levee you will see constructions of wood, railroad ties, and cast-off tires. They are for the Christmas bonfires, which can be seen blazing for miles on Christmas Eve, a Latin custom of lighting the way for the Christ Child, perhaps. However, like everything else in Louisiana, the old custom changes with the times. You may see a bonfire stack with a big sign painted on it saying GO L.S.U. TIGERS. Every year there are letters to the editor about the bonfires causing pollution. Given the vast numbers of petroleum and chemical plants along River Road, a few bonfires can't make much difference. In deference to complaints, they did quit burning tires.

So pack a picnic lunch or prepare to eat some gumbo at a local café. Listen to the gentle French accent of the people you meet. Perhaps their great-grandfather was an Acadian French refugee and they are Cajuns. Remember that you are not in a big city now, and try to dress and act accordingly. Good manners and conservative behavior will be rewarded with friendliness. As you drive under moss-hung trees or see the tops of the willows waving near the riverbank, you will begin to get an idea of what Louisiana is really like.

TOUR ROUTE

Begin at the corner of St. Charles and Carrollton avenues, about eighty blocks up St. Charles from Canal Street (end of uptown tour). Mileage is clocked from here. From St. Charles keep going straight. On your left you will see a hill, the levee of the Mississippi River. The road will veer right, along a railroad track for about a mile. Then make a sharp left turn to cross the railroad track and continue along with the levee on your left. This is the beginning of River Road. Remember, mileage via River Road may be longer than via Highway 61 or I-10.

Carrollton at St. Charles is where there was once a Tchoupitoulas Indian camp. There are, of course, not as many Indians in Louisiana as there were when the French arrived. Some tribes died out; some Eastern tribes moved in. In the state today are Choctaws (in Lacombe, St. Tammany Parish, and in LaSalle Parish), Chitimacha (around Charenton), Coushatta (around Elton), Tunica-Biloxi (around Marksville), and Houmas (in Jefferson, Terrebonne, and Lafourche parishes). The most noted Indian handcrafts today are baskets by the Chitimacha, Coushatta, and Choctaw. You will find them in museum shops.

Camp Parapet, 2 miles. The powder magazine under an earth mound at Causeway Boulevard and River Road is the only Civil War military structure in New Orleans. The Federal forces took this over and had a camp here—a rather damp one, judging from letters. American forces for the Battle of New Orleans also had a camp here.

Magnolia School, 3 miles. The raised house at River Road and Central Avenue belonged to the de la Barre family and is now a school. It was built in 1857 and originally was called Whitehall. All along this route you will see these former farmhouses, now part of suburbia.

Just past the Huey P. Long Bridge is the site of Elmwood. This home was probably built around 1800 but has burned. It may be rebuilt. Archaeological digs on the site have proved it to be dated later than was once thought. Surprisingly, old privies make good digs—all the broken china, toys, and trash were thrown in and make interesting excavations.

Kenner, 10.5 miles. River Road takes you away from the levee and to Jefferson Highway. Follow this to Williams Boulevard, where the road turns right. Don't turn. Go on straight one block to the corner of Third and Minor streets.

The **Kenner City Museum,** 1922 Third Street, was the home of Sheriff Frank Clancy—who served from 1928 to 1956. Besides Clancy memorabilia there are displays on the Kenner family plantation, which was once near here. Kenner was the site of the first World Heavyweight Championship, a forty-four-minute, ten-round bareknuckle bout on May 10, 1870. Jem Mace defeated Tom Allen for the title. Kenner also has one of only three American match factories. Although it is now a suburban community (with a great affinity for politics), Kenner once was an area of small farms, after the breakup of the large plantations. The museum is open daily from 10 A.M. to 4 P.M. There is a fee. Call Kenner City Hall, 468-7200, to arrange group tours.

Kenner is revitalizing this area, to be called Rivertown, with a railroad museum, excursion trains, shops, a river overlook, amusement rides, and a docked steamboat with a theater.

Destrehan, 19 miles (504-764-9315). Destrehan is the name of a town as well as a plantation house. (All houses on this bank of the river are on your right.) The house was built in the 1780s

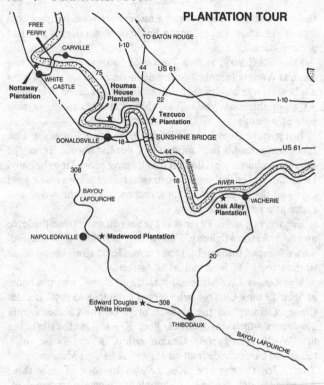

PLANTATION TOUR

and wings were added later and it was remodeled. It is open (for admission) daily from 10 A.M. to 4 P.M. Destrehan is being restored by a nonprofit group, and your contribution will help. They also hold festivals and fairs.

Destrehan Manor is somewhat bare of furniture, but a tour will give you some facts about plantation architecture.

Basically, this type of construction was governed by several factors: materials available, climate, and money. Louisiana's climate made thick walls necessary and galleries with shade a

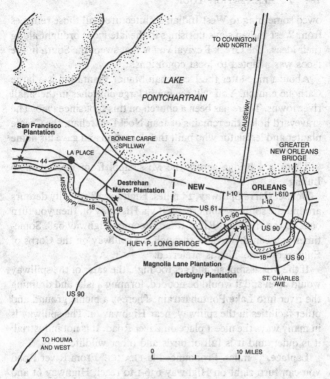

necessity. Materials included cypress wood—very hard and lasting and not well liked by termites—a cement mix made of local clays and shells and sometimes mixed with animal hair or other fiber, and locally made bricks. The bricks were usually plastered over to make them longer-wearing. Early houses had a first floor designed to keep the living quarters above water in case of flood. This also helped cool the house. Usually the house had a center hall for ventilation, a roof that sloped over the galleries, and a separate kitchen, because of the danger of fire. This early style owed something to West Indian architecture—all those refugees from West Indian slave uprisings in the late 1700s brought along their ideas. The Greek Revival vogue that swept the South in the 1800s was adapted to local conditions.

About 1 mile after the Destrehan Manor Plantation is a large Catholic church. You will see many large churches in the small river towns. There has been a church on this spot since 1740. The graveyard holds the remains of Jean Noël Destrehan, the Creole planter and legislator who built the plantation and gave his name to the town.

There is a bridge across the Mississippi from Destrehan to Luling.

Bonnet Carré Spillway, 25 miles. Highway 48 actually detours around the spillway and crosses it via Highway 61, then you turn back to the river and River Road becomes Highway 628. Sometimes you can drive right through the spillway on the Corps of Engineers road. This is preferred.

If the Mississippi should get too high, the gates of the spillway would open and it would be flooded, forming a lake and draining the river into Lake Pontchartrain. There is a picnic ground and other facilities in the spillway, near Highway 61. The spillway is in many ways the nicest place on River Road. It is not industrial; it is quiet; and it is full of birds and other wildlife.

Laplace, 33 miles. Pronounced la-PLAHCE. From River Road you can turn right on Highway 636-1 to reach Highway 61 and **Rousselle's Restaurant** and the **Airline Motors Restaurant** for lunch. Try the andouille (ahn-DEW-ee) sausage gumbo. Laplace now calls itself the Andouille Capital of the World, and they celebrate with a festival in the fall. Besides the heavy industry —those refineries and factories you've been passing—Laplace has many small farms and Victorian houses. After Laplace River Road is Highway 44. Return from lunch the way you went and continue on Highway 44.

Reserve, 37 miles. There is a ferry from this little town across the river to Edgard. You will also see a large sugar refinery here. If you travel this area in late fall, you will see the cane, piled in trucks, going to various sugar mills for grinding.

Earlier in the year you will see it in the fields, waving and green like big grass. At grinding time the air smells vaguely like molasses. Sugarcane is ground and the juice extracted and then boiled. Some becomes granulated sugar; some makes molasses for eating or feeding cattle. One heavy syrup is called La Cuite, and you dip spoons of it in pecans to eat. Before there were big mills and refineries, people used to boil the juice in big open black kettles. Now some people make fish ponds out of the kettles.

San Francisco, 42 miles (504-535-2341). This house is open daily from 10 A.M. to 4 P.M. The architecture could be called Steamboat Gothic, also the name of a novel by Frances Parkinson Keyes (rhymes with sighs) in which the house figures. The house dates from 1854. The name comes from *saint-frusquin,* a French phrase meaning roughly "the whole kit and kaboodle," which sounds somewhat like "San Francisco," and probably refers to what it cost the owner. The house is Victorian. The gallery is loaded with lacy trim. Inside are wall and ceiling paintings by Dominic Canova, the man who painted St. Louis Cathedral. When these houses were built, the levee was not so high, and they all had nice views of the river. Also, they were farther back from the water, which has moved sideways since then.

San Francisco is a scholarly restoration. Furniture and colors, even the knickknacks, are exact as to date. The guides ("docents" is a better word—more academic) are well informed. One change in plantation tours these days is the general upgrading of the guides, and San Francisco is a good example of the best kind.

Lutcher, 49 miles. There is a ferry from here across to Vacherie.

Manresa, 58 miles. Manresa is in Convent (called that because there used to be a girls' school here run by nuns of the Order of the Sacred Heart). Manresa is now a retreat house run by the Jesuits, for men only. Most of the buildings date from the 1830s. They were built as Jefferson College, a nonsectarian college for young men. The buildings are brick with Doric columns. If the gates are open, you may drive through. On retreats no one talks.

Surely this is one of the pleasantest places on earth to be quiet in. (However, they always post L.S.U. and Tulane scores for silent fans.)

Also in Convent is **St. Michael's Church.** Behind it is a monument to Valcour Aime, a famous Creole sugar planter of the early 1800s. He was extremely rich, and his plantation and gardens—on the other side of the river—were likened to Versailles. The house and gardens no longer exist. When his only son died, Valcour Aime stopped all his sugar experimentation and led a sheltered life.

About a mile from the church was the site of Uncle Sam Plantation, an immense complete group of plantation house and outbuildings that was swallowed by the Mississippi. All along River Road are historic markers with information about the locals. Be sure and read them. Some houses that are not open have historic markers.

Near Convent on River Road is **Hymel's Restaurant,** serving very good andouille gumbo, boiled seafood, raw oysters, and cold beer. In the grocery next door you can get andouille sausage to take home. There is another restaurant, the **Cabin,** at the junction of Highway 44 and Highway 22, a few miles on. Tour buses often stop here.

Sunshine Bridge, 69 miles. This bridge is a monument to Louisiana politics, said to run from cane field to cane field and named for a famous Louisiana governor's favorite song. Jimmie Davis, the governor, actually wrote "You Are My Sunshine."

Texcuco, 70 miles (504-562-3929). Stay on Highway 44 to see Texcuco.

Texcuco dates from the 1850s and is a raised cottage with iron gallery railings. The house is open Monday through Saturday from 10 A.M. to 4 P.M. and Sunday from 1 P.M. to 4 P.M. There is a gift shop and ten cabins and guesthouses for rent.

The area along the river is sometimes referred to by natives as "the coast." You hear this most often about the area below New Orleans on the West Bank, which is called the "lower coast." Many German settlers had farms along the river above New Orleans, and this was called the German Coast. The Germans quickly went native, however. The Hymel (of the restaurant) is pronounced HEE-mell or EE-mell. What it used to be was "Himmel," a perfectly good German name. The town of Des Allemands (dez-AHL-mons) means "Germans" in French.

Houmas House, 72 miles (504-473-4841 or New Orleans 522-2262). River Road becomes gravel shortly after the Sunshine Bridge. The gravel road is Highway 942. Houmas House is open daily (for admission) from 10 A.M. to 5 P.M. November through January it closes at 4 P.M. All these houses will close on Christmas Day, New Year's Day, and Thanksgiving Day. Call and ask if you are in doubt.

Houmas House—named for the Houma Indians who used to have a village here but often called Burnside, for the small town here now—is a proper-looking plantation house, white and columned.

The big house dates from about 1840. The rear wing—connected to the big house by a sort of enclosed driveway—dates from before 1800. The house was lovingly restored by the late Dr. George Crozat, himself from an old Louisiana family. The antiques are rare; the circular staircase is worth staring up at; the old kitchen in the rear has ancient utensils; and there are some lovely outbuildings: a garçonnière (gar-sun-YAIR) and a pigeonnière (pee-zhun-YAIR). The pigeonnière was for raising pigeons. The garçonnière was for raising young men, the sons of the family who were old enough to want a little privacy, or for guests.

There is a very good gift shop at Houmas House. Sometimes tours are scheduled to stop here in the evening, or for lunch in one of the outbuildings. If San Francisco is like a museum, Houmas House is like a grand home.

The gardens of Houmas House have also been restored. There is a formal garden behind the kitchen. The house has a belvedere on top for river gazing. The levee blocks the view from the first floor.

Houmas House was in the movie *Hush, Hush, Sweet Charlotte.*

Bocage, 75 miles. A square house, brick lower floor, eight columns across the front. Bocage dates to 1800 but was remodeled in the 1840s. Not usually open to visitors.

Hermitage, 76 miles. Hermitage was named for Andrew Jackson's home. Another square house, this time of brick. Surrounded by columns with galleries. The house dates from around 1810 but was remodeled later. Not usually open to visitors.

Belle Helène, 84 miles. It may be possible to get to Belle Helène via River Road. If the road is out, you'll have to detour. Take Highway 44 to I-10, go west, exit for Geismar on Highway 30, take Highway 73 to River Road (Highway 75), and turn left toward Darrow.

Ashland was the original name of Belle Helène. It was built in 1841 by Duncan Kenner, a wealthy financier and horse breeder. The house is open daily (for admission) from 9 A.M. to 4 P.M. and is in poor condition, "some furnished and some tore up," according to the caretaker. The Clint Eastwood movie *The Beguiled* was made here, and some strange Hollywood decorating remains. There is no floor on the first level—it was ransacked in the 1940s, long before the movie. Until something is done to Belle Helène, this will be a very odd tour stop. There are many large dogs on the grounds.

Carville, 92 miles. Here is a federal hospital for Hansen's disease, which used to be called leprosy. You can drive through the grounds, or walking tours are offered, 504-642-7771. The administration building was Indian Camp plantation house, built in 1858.

If you take the ferry across the river here to White Castle, you will see a strange little pier and building far out in the water. This is where supplies were left for the hospital.

The view from the ferry at this point is worth crossing for.

St. Gabriel, 95 miles. St. Gabriel's church land was granted by the Spanish government in 1774. The church building has had much alteration, but the turned wooden columns and painted ceiling are worth a look.

It's not often open, but you can see in the windows.

From St. Gabriel you can follow the levee on a poor road, or take Highway 30 into Baton Rouge, about 25 miles. Highway 30 becomes Nicholson Drive and takes you by the Louisiana State University campus.

THE WEST BANK

River Road is much the same on either side: factories, chemical plants, nature, poverty, and plantation houses. If you take the ferry across at Carville, you will be at White Castle. Take Highway 1 north toward Plaquemine. Nottoway is just outside of White Castle; you will see direction signs.

To reach Nottoway from New Orleans (65 miles), take I-10 West and exit at Highway 22. Take Highway 70 and follow the signs and cross the Sunshine Bridge. Take Highway 1 to White Castle and Nottoway.

Nottoway (504-545-2730). Nottoway is open daily (for admission) from 9 A.M. to 5 P.M. This home was built for John Hampden Randolph of Virginia in 1857. Henry Howard was the architect. It is named for a Virginia county. The most notable thing about Nottoway is the white ballroom: even the floor is white. This is a very large house, part of which is taken up by a restaurant, a gift shop, and even rooms available for the night. The grounds have not been restored. The house can also be rented for weddings and parties.

If you take Highway 1 toward Plaquemine, you will see a sign directing you to St. Louis Plantation in about 10 miles.

This 1850 galleried-center-hall home has been owned by the Gay family since it was built. If you happen to visit between May and November of 1984 (when the World's Fair is open in New Orleans), you can tour the house or even the working sugar plantation (for admission). It will be well worth the time.

Oak Alley (504-265-2151 or New Orleans 523-4351). From White Castle take Highway 1 to Donaldsonville, 22 miles. Then follow Highway 18 toward Vacherie. In about 19 miles you will reach Oak Alley. (From New Orleans it's about 60 miles.) Oak Alley is open daily from 9 A.M. to 5 P.M. (and a little later in summer). There is a restaurant and cabins for rent. Oak Alley has been named a national historic landmark.

When you get there, park on the other side of the highway and climb the levee to see the oaks. Looking, from here, will cost you nothing, but the avenue of oak trees with the pink-galleried house at the end is perhaps one of the prettiest residential views in the country.

Oak Alley dates from the late 1830s. Since then it has had its ups and downs. The river has gotten closer. Until Mr. and Mrs. Jefferson D. Hardin of New Orleans took over and made necessary repairs in 1914, the house had been open to natural destruction. The late Mr. and Mrs. Andrew Stewart acquired the house in 1926, and Armstrong and Koch of New Orleans, architects, can claim the present restoration.

Inside remains as the Stewarts left it. Two longtime family retainers give tours. The interior is not as grand as the exterior. There are some gardens for strolling (and many, many mosquitoes).

As you drive along River Road, you will see many old plantation homes in varying states of repair. Some even sport tin roofs. The levee will be on your left and the houses on your right.

Between Vacherie and Oak Alley you will see two homes, St. Joseph and Felicity, both of which were built by the wealthy planter Valcour Aime for daughters as wedding presents. They are columned, with dormer windows and center halls. The site of Valcour Aime's own plantation is pointed out by a marker. Oak Alley was his brother-in-law's home.

Evergreen. Private, not open to visitors. You can see Evergreen, gleaming white behind its massive iron gates, from the highway. Everything here is Greek Revival, even the privy. The house dates from 1840, and the front entrance, via the stairs, is on the second floor. About 15 miles below Evergreen was the site of the Locke-Breaux oak, an immense tree that was named president of the Louisiana Live Oak Society because of its girth.

Tchoupitoulas Plantation Restaurant (504-436-1277). Some 35 miles below Evergreen lies Tchoupitoulas (chop-uh-TOO-lus), now a restaurant. Open Monday through Saturday from 11 A.M. to 10 P.M. The food is good and the surroundings pleasant. One woman manager of the restaurant had a somewhat spicy past, and at one time there was a fantastic collection of badly painted buxom nudes in a hall and office—never on regular display. There are some outbuildings and attractive grounds.

Avondale Shipyards, a large, busy concern, is 2 miles below Tchoupitoulas. A mile later you will come to a crossroads with Highway 90. You can return to New Orleans, head on for the West, or continue on Highway 18.

Seven Oaks. In 5 miles you will reach the site where Seven Oaks once stood behind an oil station at the junction of Highway 18 and Highway 541, just downriver from the Huey P. Long Bridge. Seven Oaks dated from 1830 and was once a proud and fine house. It was neglected too long and finally suffered what is called "demolition by neglect." Too many houses have had this fate, so be aware that you are enjoying an endangered species when plantation-watching. Turn left on Highway 541, now River Road. The levee will be on your right and the houses on your left.

SHORT PLANTATION TOUR

If you only have an afternoon and want to see some country, take the Greater New Orleans Bridge over the Mississippi River and stay on Highway 90, the West Bank Expressway. You will veer right and head west. Keep going—even under the Harvey Tunnel—until you can make a right turn on Highway 18. Highway 18 will go to the river. Veer left and go upriver. At the intersection of Highway 18 and Highway 541, the Seven Oaks site, take Highway 541 upriver—veer right—and continue with the rest of this tour. The short plantation tour involves only about 30 miles of driving in all.

Derbigny Plantation. The Derbigny Plantation is 2 miles from the Seven Oaks site on Highway 541. It dates from around 1840. It is a simple Louisiana raised cottage, similar to some in the

Garden District. Derbigny is a typical small plantation house, but it has all the usual details: thick cypress flooring, wavy glass in the original windowpanes, tall windows for walking out on the front gallery, and a center hall with symmetrical rooms on either side—in this case, two on either side. Not open for tours at present.

Magnolia Lane. Magnolia Lane, just past Derbigny, dates back to 1784. You can see signs of its age in the first story of brick and plaster with a carriage entrance underneath in the rear.

Magnolia Lane was, for years, a nursery. Strawberries were first cultivated in Louisiana here, and the magnolia trees of Magnolia Lane have reforested many barren lawns. Not presently open.

After Magnolia Lane keep on Highway 541. In 3 miles you will get back on Highway 18. Turn left and within 1 mile you will get to Highway 90. Turn right again to go over the bridge. Stay on Highway 90, which will turn right on the other side of the river and go toward New Orleans. It is called Jefferson Highway here. When it leaves Jefferson Parish and enters Orleans Parish—about 5 miles—it becomes Claiborne Avenue. You will soon come to the intersection of Claiborne and Carrollton avenues. If you turn right on Carrollton, you'll get to the corner of Carrollton and St. Charles avenues, where the River Road plantation tour began.

BAYOU LAFOURCHE

This area of plantation homes can be reached by starting at Donaldsonville (about 60 miles from New Orleans, take I-10 West, exit at Highway 22, take Highway 70 and cross the Sunshine Bridge). At the foot of the bridge on the West Bank is a restaurant, **Lafitte's Landing,** in a house dating from around 1800.

The Sunshine Bridge is called that because it was a project of Louisiana governor James H. Davis, who wrote the song "You Are My Sunshine."

This part of Louisiana is on the edge of "Cajun Country."

The Cajuns, or Acadians, are those descendants of the French colonists driven from Nova Scotia by the English in the late 1700s. Many came to Louisiana. Remember Longfellow's *Evangeline*? The Cajun accent is lilting and rather French, with French words in the Cajun French dialect thrown in. There are lots of Cajun jokes, mostly about Cajun cunning or love for wine and women. There are lots of Cajuns, still speaking French. The Cajun area is around Lafayette, St. Martinville, down to the Gulf, and up to around Alexandria. Bayou Lafourche will take you into Cajun territory for a sampling of good scenery, good people, and good food.

At Donaldsonville take Highway 308, along Bayou Lafourche (lah-FOORSH). On the other side of the bayou is Highway 1, which runs right with Highway 308 all along the bayou. Highway 308 is a little quieter and more rustic, but there are bridges at intervals crossing the bayou, so you can take one road or the other. For this tour we will stay on Highway 308.

Many of the plantations along Bayou Lafourche were built by settlers from the Carolinas and Virginia. They were often Protestants—Episcopalians—but they were accepted by their Roman Catholic neighbors. One extensive family from the Carolinas, the Pugh (pew) family, owned numbers of plantations in this area. This gave rise to a little ecclesiastical humor: Why is Bayou Lafourche like a church? Because there are Pughs on both sides of it.

The earliest serious settlers of this area were Spanish, many from the Canary Islands. Now, however, everyone native to this part of Louisiana has the same slight French accent.

Belle Alliance. This plantation is about 7 miles from Donaldsonville on the Highway 308 side of the bayou. It dates from the 1840s. The side porches of the second-story living quarters have frilly ironwork supporting their roofs. There are square columns across the front. Private, not open to visitors.

Napoleonville. Take the bridge over the bayou at Napoleonville (in about 8 miles) and turn right. In one block you will find

Christ Episcopal Church across the street from the bayou. This ivy-covered red-brick church dates from about 1853 and is surprisingly English in character. A look into the cemetery will demonstrate how Anglo-Saxon the congregation was.

Drive around Napoleonville. If you like, you could take Highway 410 about 10 miles to Lake Verret for the fishing and scenery. Also, almost next to Christ Church is a bakery where you can buy some french bread. Then retrace your route one block from the church back to the bridge and turn left over the bridge to Highway 308 again.

Madewood (504-369-7151 or New Orleans 524-1988). Open daily (for admission) from 10 A.M. to 5 P.M. When you are across the bridge, turn right on Highway 308 and keep the bayou on your right side. In 2 miles you will come to Madewood. (If you come from New Orleans it's 75 miles.) The house bears that name because the wood to build it came from the land and was trimmed on the place. In many ways plantations are amazing. Just a look at the tremendous beams in the attic at Madewood —fastened and joined without nails—makes you admire the workmen.

Madewood was built by Colonel Thomas Pugh. For years he chose the cypress and cut the timbers, made the bricks and planned. Then, when construction was finished, he did not live long to enjoy his house. His wife, Eliza, took over and even managed to keep the house unharmed during Union occupation in the Civil War.

The house is two-storied, with white columns across the front and with two side wings. The old kitchen has some beautiful antiques, and the rest of the house has been furnished in period furniture by the Marshall family, which now owns Madewood. Other things to see include the staircase, the built-in closets—a rarity for that time—and the little cemetery.

Madewood has an annual Arts Festival in April, with opera, gospel music, and all manner of dance and entertainment. At Christmastime there is a Christmas Heritage Celebration with a grand dinner. Madewood has original fund-raising events. Call and see if any are scheduled during your trip.

One nice thing plantation houses have nowadays is seasonal decorating. Add that to the bonfires (also on Bayou Lafourche), and late December becomes a good time for touring.

After seeing Madewood, proceed down the bayou 12 miles to a bridge. Cross to Highway 1 and turn right. Proceed 1 mile to the Edward Douglass White House, on your left across from the bayou.

Edward Douglass White House. Open to visitors (for admission). Picnic tables on grounds. Edward Douglass White, Jr., was born in 1845 and was named to the U.S. Supreme Court in 1894. He was Chief Justice from 1910 till his death in 1921. This raised cottage, the White family home, has a museum to the Chief Justice and dates to around 1800 or a little earlier.

After visiting the Edward Douglass White House return on Highway 1—this side of the bayou—6 miles to Thibodaux, retracing 1 mile of your route.

Thibodaux. Thibodaux is the final test of your Louisiana pronunciations. Actually, you pronounce it TIB-uh-DOE. If you hear someone saying THIGH-bo-DACKS, you will be able to correct him and endear yourself to Louisiana citizens, who are far too accustomed to having their names mispronounced.

Another thing to remember: don't expect Cajuns to understand your French, whether it's fluent Parisian or leftover high school. Cajun French is a patois (pat-TWAH), or dialect. Some words go back to the French spoken in France in the 1600s. Some words are Spanish, Indian, or just American. Of course, there are a lot of people around who speak a pure French, too. But for run-of-the-mill bourré (boo-RAY) games—a very tough gambling game which you are advised to avoid—Cajun French suffices. You will be able to hear it on your radio, and maybe even some Cajun music, which sounds like country and western, only with French words and more fiddles and concertinas.

French Louisiana has its own language, music, customs,

superstitions, and cuisine. It takes a determined people to survive the twentieth century with a culture that intact.

Nicholls State University is in Thibodaux, and there are motels and restaurants. (Thibodaux is about 47 miles from New Orleans, via Highway 90 West and Highway 1.)

If you continue south on Highway 308 from Thibodaux, you will reach **Laurel Valley Plantation,** off the highway on Parish Road 33. This is the largest surviving nineteenth-century sugar plantation complex in the country. Tours for groups can be arranged by calling 504-446-8111.

When you return to New Orleans, be sure you drive carefully: Louisiana drivers are creative, to say the least.

Keep your eye open for festivals and fairs—that's a good way to get some home cooking, hear some good music, and meet new people. *"Laissez les bons temps rouler!"* as they say—in English that's "Let the good times roll!"

BATON ROUGE

New Orleanians have always thought of Baton Rouge as either the place where politicians go when they leave town, or that spot up the river where you have to go to see the L.S.U. Tigers play home games.

Although it's only 70 miles away, Baton Rouge is different from New Orleans. It's not very French. Baton Rouge seems more Southern, more like a small town. Actually it wasn't even part of the Louisiana Purchase.

The Florida Parishes of Louisiana, where Baton Rouge lies, form the tip of the state's boot shape. This was part of West Florida under the Spanish and English.

The name "Baton Rouge" means "red stick" and comes from a reddened tree trunk that the Houma and Bayou Goula Indians erected to make their boundary line. It was visible from the river to early French explorers.

In 1719 the French built a fort here. From 1763 to 1779 it was English, then it was Spanish until 1810, when the American-born residents threw out the Spanish and founded the Republic of West Florida. The Louisiana governor quickly claimed the territory, and it was part of the state when Louisiana joined the Union in 1812. Baton Rouge became the state capital in 1849.

Baton Rouge today has so many things to see and do that it's worth a trip up the river—even out of the football season and when the legislature isn't in session. The Louisiana Office of Tourism is located here, and there's a toll-free number out of state: 800-535-8388. There is an information desk on the main floor of the Louisiana State Capitol Building (which you can see from the interstate). Stop there and get a city map, brochures, and advice. Meanwhile, here are some of the bonuses of a trip to Baton Rouge:

Rural Life Museum. Located just off the Essen Lane exit from I-10 coming in from New Orleans, 4560 Essen Lane. Open weekdays from 8:30 A.M. to noon and from 1 P.M. to 4 P.M. Phone 504-766-8241. You must make an appointment to see this.

If they graded Louisiana museums, this one would get an A. There are no fancy audiovisual displays. The main hall resembles a barn. The guides are knowledgeable and also will leave you alone. But what a place to wander in! From all over the state old rural buildings have been collected: an overseer's house, a pioneer cabin, a blacksmith shop, a country church. And they're all furnished, down to the last shoe-button hook on a dresser. The inhabitants may just have walked out. But you step right into the nineteenth century. In the main hall are more displays, cotton-ginning equipment, old carriages, doctor's instruments. It's a grand attic of collectibles, and it's located on the Burden Research Plantation of the L.S.U. School of Agriculture. The family who owned the plantation started the collection themselves, and L.S.U. is keeping up the good work. There is no charge, but donations are gratefully accepted, and they have a museum guide for sale.

Louisiana State Capitol. You can't miss this from the highway: it's the tallest state capitol in the nation. It dates from 1932, and it's an incredible Art Deco thirty-four-story wonder. It's chock-full of statues, murals, bas-relief work, bronzes, and everything else an architect could think of. Even the exterior has huge caryatids on the upper floors. When you walk up the front steps (one for each of the forty-eight continental states: Alaska and Hawaii are inscribed on the top level together), you can turn and see the grave of Huey Long, along with his statue.

Huey Long was governor of Louisiana for only three years, 1928 to 1931. Then he served in the U.S. Senate until 1935, when he died of a gunshot wound received in the capitol building that serves as his monument. The bullet holes are in the marble to the rear of the first floor by the governor's elevator.

You must understand that in Louisiana, politics ranks somewhere above football in the list of favorite local pastimes. The Louisiana legislature in session is something to behold: lobbyists, newsmen, visiting school kids, sometimes bands or singing groups, and politicians of every shape, size, sex, and color mill madly in the marble halls, duck into committee rooms in the basement, and range throughout the thirty-four floors buttonholing the civil servants and state officials who work there year round. It is possible that you may be able to watch the legislature in session. Ask at the information desk—and be sure to take the tour of the first floor, then ride the elevator up to the twenty-seventh-floor observation deck.

You can get a view of the capitol grounds, the Mississippi River, and Baton Rouge itself.

Back at ground level you can get an overview of the state by listening to the myriad of Louisiana accents: Southern drawls from the Florida Parishes, the almost-Texas twang of the northern part of the state, Cajun patois from Lafayette, and the Brooklynese of New Orleans' ninth ward. Hill country and delta, bayou and creek, Protestant and Catholic, yes even Republicans these days (for years Louisiana was a one-party Democratic state)—somehow they get things done, and they do it with the flamboyance and panache that their fans, the voters, have come to expect.

Also on the grounds of the capitol are the **Arsenal Museum,** with military artifacts and documents inside the 1835 building, and the **Old Pentagon Barracks** (the fifth side is open to the river), built in 1822 and now offices and apartments for state officials. There's even a rose garden to stroll through.

Elsewhere in Baton Rouge is the **Louisiana Arts and Science Center** and **Riverside Museum,** located in the old railway depot. There's an art collection and a model of the Mississippi River, plus changing exhibits. The **Centroplex Auditorium** is across the street.

Magnolia Mound. Baton Rouge even has a first-class small plantation house museum, Magnolia Mound at 2161 Nicholson

Drive. This eighteenth-century house is lovingly restored and furnished in period antiques. The docents are well informed. In the kitchen building they give demonstrations of early cooking techniques. Sometimes there are also crafts demonstrations. This is a well-planned and well-run display of life in very early Baton Rouge. Open (for admission) Tuesday through Saturday from 10 A.M. to 4 P.M. and Sunday from 1 P.M. to 4 P.M. There is a very nice gift shop. Phone 504-343-4955.

Mount Hope Plantation. This cottage was built in 1817 and is open (for admission) daily from 9 A.M. to 5 P.M. The owners of Mount Hope can also rent you a room (there are two available) in the house for a night, or you can rent it for a party. It is located at 815 Highland Road. Phone 504-766-8600.

Louisiana State University. Besides the allure of **Tiger Stadium** (surely one of the steepest stadiums around), L.S.U. has several good museums on its campus. (You can pick up a map of the campus.)

First go to the **Memorial Tower,** it's a carillon in the middle of the campus. On the main floor is the **Anglo-American Museum** with a series of furnished rooms representing eras of decor in American history. The collection is good, and the rooms are well detailed and explained. There are changing exhibits here also, and a collection of silver and portraits. The museum is open weekdays from 8:30 A.M. to 4:30 P.M. and Saturdays from 9 A.M. to 4:30 P.M. and Sundays from 1 P.M. to 4:30 P.M.

The **Museum of Natural Science** has life-sized dioramas of Louisiana wildlife scenes with stuffed animals, birds, and reptiles in natural settings. A very good way to learn about the considerable wildlife of the state. Louisiana is on the Mississippi Flyway, and bird migrations and species in the state come in huge numbers. L.S.U. is a major center for ornithology, and the museum collection illustrates this. The museum is open weekdays from 8 A.M. to 4:30 P.M. and weekends from noon to 4:30 P.M.

There is even a **Geoscience Museum** in the Geology Building. There are mineral and fossil displays and special exhibits on things like "West Indian Folk Architecture" or the "Evolution of the Beer Can." The museum has displays throughout the four floors of the building, and is open weekdays from 8 A.M. to 4:30 P.M.

Baton Rouge and L.S.U. often have concerts or performances, so check the local papers, the *State Times* and the *Morning Advocate*. There are other museums and buildings of interest in the city (get your brochures at the state tourist center in the capitol), and L.S.U. even has two Indian mounds right on the campus. You'll find plenty to do.

EATING OUT

Baton Rouge has several good restaurants (politicians do not live on steak alone) that are worth trying.

Didee's, 115 South Twelfth Street (504-344-7578). Open only in the evening, so be sure and call to check their hours. The neighborhood is not high-rent; the exterior has a hand-lettered sign saying IT'S NOT MUCH BUT IT'S ALL I GOT AND I SHARE IT WITH YOU, but inside the kitchen, wonderful things are done to ducks by the family who owns this café. Baked duck is the specialty, but there's dirty rice, a great brown oyster stew, and delicious gumbo. Try it. (But park right at the door.)

Mike Anderson's, 4332 Highland Road (504-766-7823). Near the L.S.U. campus. Has the largest serving of onion rings you have ever seen. Also good fried catfish and hush puppies (fried corn bread dumplings once supposedly used to quiet noisy dogs by either moonshiners, poachers, highway robbers, or whomever your Southern raconteur chooses). Fine for a near-campus lunch.

Gino's, 4542 Bennington Avenue (504-927-7156). Amazing! A really good Italian restaurant in Baton Rouge. Sicilian cooking, a decent wine list, and a tomato sauce that Mama Marino—who cooked it—can be proud of. This is a dress-up restaurant, Baton Rouge style. You can probably get in without a tie.

Sabin's Fine Foods, 9716 Airline Highway (504-926-0708). Here's where the steaks are, and also some good seafood dishes.

The bartender makes all sorts of frozen sweet drinks. For this place you need a tie.

LODGING

Baton Rouge has motels from every chain. Just pick your favorite. It's probably wise to make a reservation, especially during football season. The town is easy to get around in, once you have a city map—which you can get at the tourist center in the capitol. The majority of wide streets where motels are located are numbered highways, and your state road map will get you there.

Audubon Park Commission

THE AUDUBON ZOO in Audubon Park is one of the best small zoos in the country, with well-designed moated enclosures and habitats.

LONGUE VUE gardens and house include a decorative-arts museum and beautifully planted fountains and walkways. *Longue Vue*

Louisiana Office of Tourism

CHALMETTE NATIONAL PARK SITE was the scene of the Battle of New Orleans in 1815. Exhibits are inside the Beauregard Plantation House.

HOUMAS HOUSE PLANTATION in Burnside, Louisiana, typifies the Greek Revival beauty of Louisiana mansions. *Louisiana Office of Tourism*

THE LOUISIANA STATE CAPITOL in Baton Rouge was the location of the shooting of Huey P. Long, and he is buried on its grounds.

SAN FRANCISCO PLANTATION on the Mississippi above New Orleans is an exquisite example of Victorian architecture.

SHADOWS ON THE TECHE in New Iberia, Louisiana, has lovely garde around it on the banks of Bayou Teche.

THE WASHINGTON PARISH FREE FAIR in Franklinton has the Mile Bran Settlement collection of historic buildings as a popular spot during t fair each October.

Louisiana Office of Tourism

THE LOUISIANA STATE CAPITOL in Baton Rouge was the location of the
shooting of Huey P. Long, and he is buried on its grounds.

SAN FRANCISCO PLANTATION on the Mississippi above New Orleans is an
exquisite example of Victorian architecture.   *Louisiana Office of Tourism*

Louisiana Office of Touri.

SHADOWS ON THE TECHE in New Iberia, Louisiana, has lovely garde around it on the banks of Bayou Teche.

THE WASHINGTON PARISH FREE FAIR in Franklinton has the Mile Bran Settlement collection of historic buildings as a popular spot during fair each October. *Louisiana Office of Tour.*

NEW IBERIA

This is not exactly a plantation tour, a Cajun country tour, or a nature excursion: it just happens to have a little of all of those things. This is also one trip that your kids will truly enjoy. After two days of this regime, they'll probably call each other "cher" ("dear" in French, often heard in this region).

New Iberia is 20 miles from Lafayette and less than 150 miles from New Orleans. It was settled by Canary Islanders before 1800. It is situated on Bayou Teche (which is probably an Indian word for "snake") and was once an important shipping point. There is rice, sugarcane, salt, and oil in the area.

To reach New Iberia from New Orleans you can take Highway 90 to Raceland, then Highway 1 to Thibodaux, Highway 20 to Morgan City, and Highway 90 again to the junction with Highway 14, which leads you right into town. Or take I-10 to Lafayette, then Highway 90 to New Iberia.

Where Highway 90 meets Highway 14 there is a Holiday Inn and also a little nineteenth-century cabin that is a Louisiana State Tourist Office. They will have maps and brochures and any information you might need.

You are in the Louisiana French country, where you will hear French on the radio—from singers as well as announcers, from people on the street and in restaurants, and even at Mass. You will notice that the food has a little more pepper. This is also near farming and oil country, so you'll see a lot of pickup trucks and faded jeans and boots. But the first thing you should do is very elegant, and that is visiting Shadows on the Teche.

Shadows on the Teche. The National Trust for Historic Preservation now owns and operates this home (one of only eight

American houses so fortunate). It is located on Bayou Teche at 117 East Main Street and is open (for admission) daily from 9 A.M. to 4:30 P.M.

The house is brick and was built in 1831 by David Weeks. It is furnished with period antiques (some from the Weeks family) and there is Weeks family silver and some portraits as well as clothing. Mr. Weeks was about seven feet tall and Mrs. Weeks was very tiny. The kids will enjoy seeing Mr. Weeks's trousers and Mrs. Weeks's little shoes.

Shadows was owned in this century by Weeks Hall, a bon vivant artist and writer who knew everybody who was anybody. Most of them came to visit and signed a downstairs door. The kids can look at Walt Disney's name. Once one of the servants painted the door, but Weeks Hall invited everybody to come back and sign again, and they all did.

There are kitchen utensils, interesting details about the construction, and a lovely formal garden, plus guides who are prepared to answer all questions as well as go through their routine.

This is not the largest house in Louisiana or the most expensive, but it seems to have been the most loved.

Konriko Rice Mill and Company Store. This is a real working rice mill, and it is open for tours. The rice is stored in a huge silo and comes in at the top floor. Gradually it is milled by machinery to the familiar white. Konriko also packages a Wild Pecan Rice, a special breed with a nutty flavor. Then they have bran rice (sort of toasted) and brown rice (not milled all the way). They even package assorted spices. And you can watch everything! It's all very noisy, dusty, and informal—but fascinating.

If you are a jazz fan, you may wish to know that the great Bunk Johnson had a job here once after he put down his horn in New Orleans and before he was discovered again circa 1940 to spark the revival of interest in New Orleans jazz.

Next to the rice mill is the Konriko Company Store, which has all sorts of gifts, rice, candies (including jalapeño jelly beans), and a brisk mail order business. Inside the store is a little movie theater where you can see a film on the Cajuns, the Acadians who settled the area in the eighteenth century when England occupied Nova Scotia and forceably removed the French colonists. The Konriko mill and store are at 307 Ann Street.

Avery Island. This incredible "island" sits on salt domes—the geologic formation that covers huge rock salt deposits. There is a salt mine here, a **Jungle Garden,** and also the factory where Tabasco sauce is made.

Take Highway 14 to Highway 329 and you will reach Avery Island in 8 miles. The gardens are open (for admission) daily from 9 A.M. to 5 P.M. Phone 318-365-8173. The factory is open daily from 10 A.M. to 4:30 P.M. Try to visit on a weekday, when it's in full operation.

Avery Island's salt was known to early Indians, whose relics have been found. There are also fossil deposits. Near the end of the eighteenth century it was acquired by a Mr. Marsh from the Spanish government. The island has continued in the possession of his descendants, the Averys and the McIlhennys.

Edward McIlhenny was a naturalist. He worked hard to establish wildlife refuges in Louisiana and in 1893 began his snowy egret colony and saved the bird from extinction. Now there are numerous rookeries and a huge nesting platform, incredible at sunset. McIlhenny also involved himself with the gardens, importing different varieties of plants. Today they are a feast for the eyes, at any time of year. There is a driving tour through the gardens, and you will be given a map. The most vivid time of year for a visit is early spring: azaleas, camellias, and irises are in bloom, and the egrets are in residence.

The Tabasco factory makes the famous sauce, named for the state in Mexico where the original seeds were found. It was first bottled in 1868. The peppers are aged with salt and vinegar in huge wooden vats. The sauce is not cooked. You can tour the vat area (notice the foot-operated water fountains along the side walls for emergency splashes) and see the bottling, labeling, and packing. You even get a tiny bottle of Tabasco as a souvenir. The factory is in an attractive brick building meant to look nineteenth century. The operation is strictly up to the minute.

Between the gardens and the factory the kids should be occupied for several hours. Bring your binoculars for the birdwatching.

Other large gardens in the vicinity may also be open for touring.

Loreauville. Take Highway 86 out of New Iberia 10 miles to Loreauville, and at 401 East Main Street you will find the **Heritage Museum Village.** Actually it's all in the very long and narrow backyard of a modest home. There are farm implements outside, small display areas showing an old school, a jail, a tiny church. Inside are rooms of Victorian furniture. It's all very low-key—you have to ring an outside bell to find someone to take your admission. The displays are arranged in chronological order and somewhat identified. Since most of the exhibit is outdoors, it is a little weather-beaten, but it's fun. Open daily from 9 A.M. to 5 P.M.

St. Martinville. Remember the poem *Evangeline*? Well, the real Evangeline's name is supposed to have been Emmeline LaBiche, and St. Martinville is where she came and where her long-lost "Gabriel" died.

St. Martinville is 9 miles from New Iberia on Highway 31. St. Martinville seems more French than all the rest of Acadiana. On Saturday evenings there is a French Mass at the 1832 **St. Martin of Tours Church.** The statue of Evangeline nearby was posed for by Dolores Del Rio when she starred in the movie of the same name in 1927.

St. Martinville's town reception center is in the old post office building on Main Street at Evangeline Boulevard. **La Maison Duchamp** was built in 1876 as a town house for a planter. It is open (for admission) Monday through Saturday from 10 A.M. to 1 P.M.

According to tradition French aristocrats settled around St. Martinville when fleeing the revolution. The French spoken here is supposed to be purer than in other areas.

Longfellow-Evangeline State Commemorative Area. Just north of St. Martinville on Highway 31 is this pleasant state park on the banks of the Teche. On the grounds is the **Acadian House**

Museum, a Cajun cabin with an outside stair to the second floor, where the young men stayed. You will see this style of house throughout the countryside. This one was built in 1765. The smokehouse, kitchen, and herb garden are reconstructions. This is a nice way to learn how simple people adapted their housing to their needs. There is also a fine handcraft shop. Acadian weaving is an old craft that is still practiced. There is even a special brown cotton used for extra sturdy fabric or to give color.

Catahoula. Take Highway 96 out of St. Martinville to Catahoula. On the way you will see a marker for the Oak and Pine Alley, which planter Charles Durand was supposed to have had set with spiders whose webs were sprayed with gold dust for his daughters' double wedding. At the marker you will also see a Station of the Cross.

These hand-painted small shrines are hung on trees along the highway to Catahoula. They have been there for some time and are regularly repainted.

If you continue past Catahoula on Highway 96, you will come to the levee of the Atchafalaya Swamp. This basin of land stretches on either side of the Atchafalaya River, which flows from the Mississippi River down to Morgan City. The Atchafalaya and the Mississippi diverge just near that point on the map where the top of the foot forms a corner with the Louisiana boot. Actually the Mississippi River would like to follow the Atchafalaya's path to the Gulf—it's much straighter—so the U.S. Army Corps of Engineers has its hands full keeping that from happening.

Meanwhile, conservationists fight to protect what remains of the wild Atchafalaya Basin.

You can drive on the gravel road on the levee here and see something of this watery land, teeming with wildlife, especially crawfish.

If you have no boiled crawfish to nibble on, stop at one of the country stores and get some hot boudin (meat-and-rice sausage) and a nice cold beer.

While you drink your beer you can contemplate the fact that Louisiana is the only state with an official state dog: the

Catahoula hog dog, a short-haired blue-eyed spotted hound, supposedly a cross between Indian dogs and sixteenth-century Spanish dogs.

EATING OUT

This is a land of special food and special restaurants. Without even going into Lafayette (which you should do if you have time —the tourist center is on Highway 90 at Sixteenth Street), here are three extraordinary places to eat.

Patout's, 1846 Center Street, right on Highway 14 as you enter New Iberia (318-365-5206). In this pleasant, rambling house Alex Patout and his sister Gigi serve up fresh seafood, very good gumbo, lots of fresh vegetables, and homemade bread and butter.

Chez Marcelle, in Broussard, just off Highway 90 above St. Martinville, 120 North St. Julien Road (318-837-3100). Marcelle Bienvenue is a St. Martinville native. She's the person Time-Life found when they needed help on a Louisiana cookbook. Imaginative recipes in a grand Victorian home in the cane fields.

The Yellow Bowl, Highway 90 in Jeanerette, about 15 miles below New Iberia (318-276-9132). Oh my! What fried crawfish tails! There's also étoufée, lots of other fried seafood—and the dining room will be filled with what seems to be every family in driving distance.

LODGING

There are motels in and around New Iberia, but the Holiday Inn at Highway 90 and Highway 14 seems centrally located. It's standard.

If you wish to try spending the night on a plantation, you have two choices:

Mintmere is an 1857 Greek Revival cottage at 1400 East Main Street in New Iberia. It is open (for admission) daily from 10 A.M. to 4 P.M. and has rooms to rent. Phone 318-364-6210. Also on the grounds here is the **Broussard House,** a much earlier home with the mud-and-moss construction material called bousillage (BOO-see-yahge).

Albania Plantation on Highway 182 south of Jeanerette has a cottage to rent on the grounds. Albania was built in 1842 by a French Royalist refugee, Charles Grevemberg. The house also holds a doll collection. Phone 318-276-4816.

Wherever you spend the night, here's hoping you *fais do-do* (fay dough-dough). That means "go to sleep." It also means a dance, or a party. Well, whatever you're in the mood for, you're likely to find it around here.

CALENDAR OF EVENTS AROUND LOUISIANA

Everyone in the Western world punctuates the year with festivals: Christmas, Halloween, Independence Day. When you can join someone in celebrating, you can learn more about him, and you can learn something of the customs of other people.

In Louisiana you will find that many of the festivals have come from folk traditions not common elsewhere in America. Of course, Louisiana offers events that please everyone—football games, golf tournaments, tours of old homes, fishing rodeos. But the special ways that communities celebrate saints' days, the blessing of the shrimp fleet, pirogue races, and Mardi Gras are seldom found elsewhere.

If you are interested in a particular event, write to the Louisiana Tourist Development Commission, P.O. Box 44291, Baton Rouge, Louisiana 70804, or to the Greater New Orleans Tourist and Convention Commission, 334 Royal Street, New Orleans, Louisiana 70130. They will be able to give you the current address of the festival headquarters.

For more festive, and expensive occasions you might consider attending a charity benefit. In New Orleans everyone seems to be raising money with dances, balls, and gourmet cooking, in interesting locations—the zoo, parks, banks, historic houses, and on boats. It's one way to help a good cause while dressing up and meeting local folks. Check the newspapers for what is available during your stay.

If you go into a small Louisiana town for a festival, do not expect elaborate events and pageants and luxury accommodations. However, you will find friendly people celebrating something they enjoy, and it won't be long before you'll feel just like one of the family. And that's the kind of vacation you'll remember for a long, long time.

JANUARY

Sugar Bowl Football Game, January 1, the Superdome, New Orleans. For tickets, write the Mid-Winter Sports Association, 510 International Building, 611 Gravier Street, New Orleans, Louisiana 70112. Sugar Bowl events include yacht races, tennis, and a basketball tournament. If the Super Bowl is held here, it will also be in the Superdome. The few local tickets usually go to Saints ticket holders (that's even if the Saints aren't playing).

Twelfth Night, January 6. Twelfth Night is the Feast of the Epiphany, when the Three Wise Men reached Bethlehem. In Louisiana you celebrate Twelfth Night, or Kings' Day, by having a King Cake, a brioche or sweet bread in a wreath shape. Hidden in the cake is a doll or a bean. Whoever gets the bean is crowned king or queen of the party or gets to give a party the next week. The King Cake parties go on until Ash Wednesday, the beginning of Lent. Twelfth Night also begins the Mardi Gras season in New Orleans. Private balls are held until Mardi Gras Day—the day before Ash Wednesday. Since Easter falls on the first Sunday after the first full moon of spring, and Ash Wednesday is about six weeks before Easter, the date of Mardi Gras can vary. No Mardi Gras balls are open to the public. If you really want to go to one—black tie required—put an ad in the personals column of the *Times-Picayune* in advance, and some ball will probably send you an invitation. However, the Krewe of Clones of the Contemporary Arts Center has a party after their parade for which you can buy tickets.

FEBRUARY

Mardi Gras usually falls in February. The parades start weeks ahead of Mardi Gras Day. Reservations must be made in advance for Mardi Gras in New Orleans, and rates are higher, as they are around Sugar Bowl or Super Bowl time. Mardi Gras is also celebrated in the New Orleans suburbs, in Lafayette, Covington, Bogalusa, Slidell, and in Mobile, Alabama, and on the Mississippi Gulf Coast. Around Mamou, Louisiana, in the Cajun country, you will find Mardi Gras sometimes is celebrated by masked riders on horseback going from farm to farm to "steal" enough chickens for a Mardi Gras gumbo.

MARCH

St. Patrick's Day, March 17. The patron saint of the Irish is honored with a parade in the Irish Channel of New Orleans, complete with jazz bands. Restaurants serve green beer—colored by harmless dye—and green corn bread and cabbage. They throw cabbages from the parade floats.

St. Joseph's Day, March 19. The patron saint of the Italians has a parade in New Orleans and is honored with St. Joseph altars. You can go to one (check the addresses in the personals column of the *Times-Picayune*). You will find a massive display of Italian foods, including pastries and breads, some in the shape of a lamb. Also, you can get a lucky bean—a blessed fava bean —for luck through the year. Usually some children are asked to represent saints, and they eat first. Then the family and guests eat, and then the remains go to the poor. There is a huge altar in front of the Piazza d'Italia on Poydras Street in New Orleans every year. In the country, across Lake Pontchartrain, no St. Joseph altar is complete without strawberry wine. The altars honor St. Joseph for answering prayers to stop a famine in Italy in some past century.

The **Italian Open Golf Tournament,** with muffaletta sandwiches and wine on the course, is held each year in City Park in New Orleans at this time also. And on St. Joseph's Night the black Mardi Gras Indian maskers parade—you can catch them around North Claiborne and Orleans avenues.

Audubon Pilgrimage, St. Francisville, Louisiana. During a tour of homes the antebellum homes in a small town are all open to visitors—for a fee—and the guides are local people, often the family who lives in the house. There may be a dinner at the local church. Other towns with home tours in the spring are Natchez, Mississippi—the Natchez Pilgrimage with pageants and a ball—and Clinton, Louisiana.

St. Francisville, Jackson, and Clinton, Louisiana, are all very pretty small towns around Baton Rouge. They were settled in the nineteenth century and have many lovely plantation homes, some built prior to 1800. This area is known as the Felicianas, and East and West Feliciana parishes cover the territory.

Taking Highway 61 from New Orleans to Baton Rouge, you might stop and see the **Louisiana State Capitol,** the old **Louisiana State Capitol,** and the **Magnolia Mound Plantation** home—all in Baton Rouge. Continue on Highway 61 to St. Francisville. Here you can see **Rosedown,** a beautiful restoration of a plantation home and gardens, admission charged. You can visit **Oakley House,** where Audubon taught and painted and which is now part of a state park.

The **Cottage and Asphodel plantations** are both open and accommodations are available. Don't miss the homemade bread at Asphodel. See Grace Episcopal Church in St. Francisville—dates from 1858—and then take I-10 to Jackson and to Clinton, and Highway 67 back to Baton Rouge. Some homes are open to visitors year round, but the annual "homes tour," or "pilgrimage," will afford you more places to see. The round trip from New Orleans is about 250 miles.

APRIL

Spring Fiesta, 546 St. Peter Street, New Orleans. Spring Fiesta begins on the first Friday after Easter and lasts nearly three weeks. There is a parade, and tours of homes, gardens, and plantations. In April the azaleas are in bloom, and Louisiana is covered with pink.

During the spring the gardens of Louisiana are lovely. **Longue Vue Gardens** in Metairie, a suburb of New Orleans, is open—$5.00 admission—as are the **Jungle Garden** of Avery Island, the **Dutch Gardens** near Newellton—specializing in tulips—**Hodges**

Gardens near Many, and **Zemurray Gardens** near Ponchatoula. City Park and Audubon Park both have horticultural exhibits.

Ponchatoula Strawberry Festival. Ponchatoula, Hammond, Independence, Amite, Covington, and Folsum are all small towns north of Lake Pontchartrain. (Take I-10 to Laplace to Highway 55 North.) At the Strawberry Festival there will be music, a parade, and a strawberry-eating contest. There is no contesting the fact that Louisiana strawberries are the best on earth. Hammond has a **Heritage Day Festival** in early May.

Amite has an **Oyster Festival** in spring (there is an oyster-packing industry here). Amite sometimes schedules a tour of homes during the festival. One home worth seeing is **Blythewood,** built by D. H. Sanders around 1900, with a fine double staircase.

Covington and Folsum are in the Louisiana horse country. Folsum hosts bluegrass music festivals from time to time. This is pretty country in the springtime; you can buy flats of berries from roadside trucks and visit the **Zemurray Gardens** on Highway 40, off Highway 55. Independence has an **Italian Festival** in April—many Italian immigrants came here and became vegetable and strawberry farmers. Other immigrants to the area included Hungarians, in Albany. There are small museums and nice gift and antique shops throughout the region. There are also several good restaurants. For Italian food, try **Ardillo's,** off Highway 55 at Amite. And, if you are adventuresome, take Highway 51 to Tickfaw, rent an inner tube, and float down the Tangipahoa River. (There are tube-rental signs directing you.)

MAY

Breaux Bridge Crawfish Festival, Breaux Bridge. Breaux Bridge is just a few miles from Lafayette, in the heart of the Cajun country. The crawfish festival has had, in the past, both crawfish-picking and crawfish-eating contests, crawfish races, a parade, and lots to eat and drink. The festival is held in even-numbered years. There should be some Cajun music to dance to —a sort of country music with French lyrics. Bands may include triangles and concertinas.

New Orleans Jazz and Heritage Festival, New Orleans. This is usually held in May and combines top-name jazz stars with traditional New Orleans musicians and folk musicians from elsewhere in the state. Gospel singers, Cajun bands, blues guitarists, and ragtime bands entertain on the center oval of the Fair Grounds Race Track on two weekends for the Jazz and Heritage Fair, which also offers local foods and crafts. There are concerts of big-name artists, dance bands on the *President* riverboat, and the **Archive of New Orleans Jazz** at Tulane University hosts a **Hot Jazz Classic** with performances and seminars. Write for tickets to the New Orleans Jazz and Heritage Festival, P.O. Box 2530, New Orleans, Louisiana 70176. One bonus of the festival is that out-of-town musicians will be turning up at late-night jam sessions throughout town during the festival.

Pirogue Races, Lafitte. The pirogue (PEE-rogue) is a dugout canoe. In the hands of experts it skims over the water of Louisiana bayous. On Bayou Barataria during the Pirogue Races the other boats are all decorated with streamers; there is a beauty queen and lots of beer and music. Plus you get to drive to Lafitte through some typical Louisiana swamp country, and you can eat at the **Barataria Tavern** (very good seafood).

Jambalaya Festival, Gonzalez. Jambalaya is made with rice, seasoning, and meat and seafood. Every year they have a contest at Gonzalez to see who cooks the best jambalaya—there is enough jambalaya to feed an army of visitors.

JULY

New Orleans Food Festival, New Orleans. Foodfest features not only a gourmet meal—available at a high price—but also a weekend of eating, from booths set up in the Rivergate Exhibition Hall at the foot of Canal Street. You can buy tickets to use at each booth, and you can taste jambalaya from the champion cook of Gonzalez, raw oysters, cochon de lait, and all sorts of Louisiana specialties. Go early because the festival is literally eaten up by the onlookers.

La Fête. The New Orleans summer celebration has fireworks on the Mississippi July 4 and a program including parades, performances, tours, and a cooking school each year. Call them at 504-525-4143 for information. The Bastille Day celebration, with a waiters' race and music, is held July 14 or the preceding weekend, during La Fête.

JULY–AUGUST

Fishing rodeos, in Grand Isle, Cameron, Empire, and Golden Meadow, plus other towns. You enter a fishing rodeo for a small fee, and then during the rodeo dates you catch the biggest fish you can. The winner in each classification gets a prize and a trophy. Also there are booths to display the big fish, usually a parade, and lots to eat and drink. If you are a serious fisherman, you won't want to miss a chance at big-game fishing off the Louisiana coast.

Delcambre Shrimp Festival and Fair, Delcambre. Shrimp festivals begin with a blessing of the fleet, usually by a bishop. There will be parades, things to eat and drink, and contests in eating or peeling shrimp.

SEPTEMBER

Louisiana Shrimp and Petroleum Festival, Morgan City. This is the big shrimp festival, with the biggest parade. Probably there will be events, and maybe a name star appearing, at the **Morgan City Auditorium,** one of the nicest and best auditoriums in any small city in the country. The Morgan City money comes from oil; most of the servicing of the offshore oil rigs in the Gulf of Mexico is done from Morgan City.

New Orleans Saints, New Orleans. The Saints' professional football team exhibition games begin in late summer, and football goes into full swing.

OCTOBER

Festivals Acadiens, Lafayette. Cajun music, food, and crafts all over the city. Lafayette is the capital of the Louisiana petroleum industry and somehow mixes Texas-style largesse with French finesse. There is a tourist office on Highway 90 at Sixteenth Street, and there are museums, parks, and the University of Southwestern Louisiana. Lafayette has a Mardi Gras celebration and, in October, the **Louisiana Gulf Coast Oil Exposition,** a fair for the oil business with technical displays as well as a ball.

Louisiana Yambilee Festival, Opelousas. The yam, a sort of sweet potato, is a Louisiana product. Perhaps the best way to eat it is candied, but imaginative Louisiana cooks can think of a multitude of ways to prepare it. The Yambilee has a parade, agricultural show, and beauty contest. There is a **Jim Bowie** (the knife inventor) **Museum** here.

Louisiana Cotton Festival, Ville Platte. Part of this festival makes it unique: Ville Platte has a *tournoi* (tourn-WAH), "tournament." "Knights" in costume on horseback ride back and forth and try to catch a ring on their lance. This is an old custom that has recently been revived.

Washington Parish Free Fair, Franklinton. October is a good month for fairs, and this is the largest free fair in the nation. There are agricultural exhibits, an art show, a rodeo, and the **Mile Branch Settlement**—a collection of old homes and farm buildings with costumed guides and craftsmen. Take the causeway over Lake Pontchartrain, Highway 190 toward Covington, and Highway 25 to Franklinton. Old-fashioned country fun, and all for free.

NOVEMBER

All Saints' Day, November 1. This is the day to honor the dead, and in Louisiana this is done by whitewashing the family tombs, cutting the grass, and putting out new flowers, usually chrysanthemums. Everybody goes to the cemetery that day, as much to see their friends as to remember the dead. The custom is common wherever Latin customs are still followed in Louisiana. (Northern Louisiana is mostly Protestant, and they usually clean their cemeteries with a work party one weekend in the summertime and then have a dinner on the church grounds.)

Fair Grounds Race Track, New Orleans. The racing season opens on Thanksgiving Day and runs for 101 racing days. The **L.S.U. National Quarter Horse Show** in Baton Rouge usually falls in November also.

DECEMBER

Natchitoches Christmas Festival, Natchitoches (NACK-uh-tosh). Natchitoches, founded in 1714, is older than New Orleans. The older part of town will remind you of the French Quarter, and the Cane River—actually it used to be a navigable part of the Red River—runs through town. Everything will be decorated with thousands of Christmas lights, and there will be a fireworks display.

The road down the Cane River to Cloutierville passes many lovely plantation homes, including **Melrose,** which has an outbuilding done in African style—settlers in that section were free men of color. In Cloutierville is a **Bayou Folk Museum** in the onetime home of Kate Chopin, a nineteenth-century novelist just beginning to be appreciated for her surprisingly modern work.

During the festival you will get a chance to taste the Natchitoches culinary specialty, meat pies. These are very spicy meat concoctions fried in a half-moon-shaped pie crust. The **Kisatchie National Forest** is near here for camping and picnicking. Natchitoches also has a folk festival in July and a homes tour in October.

Plaquemines Parish Fair and Orange Festival, Fort Jackson. Louisiana oranges are the sweetest and best anywhere, especially if you can eat them straight from the orchard.

Fort Jackson, a National Historic Landmark, is in Plaquemines Parish on the West Bank of the river below New Orleans. Take Highway 23. The fort is one of a series of early coastal forts and is near the site where the explorer La Salle claimed Louisiana for France in 1682. There is a military museum and picnic facilities. The Orange Festival will have oyster-shucking contests, duck-calling contests, and maybe even nutria-skinning contests.

The nutria is a furry animal that proliferated in the state after being brought here in the 1930s. For some reason they are often hit by cars, so you'll see them on the highway. They are trapped for their fur.

The highway down to Fort Jackson winds along next to the levee of the Mississippi River (West Bank) and finally comes to a halt at Venice. There are other settlements farther on, such as Pilottown, but these can be reached only by water. Along the road you can see the evidence of the great damage done by the mammoth hurricanes that follow the path of the river out of the Gulf. There are also settlements of people in this area who originally came from Dalmatia in Yugoslavia. That is why so many oyster dealers in New Orleans have names like "Jurisich." Everyone will speak with a Cajun accent though.

Sugar Bowl, New Orleans. The Mid-Winter Sports Association Sugar Bowl events start just before Christmas with sailing, then tennis, then basketball, and finally the Sugar Bowl football game on New Year's Day.

Christmas bonfires, December 24. Along River Road above Laplace people build huge bonfires on the levee before Christmas. On Christmas Eve they are lit—to light the way for the Christ Child or St. Nicholas. There are bonfires scattered on both sides of the river and also along Bayou Lafourche. The wind from the river carries the sparks up into the night, and the reflection of the fires on the water is worth the drive, and the walk up the levee. Restaurants on Airline Highway (Highway 61) are open for gumbo and beer. Some of the bonfires are really private parties, so be sure you announce yourself and ask politely if you might watch. Also, there will be lots of firecrackers.

EMERGENCIES

Hopefully, your vacation will be tranquil and fun, but if anything should happen while you're here, you might as well be prepared with phone numbers.

Both New Orleans and Jefferson Parish are getting an emergency number system.

Dial 911 for police, fire, and ambulance service.

If that service is not yet in effect during your stay here, the phone numbers listed below will help.

Police—911 or (New Orleans) 821-2222 or (Jefferson Parish) 368-9911. Call them about crimes and traffic accidents. If the damage is minor, they may just suggest the drivers exchange names and addresses. Move cars out of intersections if they block traffic. You may need to wait for the police to get there if you call. Keep a record of the police incident number for your insurance company. You may also have to report it to your home state. The police can also provide some medical help.

If your car has disappeared in the French Quarter, you might call the **Auto Pound,** 586-5097. Parking regulations are strict, and you may have been towed away if you violated them.

If you are arrested in New Orleans, you will probably be brought to **Central Lockup** in the Police Complex on Broad Street near Tulane Avenue. If the arrest is for driving while intoxicated, you will stay there awhile and will have a stiff fine and possibly a jail sentence. D.W.I. laws are strict. Narcotics laws are also strictly enforced. Patrons of prostitutes are liable to be picked up by the vice squad and may get their names in the paper as well as an appearance in court.

Fire—991 or (New Orleans) 581-3473 or (Jefferson Parish) 368-9911.

Charity Hospital, 1532 Tulane Avenue, 568-2311. There is a twenty-four-hour emergency room here. If you can afford to, you will be asked to pay. Franchise-type emergency treatment centers, such as the Instant Care Center at 3600 Prytania Street, are open from 7 A.M. to 11 P.M. Other locations are planned throughout the metropolitan area.

Orleans Parish Medical Society, 523-2474. You can call weekdays between 8 A.M. and 4:30 P.M. for names of doctors who are members of the society. There will be a fee.

New Orleans Dental Association, 834-6449. Call if you need the name of a dentist; there is an answering service when the office is closed.

Waterbury's Rexall Drug Store, 536 Canal Street, 525-0321. This drugstore is open, with a pharmacist on duty, twenty-four hours a day.

Society for the Prevention of Cruelty to Animals, 1319 Japonica Street, 944-7445. The S.P.C.A. has a staff veterinarian and a pet-ambulance service.

WEATHER

New Orleans is surrounded by water, so it has a humid climate. The temperature is usually mild, but summer can be hot. The highest temperature ever recorded was 102° and the lowest was 6°. Most summers will have less than ten days with temperatures over 95°, and there are about as many days with below-freezing temperatures in winter.

Rain is relatively frequent throughout the year and 61.55 inches a year is considered normal.

If you want a forecast, the **Weather Bureau** number is 525-8831.

The hurricane season lasts roughly from June to September, and absolutely no prediction on the frequency or severity of hurricanes can be made. Thanks to the U.S. Weather Bureau, there is always advance warning of hurricanes, and the local government has many precautionary and safety measures at its disposal.

One old saying has it that "There are only two seasons in New Orleans: February and the rest of the year." However, don't put off coming to Mardi Gras just because February is the coldest month. If you really have a good time, you won't even notice the temperature.

In recent years heavy spring rains have caused street flooding. If you hear of a flash-flood watch, move your car to high ground.

TRANSPORTATION

AIR

New Orleans International Airport, Highway 61 in Kenner. The reason the baggage tags read MSY is that this was once Moisant Airport, named for a pioneer aviator. New Orleans has full domestic airline service from everywhere in the country. There are also many flights to and from South and Central America, so there is a full customs inspection area.

New Orleans International Airport seems to have had construction projects under way for the last decade. Allow over an hour to reach the airport when you leave, because traffic may be impossible. To get there, take I-10 West. You'll see the airport exit around Williams Boulevard in Kenner. To get into town you can either take Airline Highway (Highway 61), which becomes Tulane Avenue and runs parallel to Canal Street, or you can get on the I-10 East. Exit at St. Charles Avenue (for St. Charles going uptown), Loyola Avenue (right into the business district), Poydras Street (by the Superdome), or Orleans (which gets you to the French Quarter). If you pass the St. Charles exit going straight, you'll go over the Greater New Orleans Bridge and end up on the West Bank.

The cheapest way to get to and from the airport is by bus. Louisiana Transit buses stop on the upper ramp at the airport. They run from 5:30 A.M. to 11:30 P.M. It costs sixty-five cents to go to Tulane Avenue and Elks Place (right in the business district) and forty cents to Tulane and Carrollton avenues. Luggage can be carried on at the discretion of the driver, so if you have a lot of baggage, this may not be feasible for you. The buses run every twelve minutes from 6 A.M. to 9 A.M. and from 3 P.M. to

5:40 P.M. Otherwise they run about every half hour. The two New Orleans stops are where you board if you are airport-bound. From 6 P.M. to 11:30 P.M. the buses only go as far as Carrollton Avenue.

The limousine costs $6.00 a person and runs to the airport from major hotels. Limos leave from the baggage area at the airport.

Lakefront Airport, Haynes Boulevard at Lake Pontchartrain (241-2337). Although some corporate and private planes use New Orleans International, the Lakefront is closer in to town and is preferred by private owners. Call and make arrangements if you'd like to land here.

WATER

Delta Queen Steamboat Company, 511 Main Street, Cincinnati, Ohio 45202. Write or call (1-800-543-1949) for information on the two cruise ships that ply the Mississippi River for two- to fourteen-night trips: the *Mississippi Queen* and the *Delta Queen.* Ports include Memphis, Tennessee; St. Louis, Missouri; St. Paul, Minnesota; Cincinnati, Ohio; and Pittsburgh, Pennsylvania; as well as New Orleans. Old-time luxury.

RAIL

Union Passenger Terminal, 1001 Loyola Avenue (528-1660). Amtrak trains call on New Orleans, and there are overnight ones to California, Chicago, and Washington. From time to time local railway buffs will schedule a steam train excursion, which should be listed in the "Calendar" section of the *Times-Picayune.* Sometimes at Mardi Gras or for other special events train tours will schedule into New Orleans. A New Orleans to Mobile, Alabama, route is planned for regular service.

BUS

Greyhound Bus Lines, 2101 Earhart Boulevard (525-9371). The Greyhound buses park at the Union Passenger Terminal and leave from there. The passenger terminal has some nice murals and is right on the edge of the business district. Easy to look at and easy to get to.

Trailways Bus System, 1314 Tulane Avenue (525-4201). Trailways is located next to the public library and near Charity Hospital.

Regional Transit Authority (569-2700). New Orleans in-town transit is quick and convenient. Call, tell them where you're coming from and where you're going, and they'll give you the best route.

CAR

You can get a Louisiana map by writing the Greater New Orleans Tourist and Convention Commission, 334 Royal Street, New Orleans, Louisiana 70130; or the Louisiana Office of Tourism, P.O. Box 44291, Baton Rouge, Louisiana 70804; or the Chamber of Commerce, 301 Camp Street, New Orleans, Louisiana 70130.

If you want to rent a car while you are here, reserve one in advance. Call 1-800-555-1212 (WATS information) and get the reservation number for Avis, Hertz, Budget, Airways, or any other chain you know. If they don't have a booth in the airport, they will have a van to pick you up and bring you to their office.

Driving in New Orleans is difficult, mostly because of the other drivers. It sometimes seems that as soon as a raindrop falls, every nut with a driver's license grabs his car keys and sets out.

You may turn right on a red light. School zones are 20 miles an hour and strictly enforced (from about 7:45 A.M. to 8:45 A.M. and from 2:45 P.M. to 3:45 P.M.). Divided streets have a 35-mile-an-hour speed limit. Most smaller streets are 25 miles an hour.

The interstate is crowded at rush hour, and traffic over the Greater New Orleans Bridge is very slow at that time.

TAXICABS

In New Orleans you can hail a cab on the street, or call one to pick you up. **United Cab,** 522-9771, is a large local company.

A cab ride to or from the airport will cost one to three people a total of $18.75. The fourth and fifth person in the cab pay $6.00 each.

Taxicab meters begin with ninety cents, which will take you a quarter of a mile. Then it is twenty cents each additional minute or quarter of a mile. If you have a complaint about a cab, get the C.P.N.C. (Certificate of Public Necessity and Convenience) number posted both outside and inside the cab. Call the **Taxicab Bureau** at 586-4621.

BICYCLE

The **Bikesmith,** 4700 Freret Street (891-8585). If you rode your bike here and need some repairs, the Bikesmith can send out their repair van. Or go by their shop. They are knowledgeable and used to dealing with long-distance bike riders.

GONDOLA

Mississippi Aerial River Transit will have an aerial gondola system on cables across the Mississippi River to the site of the World's Fair. The East Bank terminal will be located near the New Orleans Convention Center, at Julia Street and the river; the West Bank terminal will be at Lamarque Street and Teche Street in Algiers. Round-trip tickets are $3.50 and the trip takes four minutes.

CLOTHES AND SHOPPING

When you pack for your New Orleans vacation be sure you bring two things: comfortable shoes and an umbrella or raincoat. You're going to walk a lot, and it most likely will rain.

New Orleans has relatively few clothing rules. Some restaurants may require coat or coat and tie for gentlemen, especially in the evening. At Mardi Gras balls ladies need dresses to the ankles and men must wear black tie (as spectators) or white tie (as members of the floor committee). Judging by signs on the doors of neighborhood restaurants, tank tops, cut-off jeans, and bare feet are unwelcome at lunch and dinner.

If you come in the winter (especially in February), be prepared for cold weather. Even if the thermometer doesn't get that low, the humidity is high, so the wind will be piercing and damp. In the summer you may need a hat for the sun.

One New Orleans fashion that continues over the years is the white linen suit for men. You will see men wearing them throughout the hot months. If you wish to purchase one, you can do so at **Terry & Juden,** 135 Carondelet Street, or **Perlis' Men's Store,** 6070 Magazine Street. Perlis has their own line of cotton polo shirts with a crawfish emblem that makes a nice souvenir.

Canal Street has many clothing shops, from **Saks Fifth Avenue** and **Brooks Brothers** branches to the local department stores: **D. H. Holmes, Godchaux,** and **Krauss** (which has a great fabrics department). There are many boutiques in the French Quarter, and there is an attractive shopping center, **Uptown Square** at Broadway and the river.

Other shopping areas include St. Charles Avenue above Lee

Circle and the Riverbend area at Carrollton and St. Charles avenues.

There are also some good discount places: **Lynley Designs,** 2628 Jefferson Highway, is an outlet for children's clothing, as is the **Outlet** at 4001 Earhart Boulevard. For men's clothing there are two **Haspel Factory Outlets,** one near the giant Lakeside Shopping Center in Metairie at 3515 Nineteenth Street and the other on the West Bank at 3767 General de Gaulle Drive.

Feet First has discount ladies' shoes at 7725 Maple Street uptown, 518 Chartres Street in the French Quarter, and 3750 Veterans Highway in Metairie. **Uptown Izzy's** has discount designer clothing at 833 Conti Street in the French Quarter, 8219 Oak Street uptown, and 3750 Veterans Highway. **Designers Anonymous** at 3020 Severn Avenue in Metairie also carries discount designer clothes, as does the **Uptown Apparel Company** at Uptown Square.

Sam's Women's Apparel, a Southern discount chain, has several local branches, and there are also **Marshall's** and **Solo's** in the Elmwood Shopping Center at Clearview near the Huey P. Long Bridge with two stores full of all sorts of discount clothing.

There is an excellent local jewelry designer, **Mignon Faget,** who has a shop at 710 Dublin Street and a location in the Godchaux store at Lakeside Shopping Center. She does casting of shells in gold and silver as well as other designs.

Yvonne LaFleur designs clothing and hats. Her shop is on Hampson Street at Dublin Street, off Carrollton Avenue.

If you need to do some washing or have some dry cleaning done while you are in New Orleans, a good French Quarter name to remember is the **Washing Well,** 841 Bourbon Street, 523-9955. They are open daily except Sunday and will wash, fold, and iron your clothes or do your dry cleaning. On weekdays there is four-hour service.

WHERE TO STAY

Accommodations of any sort are available in New Orleans, from the huge chain hotels to the smallest guesthouses. There are listings in this chapter from every category. Not every place in town is included—and not all the ones excluded are bad—but a variety of selection is given.

The Greater New Orleans Tourist and Convention Commission, 334 Royal Street, New Orleans, Louisiana 70130, will send you a brochure on accommodations if you write. Almost every major chain has representation here, and if you call WATS information, 1-800-555-1212, they will give you the chains' reservation number for your area code. The New Orleans numbers given are in area code 504.

ALL THE RATES QUOTED HERE ARE SUBJECT TO CHANGE. There may be seasonal decreases or across-the-board increases. One thing you must remember about New Orleans: THERE WILL BE INCREASED RATES AND A MINIMUM STAY REQUIRED FOR SPECIAL EVENTS! The pattern will vary from hotel to hotel, but generally Mardi Gras, the Sugar Bowl at New Year's Eve, the Super Bowl, and the months of the World's Fair will bring higher rates and minimum-stay requirements. These may also apply during the Jazz Festival.

Make your reservations early: hotels fill up quickly at popular periods and the least expensive rooms will go first. Some hotels will require you to pay part of the bill in advance. Be sure that you ask for all their requirements when you reserve your room. And double-check to be sure they accept your credit card. Ask about discounts: for senior citizens, in the summer, or for weekly or family rates.

Prices are given throughout this chapter to give you an idea of relative cost: which ones are luxury and which inexpensive. If you are bringing kids or pets, be sure and ask what that hotel's rules are. If you can settle all the details in advance, you'll be more relaxed during your stay.

The abbreviations for credit cards are: American Express: AE; Carte Blanche: CB; Diner's Club: DC; Master Card: MC; VISA: V. Some hotels will guarantee your room with a credit card, others will require a cash deposit but let you charge the rest when you check out. It would be best if you called or wrote in advance. The ZIP code for New Orleans begins with 701.

New Orleans hotels have a 10 percent tax on room rates, so figure that into your budget. However, whatever your budget might be, there's something here that fits it.

GUESTHOUSES

These tiny hotels can have elegant rooms and personal service. They also can be very romantic, and you might meet some interesting fellow guests. If you want to immerse yourself in New Orleans atmosphere twenty-four hours a day, you'll have the best chance of doing that if you stay in a guesthouse.

French Quarter

Andrew Jackson Hotel, 919 Royal Street (561-5881). 19 rooms, all air-conditioned, with TV. Rooms from $55 to $115. Like the other French Quarter guesthouses, this is housed in a redone Victorian building. Credit cards: AE, MC, V.

Corn Stalk Hotel, 915 Royal Street (523-1515). 14 rooms, all air-conditioned, with TV. Singles $60, doubles $65. Parking $3.00. Continental breakfast (coffee and a croissant or sweet rolls). Some rooms furnished with antiques, some balconies. Credit cards: AE, MC, V.

French Quarter Maisonettes, 1130 Chartres Street (524-9918). 7 rooms from $36 to $42. Extra person $7.00. No children under twelve, but will take well-trained pets. Another French Quarter mansion, this one with lovely patio. An exceptionally good value.

Lafitte Guest House, 1003 Bourbon Street (581-2678). 14 rooms. Singles from $64 to $94, doubles from $75 to $105. Free parking. Continental breakfast. Credit cards: AE, MC, V.

Lamothe House, 621 Esplanade Avenue (947-1161). 20 rooms. Free parking. All air-conditioned, with TV. Rooms $75, suites $90 to $100. Lovely mansion, many antiques. A longtime New Orleans favorite, now under new ownership and just refurbished. Continental breakfast in Victorian dining room. Credit cards: AE, MC, V.

Maison Chartres, 508 Chartres Street (529-2172). 16 rooms, all air-conditioned, with TV. Pool and patio. Continental breakfast. Rooms from $65 to $85, extra person $10. Pleasant decoration of rooms. Credit cards: AE, DC, MC, V.

Maison de Ville, 727 Toulouse Street (561-5858). 21 rooms (14 on Toulouse Street and 7 at 509 Dauphine Street in the Audubon Cottages). Pure elegance, lots of antiques. Singles from $90 to $105, doubles from $100 to $115, suites $180. The Audubon Cottages include what was once John James Audubon's New Orleans home. The cottages surround a central court with pool. One bedroom $250, two bedroom $350. No credit cards. If you can afford it and you want a really special vacation, stay here.

Noble Arms Inn, 1006 Royal Street (524-2222). 16 rooms with kitchenettes, all air-conditioned with TV. Rooms from $45 to $72, extra person $6.00. Suite (sleeps six) $135. Children under twelve free. Laundromat on premises. If you want to stay in the French Quarter and you brought the kids, consider this pleasant apartment hotel. Credit cards: AE, CB, MC, V.

Olivier Guest House, 828 Toulouse Street (525-8456). 40 rooms with kitchenettes. Free parking. Pool. Singles from $40 to

$85, doubles from $55 to $85, suites from $125. Nice blending of modern apartments in old French Quarter house. Some antiques, lovely staircase. Many European guests. Continental breakfast. Another perfect choice if you have the kids along. Credit cards: AE, CB, DC, V.

Soniat House, 1133 Chartres Street (522-0570). 25 rooms in an 1830 town house. All redone with antiques. Singles from $70 to $90, add $10 for double occupancy. Suites from $100 to $250. Continental breakfast. Credit cards: AE, MC, V.

Villa Convento, 616 Ursulines Street (522-1793). 24 differently decorated rooms, some with balconies, from $40 to $95. All air-conditioned, with TV. Continental breakfast. Elevator. Very homelike and elegant, too. Family-run. Credit cards: AE, MC, V.

Uptown

Columns Hotel, 3811 St. Charles Avenue (899-9308). 22 rooms, some with shared bath, priced from $35 to $75. A popular restaurant and bar are located here. The film *Pretty Baby* used this location. First-floor rooms and public area have been restored and are lovely. Unrestored rooms are not. The first-floor rooms may be noisy when bar is in full swing. Credit cards: AE, MC, V.

Hedgewood Hotel, 2427 St. Charles Avenue (895-9708). 14 rooms, all air-conditioned. Rates are $25 with shared bath, $40 with private bath. This old home has its original woodwork, which is worth seeing. Some rooms are furnished in antiques. Can be elegant. No credit cards. A good value.

Old World Inn, 1330 Prytania Street (566-1330). 18 rooms (12 share baths). Rates begin at $25 and go to $57.50 for a 2-room suite. Continental breakfast, lounge. Special weekly rates. This area of Prytania Street is very close to the World's Fair location and to the business district. Several guesthouses are located here, with dedicated owners who have done a lot of their own renovation work. Credit cards: V.

Park View Guest House, 7004 St. Charles Avenue (861-7564). 22 rooms (13 share baths). Single rates from $28 to $45, doubles from $38 to $55. A huge Victorian house next to Audubon Park. Originally built as a guesthouse. Credit cards: AE, MC, V.

Prytania Park Hotel, 1525 Prytania Street (524-0427). 60 rooms in four buildings on a central court. Some rooms will have microwave ovens, refrigerators, a living-dining area, and pull-down (Murphy) beds. Packaged foods, from the owner's restaurant, will be available for the microwaves. Trendy modern furnishings, also from the owner's establishment. Projected room rates range from $33 to about $60. Credit cards: AE, CB, DC, MC, V.

St. Charles Guest House, 1748 Prytania Street (523-6556). 38 rooms in four buildings, 19 with shared baths. Rates from $20 to $50. All rooms have ceiling fans and air-conditioning. Continental breakfast, pool and patio. Another guesthouse on Prytania Street with hardworking owner. This is not a neighborhood for nighttime strolls, but Prytania Street is only one block off the St. Charles Avenue streetcar line. Credit cards: AE, MC, V.

St. Charles Inn, 3636 St. Charles Avenue (899-8888). This is actually a modern hotel, with 40 rooms over the popular Que Será bar and restaurant. Parking is $1.50 a day. Singles $51, doubles $61. Continental breakfast. Right on the streetcar line. Credit cards: AE, CB, DC, MC, V. This hotel plans to increase its number of rooms.

Uptown Inn, 1550 Foucher Street (899-1000). 33 rooms, all with two double beds. Rates are $45 for one, $10 for each additional person. All air-conditioned, with TV. There are 3 suites with kitchens. Spartan decoration in a redone apartment building, but just off the streetcar line. Parking $1.50. Credit cards: MC, V.

SMALL HOTELS

These establishments will give you all hotel services, but they are not sized for large conventions. So if you don't care for guesthouses and don't want a huge facility, these may be what you are looking for.

French Quarter

Bienville House, 320 Decatur Street (529-2345). 82 rooms, all air-conditioned, with TV. Pool, restaurant. Free parking. Singles from $55 to $65, doubles from $75 to $95. Extra person $8.00, children under sixteen free. Modern motel, but with patios and balconies. Credit cards: AE, CB, DC, MC, V.

Burgundy Inn, 911 Burgundy Street (524-4401). 65 rooms, all air-conditioned, with TV. Includes the Hansel and Gretle *(sic)* Guest House. Singles from $45 to $55, doubles from $55 to $66, suites from $95 to $155. Bar and restaurant in building. Two pools. Children under twelve free. Free parking. Credit cards: AE, MC, V.

Chateau Motor Hotel, 1001 Chartres Street (524-9636). 42 rooms, free parking. All air-conditioned, with TV. Singles from $40 to $60, doubles from $50 to $85. Extra person $5.00. Children under twelve free. Daytime café. Pool. Credit cards: AE, CB, MC, V. In the quiet section of the French Quarter.

Dauphine Orleans Hotel, 409 Dauphine Street (586-1800). 109 rooms, all air-conditioned, with TV. Free parking. Singles from $69 to $79, doubles from $79 to $89, suites from $105 to $130. Extra person $10, children under twelve free. Affiliated with Master Hosts. Pool. Credit cards: AE, CB, DC, V.

Le Richelieu Motor Hotel, 1234 Chartres Street (529-2492). 88 rooms, free parking, all air-conditioned, with TV. Singles from $55 to $70, doubles from $65 to $80, suites from $85 to $300. Extra person $10. In quiet part of French Quarter, blends in well with area. Coffee shop, bar, pool. Credit cards: AE, CB, DC, V.

Marie Antoinette Hotel, 827 Toulouse Street (525-2300 or 1-800-535-9730). 94 rooms, all air-conditioned, with TV. Louis XVI Restaurant is located here. Singles from $65 to $95, doubles from $75 to $115, suites from $150 to $225. Extra person $5.00. Affiliated with Century Management, which has several small French Quarter hotels. Credit cards: AE, CB, DC, V.

Place d'Armes Motor Hotel, 625 St. Ann Street (524-4531). 74 rooms, all air-conditioned, with TV. Just around the corner from Jackson Square. Singles from $60 to $75, doubles from $70 to $106, suites from $140. Extra person $10. Children under twelve free. Coffee shop, pool. Very nice, has quiet charm. Credit cards: AE, DC, MC, V.

Prince Conti, 830 Conti Street (529-4172). 50 rooms, all air-conditioned, with TV. Free parking. Singles from $60 to $80, doubles from $70 to $100, suites from $100 to $150. Extra person $10. Continental breakfast. One of the first French Quarter motels, now affiliated with Century Management (1-800-535-9111). Some rooms have antiques.

Provincial Motel, 1024 Chartres Street (581-4995). 96 rooms, all air-conditioned, with TV. Has its own WATS line (1-800-535-7922). Singles from $65 to $70, doubles from $70. Suites $80 to $90. Restaurant, pool, bar, free parking. This hotel blends in very nicely with a quiet part of the French Quarter. Family-owned. Credit cards: AE, CB, DC, MC, V.

St. Louis Hotel, 730 Bienville Street (581-7300 or 1-800-581-7300). 66 rooms, all air-conditioned, with TV. Restaurant, lounge. Singles from $100 to $125, doubles from $110 to $140, suites from $175 to $400. Parking $5.50. What a beautiful building! Very elegant. The restaurant, **L'Escale,** is extremely good, and the patio is exquisite. An award-winning French Quarter design. Credit cards: AE, DC, MC, V.

Business District

Le Pavillon Hotel, Baronne and Poydras streets (581-3111 or 1-800-535-9095). 226 rooms, all air-conditioned, with TV. Singles from $62 to $70, doubles from $72 to $80, suites from $95 to $375. Parking $4.00. Restaurant, lounge, pool. Was once the Desoto Hotel, frequented by Huey Long. Renovated. Credit cards: AE, CB, DC, M, V.

Sugar House, 315 Julia Street (525-1993 or 1-800-421-6045 outside Louisiana). 227 suites, all air-conditioned, with TV. All have wet bars. Rates begin at $120. Restaurant, lounge, pool, meeting space. Parking for a fee. All major credit cards. This project, designed by the World's Fair architects, August Perez and Associates, is scheduled to open in May 1984.

Warwick Hotel, 1315 Gravier Street (586-0100). 171 rooms, all air-conditioned, with TV. Affiliated with Downtowner chain. Singles $39, doubles $45, suites $90, parking $4.00. Once an apartment building, right near city hall, the public library, etc. The restaurant here usually has very good food. This is a standard hotel, has a small lobby, but is quite a good value for the money. Credit cards: AE, CB, DC, MC, V.

Windsor Court, 1 Poydras Street (523-6000). 330 suites, all air-conditioned, with TV. Most have kitchenettes. Rates begin at $125. Restaurant, lounge, pool, and health club, meeting space. Parking for a fee. All major credit cards. A luxurious, suites-only hotel opening February 1984.

Uptown

Avenue Plaza Hotel, 2111 St. Charles Avenue (566-1212 or 1-800-535-9575). 85 rooms, all air-conditioned, with TV and some wet bars and refrigerators. Another apartment building turned hotel. Singles $60, couples $70, extra person $12.50. Suites $150. Parking $3.00. Avenue Café restaurant. Credit cards: AE, CB, DC, MC, V.

Beauregard Hotel, 1319 St. Charles Avenue (522-0187). 136 rooms, all air-conditioned, with TV. This new hotel, done by a couple much interested in historic preservation, combines five Greek Revival town houses with some reproduced nineteenth-century buildings around a series of courtyards. Balconies and attention to decoration. Pool, restaurant. Average room rate from $68 to $70, suites $90 to $100. Credit cards: AE, CB, DC, MC, V.

Pontchartrain Hotel, 2031 St. Charles Avenue (524-0581). 73 rooms, all air-conditioned, with TV. Singles from $75 to $125, doubles from $85 to $155, suites from $175 to $410. A stay at the

Pontchartrain is like a short course in how to run the best small hotel in the country. Simply elegant, in all ways. The Coffee Shop (where politicians gather for breakfast), Caribbean Room Restaurant, Bayou Bar. Antiques in suites. Treat yourself to a stay at the Pontchartrain at least once in your life. Credit cards: AE, CB, DC, MC, V.

St. Charles Hotel, 2203 St. Charles Avenue (529-4261 or 1-800-535-9676). 132 rooms, all air-conditioned, with TV. Free parking. Once an apartment building but all redone. Singles $50, doubles $60, suites $85. Savoir Faire Restaurant is here, plus a piano bar. Credit cards: AE, CB, DC, MC, V.

BIG HOTELS

This category includes the biggest in town, the places where national conventions gather. The French Quarter ones are somewhat smaller but are still large enterprises.

French Quarter

Monteleone Hotel, 214 Royal Street (523-3341). 600 rooms, all air-conditioned, with TV. Singles from $75 to $95, doubles from $85 to $120. Suites from $155 to $450. Extra person $15. Children under twelve free. Restaurant, lounge, nightclub. Rooftop bar in summer. Pool. Credit cards: AE, CB, DC, MC, V. An older hotel.

Royal Lafayette, 717 Orleans Street (523-2222). 220 rooms, all air-conditioned, with TV. Singles from $80 to $125, doubles from $95 to $140, suites from $155 to $425. Extra person $15. Children under twelve free. This building houses the old Orleans Ballroom. Bar. Pool. Restaurant. Credit cards: AE, CB, MC, V.

Royal Orleans Hotel, 621 St. Louis Street (529-5333 or 1-800-535-7988). 388 rooms, all air-conditioned, with TV. Singles from $90 to $120, doubles from $125 to $140. Suites from $225 to $350. Parking $4.50. Children under twelve free. Rib Room Restaurant. Bar. Esplanade Lounge with pianist. Rooftop pool and bar. The Royal Orleans is the hotel that occurs to most Orleanians when they think of French Quarter hotels. A carefully run establishment with a fine catering department for large affairs. Credit cards: AE, DC, MC, V.

Royal Sonesta Hotel, 300 Bourbon Street (586-0300 or 1-800-343-7170). 494 rooms, all air-conditioned, with color TV. Bar, restaurant, oyster bar, central courtyard, and sumptuous lobby. Good executive chef. Singles from $85 to $155, doubles from $95 to $155. Extra person $20. Children under sixteen free. Parking $4.75. Credit cards: AE, DC, MC, V.

Business District

Fairmont Hotel, 123 Baronne Street (529-7111). 830 rooms, all air-conditioned, with TV. Singles from $80 to $110, doubles from $100 to $130, suites from $175 to $850. Blue Room nightclub, Sazarac Bar, lounge, restaurants, pool, tennis courts. Once the Roosevelt Hotel, this is an old New Orleans landmark that has been somewhat refurbished. Credit cards: AE, CB, DC.

Hyatt Regency, 500 Poydras Plaza (561-1234). 1,195 rooms, all air-conditioned, with TV. Singles from $70 to $99, doubles from $99 to $119, suites from $225 to $475. Parking $5.00. Restaurant, pool, bar, shops. Right next to the Superdome. May have good local piano players in atrium lounge. Credit cards: AE, CB, DC, MC, V.

The Iberville at Canal Place, Iberville at North Peters Street (525-2536). 446 rooms, including 46 suites, all air-conditioned, with TV. A Trusthouse-Forte hotel. Restaurant, bar, health club, shops. Singles from $120 to $150, doubles $140 to $170, suites $275 to $850. All major credit cards. This hotel is supposed to open in the summer of 1984.

International Hotel, 300 Canal Street (581-1300). 375 rooms, all air-conditioned, with TV. Singles from $79 to $98, doubles from $100 to $115, suites from $250. Parking $6.50. Restaurant, lounge, pool. Not as grand as the rest in this group, but not far from the World's Fair site. Credit cards: AE, CB, DC, MC, V.

New Orleans Hilton and Towers Hotel, Poydras Street at the Mississippi River (561-0500). 1,600 rooms, all air-conditioned, with TV. Singles from $82 to $100, doubles from $104 to $122, suites from $240 to $425. The Towers luxury accommodations right on the Mississippi have singles at $110 and doubles at $132. Suites are also available (call for rates). Pool, tennis courts, racquetball, bars, restaurants, Pete Fountain's Night Club, shops. Very near the World's Fair. A giant. Credit cards: AE, CB, DC, MC, V. Parking $7.50 a day, extra charge for in and out.

New Orleans Marriott Hotel, 555 Canal Street (581-1000). 1,330 rooms, all air-conditioned, with TV. Singles from $85 to $115, doubles from $105 to $135, suites from $190 to $575, extra person $15. Children under sixteen free. Restaurants, bars, entertainment, swimming pools. Credit cards: AE, CB, DC, MC, V.

Ramada Hotel, 1732 Canal Street (525-5525). 1,036 rooms, all air-conditioned, with TV. Singles $45, doubles $53, extra person $8.00. Children under eighteen free with parents. Restaurant, lounge, café. Parking $5.00. This remodeling of an old apartment house has some very spiffy decorating in the public areas. All major credit cards.

Sheraton New Orleans, 500 Canal Street (525-2500). 1,700 rooms, all air-conditioned, with TV. Singles from $78 to $104, doubles from $98 to $124, suites from $250 to $500. Parking $6.00. Restaurants, lounge, pool, nightclub. May have local pianists in Gazebo. Has hired good executive chef. Credit cards: AE, CB, DC, MC, V.

MOTELS

Every chain that you can name has a New Orleans motel. If you want to stay in one, call WATS information (1-800-525-1212) for their reservations number in your area. Slidell is *not* in New Orleans, and when the expressway traffic is bad, it could take you a long time to get into town. Metairie is closer in than Kenner.

The West Bank is another place that may cause you traffic problems getting into town.

If you do stay at an outlying motel, you can park your car reasonably in the French Quarter at the D. H. Holmes department store garage on Iberville Street. You park yourself, and they are open till midnight, with lower nightly rates. You can park a van safely at the Superdome garage, then take the shuttle bus (thirty cents) to Canal Street.

These are three motels that seem to offer the usual amenities at low prices. One is close to the center of town, and, if you want a motel, you might consider them.

Days Inn, 1630 Canal Street, New Orleans (586-0110). 216 rooms, air-conditioned, with TV. Singles $49.88, doubles $54.88, extra person $5.00, children under eighteen $1.00. Free parking, pool, restaurant (where kids under twelve eat free). All major credit cards.

Days Inn, 1300 Veterans Boulevard, Kenner (469-2531). 371 rooms, air-conditioned, with TV. Singles $30.88, doubles $35.88, extra person $12, children under eighteen $1.00. Free parking, pool, restaurant (where kids under twelve eat free). All major credit cards.

Days Inn, 5801 Read Boulevard, New Orleans East (241-2500). 143 rooms. Singles $35.88, doubles $39.88, extra person $4.00, children under eighteen $1.00. All rooms air-conditioned, with TV. Restaurant, pool. All major credit cards.

BED AND BREAKFAST

If you like, you can stay in a private home and even have breakfast the next morning. European travelers know what to expect from bed-and-breakfast places, but they may be new to some Americans. The rates vary according to the luxury of the accommodations, and some effort should be made to match compatible hosts and guests.

Bed and Breakfast, Inc., 1236 Decatur Street, New Orleans,

Louisiana 70116 (525-4640). A member of the American Bed and Breakfast Association. Singles begin at $15, doubles at $25, up to $110. Some are in separate apartments in houses, some at guesthouses with owner living on the premises. Write for a form.

New Orleans Bed and Breakfast, P.O. Box 8163, New Orleans, Louisiana 70182 (949-6705). Priced from $20 to $125 for a couple, some shared and some private baths. May have some listings around Louisiana.

BUDGET SPECIALS

If you really don't care what sort of room you sleep in and plan to be out touring or partying, and if you are young or adventuresome, these choices may be up your alley.

La Salle Hotel, 113 Canal Street (523-5831). 64 rooms, all air-conditioned, with TV. 18 rooms share baths. Singles from $22 to $30.50, doubles from $23.50 to $34. Suites $30 for four, shared bath. Extra person $4.00, children under twelve free. Laundry room available. Commercial hotel next to the Saenger Theater. Lots of European guests, not fancy but a good value. Credit cards: AE, CB, DC, MC, V.

L'Auberge Hotel and Guest House, 717 Barracks Street (523-1130). Ten or eleven people, some of whom may share rooms as well as baths. Per person $25 a night. Two kitchens available for guests' use. Two baths. All rooms have ceiling fans and air-conditioning.

Marquette House International Hostel, 2253 Carondelet Street (523-3014). Member of International Youth Hostel Association. 60 beds, kitchen use. Members $6.25, nonmembers $8.25. Not an area for strolling.

YMCA International Center, 936 St. Charles Avenue (568-9622). 250 rooms, all air-conditioned. Men, women, and children. Some shared baths. Singles from $13.20 to $25, doubles from $18 to $28. Parking $3.00. Health club and restaurant available.

TIME-SHARES

New Orleans has numerous time-share developments: apartment buildings where each apartment is sold in weeks. Owners "own" their week in that apartment each year.

If you have a time-share week somewhere, check and see if it can be exchanged to a New Orleans site. The time-share developments nationwide are supposed to afford you the possibility of exchanging locations.

It may also be possible to rent a time-share unit for a week. The units are usually modernized apartments in a complex with a swimming pool. There will be a kitchen. You should ask about linen and maid service.

Here are two time-share developments. Both have been extensively modernized, but they do have some New Orleans amenities.

Chateau Orleans, 240 Burgundy Street (524-8412). This one is located in the French Quarter and has an attractive courtyard. There is a swimming pool.

Woodhouse Row, 800 St. Charles Avenue (561-8200). This location is around the corner from Julia Row, the 1830 town houses being restored. The neighborhood is somewhat seedy but is right in the business district. Woodhouse Row has many nice architectural features. There is free parking. A swimming pool is being added.

CAMPING

If you have brought your recreational vehicle with you to New Orleans, you will need a trailer park. If you are intent on sleeping in a tent during your stay here, you'll need a campground.

If you are planning on combining your New Orleans vacation with some camping in the woods, read the chapter on "Sports." The Sierra Club's *Trail Guide to the Delta Country* and pamphlets on the Louisiana State Wildlife Management Areas are mentioned, and information on local outfitting shops that organize expeditions will also be found in that chapter.

TRAILER PARKS AND CAMPGROUNDS

Parc d'Orleans I and II, Chef Menteur Highway (241-3167 and 242-6176). Number I, at 7676 Chef Menteur Highway, has 75 sites and Number II, at 10910 Chef Menteur Highway, has 120 sites. Both will take recreational vehicles or tent campers. Both have swimming pools and shuttle bus transportation ($1.50 a person) into town. Chef Menteur Highway is on Highway 90, and there are several trailer parks located on this road, which runs east of New Orleans.

Riverboat Travel Park, 6232 Chef Menteur Highway (246-2628). No tent campers but all other amenities, pool, shuttle bus, etc.

STATE PARKS

Write for a brochure on state parks to Department of Culture, Recreation and Tourism, Office of State Parks, P.O. Drawer 1111,

Baton Rouge, Louisiana 70821. Two pretty parks are across Lake Pontchartrain: Fontainebleau, at Lacombe; and Fairview-Riverside, near Madisonville. Both are reached via the Lake Pontchartrain Causeway, and both have campgrounds.

Bayou Segnette State Park, Drake Avenue off Highway 90 in Westwego. This small West Bank community is just over the Huey P. Long Bridge from New Orleans and will be the site of a 600-acre park, scheduled to open in the spring of 1985. A recreation area with hiking and canoe trails, camping facilities, and a "wave pool" with an automatic wave machine is planned.

St. Bernard State Park, P.O. Box 534, Violet, Louisiana 70092 (682-2101). This 350-acre park is 18 miles southeast of New Orleans on Highway 39 in St. Bernard Parish. There are campsites, hookups, showers, a pool, lagoons, and picnic areas.

This is about as close as you can get to wilderness camping during a New Orleans vacation, but all the usual trailer park facilities are available.

RESTAURANTS

Unbelievable as it may seem, New Orleans restaurants get better every year.

Even the big hotel chains like Hilton and Sheraton seem to make an extra effort in their New Orleans' kitchens.

New Orleans, of course, has its own recognizable cuisine, but you can find good examples of almost any style of cooking here. There are two fine guides to New Orleans restaurants: Richard and Rima Collin's *The New Orleans Restaurant Guide,* which has an annual insert with updated ratings; and *New Orleans Menu Magazine*'s annual *Review of One Hundred Restaurants,* by Tom Fitzmorris. Fitzmorris as "Mister Food" may do critiques in the *Citibusiness* tabloid, and his *Menu Magazine* is published monthly and available in bookstores. He even turns up on cable television.

If you are on a strict budget, you can still eat well. Even franchises can be good in New Orleans, and sandwiches are incredibly tasty here. The business district has many lunchrooms with daily specials, and neighborhood restaurants may have talented cooks.

One way to save is to try an expensive restaurant for lunch. New Orleans' restaurant prices are still far below New York's, so you may be pleasantly surprised.

Since New Orleans is a late-night town, you will be able to get a good meal late in the evening. Just don't arrive five minutes before closing time if you want the best food.

Dress codes have relaxed in New Orleans, but the finer restaurants still require a coat and tie for gentlemen, especially for dinner. Reservations—except at Galatoire's, K-Paul's, and Antoine's—are essential. If you are coming in for Mardi Gras or a special event, write in advance.

To better enjoy dining in New Orleans you should be sure to read the chapter on "New Orleans Food." While you are here, you should try local dishes. Eat red beans and rice for lunch on Monday. Have some gumbo. Try boiled crabs and shrimp and crawfish. Have a po' boy sandwich and a long-necked Dixie or a Barq's. You will find that you will know more about New Orleans if you taste it as well as look at it.

This listing of New Orleans restaurants does not include every one. It does, however, include the ones where you can get well-prepared food, see local people, and have a memorable dining experience.

GRAND RESTAURANTS

These include the best-known New Orleans restaurants and are, in general, quite expensive. Plan to dress up.

Antoine's, 713 St. Louis Street (581-4422). Open daily from noon to 9 P.M., closed Sunday. Oysters Rockefeller was invented here. The soufflé potatoes, the fish dishes, and—remarkably— the steaks are very good, and the wine cellar is extensive. The front room has sparse decor, but the rear dining rooms can be plush. You may have to wait in line outside. This is a very old New Orleans restaurant and well patronized by locals.

Arnaud's, 813 Bienville Street (523-5433). Open daily from 11 A.M. to 3 P.M., except Saturday, and from 6 P.M. to 10 P.M., except Sunday. Arnaud's has long been a favorite local spot and has recently been totally redone, from the kitchen to the decor. Shrimp Arnaud, with a remoulade sauce, is a must. The bread pudding is good. Try some seafood dishes, perhaps pompano.

Brennan's, 417 Royal Street (525-9711). Open daily from 8:30 A.M. to 2:30 P.M. and from 6 P.M. to 11 P.M. You must have breakfast at Brennan's at least once. Eggs poached and covered with succulent sauces, crispy french bread, and oysters 2-2-2 (that gives you a sampling of three kinds of baked-oysters-on-the-half-shell recipes), plus flaming desserts. Brennan's kitchen can accommodate you well for late dining, but be sure and have reservations.

Caribbean Room, 2031 St. Charles Avenue (524-0581). Open weekdays from 11 A.M. to 2 P.M. and daily from 8 P.M. to 10 P.M. Housed in the Pontchartrain Hotel, the Caribbean Room has wonderful crabmeat appetizers. Trout Véronique, with white grapes and hollandaise sauce, is delicious. The Pontchartrain also has a coffee shop with earlier hours where the same kitchen makes simpler dishes. Politicians regularly breakfast there.

Commander's Palace, 1403 Washington Avenue (899-8221). Open daily from 11 A.M. to 3 P.M. and from 6 P.M. to 10 P.M. The Brennan family split, and one branch now has Commander's and also Mr. B's Bistro on Royal and Iberville streets. Commander's is the place to come for Sunday brunch because there is jazz music. The soup here is especially good, and you can even get a 1-1-1, which is three little cups of different soups. They have good veal and scrumptious desserts. This is the place movie stars come to in New Orleans. See if you can be seated upstairs in the Garden Room. This is a perfect lunch stop during a Garden District tour.

Galatoire's, 209 Bourbon Street (525-2021). Open daily from 11:30 A.M. to 9 P.M. (closed Monday). Everybody stands outside in line to get into Galatoire's—because it's worth the wait. If there is any one thing that signified the restaurant revolution in New Orleans, it was when Galatoire's got decent wineglasses. Otherwise the barbershop-style decor—white tile floors and mirrored walls—has never changed. Everything is fresh that day and lovingly prepared. The Trout Marguery, with a cream seafood sauce; the pompano; even the egg dishes are good. The lights occasionally blink—for some reason they have DC electricity—the waiters may make everyone sing "Happy Birthday to You" to some celebrant, the locals tend to table-hop and move their chairs around to chat with friends, but Galatoire's is a restaurant you will love.

Jonathan, 714 North Rampart Street (586-1930). Open week-days from 11 A.M. to 2 P.M. and from 6 P.M. to 10:30 P.M., Saturdays from 6 P.M. to 11 P.M. What a jewel of a restaurant! Everything about Jonathan (even the phone number) is 1930. If you like Art Deco, you will love Jonathan. However, it's worth visiting for the food. The cuisine here is imaginative, and the chef always has something new—seviche, a curry, a new way with liver. The desserts are especially good. Jonathan is a good place to go before a show at the Theatre of the Performing Arts across the street. This is another spot frequented by visiting actors.

LeRuth's, 636 Franklin Street (361-4914). Open daily from 5:45 P.M. to 10 P.M. (closed Sunday). Take the Greater New Orleans Bridge over the river, take the first exit right, continue, and at the third traffic light turn right. Go three blocks to LeRuth's. Once Warren LeRuth took out an ad in the *Times-Picayune* to announce that he was taking some tables out of the dining room so he could serve fewer people. He usually closes and takes a vacation in summer. If anyone sparked the renaissance in New Orleans cooking, it was Warren LeRuth. Let your big-splurge dinner be here, and you will treasure the memory. There is an artichoke-oyster soup, a wonderful avocado Green Goddess salad dressing, soft-shell crab, rack of lamb, and sautéed bananas as a side dish. The atmosphere is warm and friendly, and the mandarin ice may be the best dessert ever. Write for reservations far in advance.

Louis XVI, 829 Toulouse Street (581-7000). Open weekdays 11:30 A.M. to 3 P.M. and daily from 6 P.M. to 10 P.M. This is French cuisine and New Orleanians love it. There is a lot of table-side serving and carving and well-trained waiters. The rack of lamb is fabulous, and there is always an elegant cream soup. The hors d'oeuvres are especially good. The Louis XVI is at the Marie Antoinette Hotel.

Versailles, 2100 St. Charles Avenue (524-2535). Open Monday through Saturday from 6 P.M. to 10 P.M. Chef Gunther Preuss always has good food and especially good vegetable garnishes. The snails-in-french-bread appetizer, the soups, and the seafood are all good bets. Versailles is downstairs at the Carol, a condominium apartment building.

CHEF-OWNED RESTAURANTS

These restaurants seem to go in a category together: all of them bear the strong touch of their chef owners. This in no way means that they are in a class below the "Grand Restaurants" —they just seemed to fit together as a group. If you want to drop the name of "a little place we discovered in New Orleans," it would probably be one on this list.

Christian's, 3835 Iberville Street (482-4924). Open Monday through Saturday from II:30 A.M. to 2 P.M. and from 5:30 P.M. to 10 P.M. Christian Ansel, a Galatoire relative, managed to find a building to suit his name: this restaurant is located in a renovated church, visible from Canal Street in the 3800 block. Inside is a pleasant restaurant and a tiny bar. The cooking is reminiscent of Galatoire's, but there are some nouvelle cuisine dishes from time to time, perhaps chicken with blackberry vinegar. The redfish appetizer is good.

Willy Coln's, 2505 Whitney Avenue, Gretna (361-3860). Open Tuesday through Saturday from 6 P.M. to 10 P.M. Willy Coln cooks German as well as French food. There is a veal shank entrée for two with lots of fresh vegetables. The Bahamian seafood soup is interesting. He even does a choucroute garnie— sauerkraut with sausages—if you're in the mood. There is a Black Forest cake for dessert. Willy Coln's is one of several very good restaurants on the West Bank.

Crozier's, 7033 Read Lane (241-8220). Open Tuesday through Saturday from 6 P.M. to 10 P.M. Gerard and Eveline Crozier preside over their small, very French, restaurant. The pâté is good, the trout with fennel excellent, and the Tournedos Gérard (filet of beef with foie gras and a cream sauce) is divine. The menu is small, but the dishes are beautifully prepared, and Eveline and Gerard provide the proper welcoming atmosphere.

K-Paul's Louisiana Kitchen, 416 Chartres Street (524-7394). Open weekdays from 6 P.M. to 10 P.M. Paul Prudhomme learned to cook at home in Opelousas. He is a phenomenon, the sort of chef Craig Claiborne of the New York *Times* brought up to New York for his birthday dinner. This is Cajun cooking with flair and superfresh ingredients. Paul's ideal is to have a cooking school where apprentice chefs would learn to grow the vegetables and care for the rabbits, chickens, and pigs and do all the butchering, sausage making, and farm work as well as learn to create memorable dishes. Try the eggplant pirogues with seafood, try anything with crawfish (even Cajun Popcorn: fried crawfish tails), and the rabbit. Don't forget the gumbo and jambalaya. You have to stand outside in line to get in, but you will get a gold star when you clean your plate. K-Paul's is a simply decorated café, but the ceiling cartoons illustrating various dishes will keep you looking up.

La Provence, Highway 190, Lacombe (1-626-7667). Open Tuesday through Friday from 11 A.M. to 3 P.M. and from 5 P.M. to 9 P.M., Saturday from 5 P.M. to 9 P.M., and Sunday from 1 P.M. to 9 P.M. Chris Kerageorgiu has created the best reason to drive across Lake Pontchartrain for dinner, or lunch. The only problem is that one member of the party has to forego the second glass of wine to drive everyone home. The best appetizer: a cart full of charcuterie, sausages, and pâtés made by the chef. There is duck, veal, pompano, and sole, plus whatever daily special comes into the chef's fertile mind. The restaurant has a marvelous open fireplace and is especially cozy and romantic in the winter months.

Maurice's Bistro Room, 1637 Stumpf Boulevard, Gretna. Open Monday through Saturday from 6 P.M. to 11 P.M. Maurice Bitoun is at this restaurant, and his brother has **Maison André,** General de Gaulle Drive at Holiday Drive in Algiers. The Bitouns are from Algeria, and they are French. Maurice has amazing herbal and flavored sauces on birds and beef. There is always some fried parsley to munch on and some delicious toasted french-bread appetizers with a cheese-tomato topping. Maurice's Bistro is for a long leisurely meal with lots of good talk and wine.

ECLECTIC RESTAURANTS

There's a little something for everyone here. These cafés all have personality, and they are popular. And they have good food.

Bouligny, 4100 Magazine Street (891-4444). Open daily from 11 A.M. to 2:30 P.M. and from 6 P.M. to 11 P.M. Sunday brunch from 10:30 A.M. to 5 P.M. One of the new, hot uptown dining spots with a very attractive setting, part of which is a remodeled firehouse.

Café Sbisa, 1011 Decatur Street (561-8354). Open Tuesday through Saturday from 6 P.M. to midnight, Sundays from 11:30 A.M. to 2:30 P.M. and from 6 P.M. to 10 P.M. This is an attractive renovation with a restaurant on two levels. There is a grilled redfish (a dish Paul Prudhomme introduced to New Orleans when he worked for the Brennan family of Commander's) and new potatoes with sour cream to accompany it. There is other grilled seafood, plus veal. This is a trendy spot and good for late-night dining if you remember not to wander around in the neighborhood.

Clancy's, 6100 Annunciation Street (895-1111). Open weekdays from 11:30 A.M. to 2:30 P.M. and from 5:30 P.M. to 10:30 P.M., Saturdays from 5:30 P.M. to 10:30 P.M. A mesquite pit for smoked duck, lots of imaginative dishes: cold meat salads, good soups. Plus a pastry cart that will ruin any diet. Same sort of lunch crowd as Galatoire's.

Gautreau's, 1728 Soniat Street (899-7397). Open Mondays from 11 A.M. to 2:15 P.M., Tuesday through Friday from 11 A.M. to 2:15 P.M. and from 6 P.M. to 10 P.M., Saturdays from 6 P.M. to 10 P.M. Good crêpes and casseroles and fantastic chocolate desserts.

Indulgence, 1539 Religious Street (523-2209), and at Prytania Street and Washington Avenue (899-4411). Religious Street restaurant open Tuesday through Friday from 11:30 A.M. to 2 P.M. Prytania Street restaurant open Monday through Thursday from 11:30 A.M. to 2:30 P.M. and from 5:30 P.M. to 9 P.M., Fridays and

Saturdays from 11:30 A.M. to 2:30 P.M. and from 5:30 P.M. to 10 P.M., Sundays from 11:30 A.M. to 2:30 P.M. Reservations essential. Frank Bailey writes a food column for *Dixie* magazine of the *Times-Picayune*—and here is where you can taste his recipes. Fresh herbs from his garden. If you have time for a long lunch, spend it here.

Marti's, 1041 Dumaine Street (524-6060). Open weekdays from 11:30 A.M. to 2:30 P.M. and from 5:30 P.M. to 11 P.M., Saturdays from 5:30 P.M. to 11 P.M. Marti stays open later when there's a ball or performance at the Municipal Auditorium or the Theatre of the Performing Arts across the street. You can get New Orleans food at Marti's: red beans and rice, grilled andouille sausage, gumbo. The menu is on a blackboard. There is a good steak au poivre. This is another chic café. Tennessee Williams was a regular patron when he lived down the block on Dumaine Street.

Savoir Faire, 2203 St. Charles Avenue (529-4261). Open Monday through Saturday from 11 A.M. to 11 P.M. Lots of interior-decorator touches, but good cooking from the kitchen, where the chef was trained by Chef Daniel Bonnot of Louis XVI. Here you will find some nouvelle cuisine, with original crisp vegetable and seafood combinations, a good garlic soup, sweetbreads. Also there are mussels—not often seen on New Orleans menus. There are no reservations, but all the locals are happily waiting for tables as Savoir Faire becomes a fashionable uptown eatery.

The Upperline, 1413 Upperline Street (891-9822). Open Tuesday through Thursday from 11:30 A.M. to 2:30 P.M. and from 6 P.M. to 11 P.M., Fridays and Saturdays from 11:30 A.M. to 2:30 P.M. and from 6 P.M. to midnight, Sundays from 5 P.M. to 10 P.M. Grilled seafood and chicken, seafood boudin, new ways with standard New Orleans fare. Call for reservations as this is a popular spot.

GOOD-VALUE RESTAURANTS

The category holds four pleasant restaurants and, for lagniappe, a cafeteria, where you can get very good food at reasonable prices.

Berdou's, 300 Monroe Street, Gretna (368-2401). Open Tuesday through Saturday from 11 A.M. to 7:30 P.M. Reservations are necessary at Berdou's—the natives know a good thing when they see it. There are standard New Orleans restaurant dishes: pompano en papillote (in a paper sack), trout fried and broiled, and Crabmeat Berdou in a garlicky sauce. The prices are low and usually include salad, an appetizer or soup, and dessert. Mrs. Berdou has a dress code forbidding blue jeans or any denim pants, and she closes the doors promptly at 7:30. If you have the kids and want a good New Orleans meal, change their clothes and take them to Berdou's.

Delmonico's, 1300 St. Charles Avenue (525-4937). Open daily from 11:30 A.M. to 9:30 P.M. Inside this Victorian house is a Creole cooking mecca. The dining rooms are just fancy enough, without being overwhelmingly elegant. Children are welcome, and you'll see family groups. The soups are good, the dinner salad with all sorts of vegetables is delicious, and there are dinners with several courses available. There is a good catfish meunière, and the Chicken Anthony (wrapped around ham and cheese) is tasty. If you don't go overboard on before-dinner drinks and wine, you'll be pleasantly surprised at the bill.

La Cuisine, 225 West Harrison Avenue (486-5154). Open Tuesday through Saturday from 11:30 A.M. to 10 P.M. This is another spot to take the children for a good dinner. There is New Orleans Creole cooking, lots of good seafood, interesting soups, and even an oyster bar for fresh oysters on the half shell. You can even get an entrée with three kinds of trout dishes. The portions are quite large, so order carefully. Again, watch your bar bill, and you'll keep the costs down.

Feelings, 2600 Chartres Street (945-2222). Open Monday

through Saturday from 6 P.M. to 10 P.M., Sunday from 5 P.M. to 9 P.M. Feelings occupies the building that once held Luthjens dance hall. Now there is a bar, a patio, and some pleasant dining rooms. There are dinners with several courses on the menu at very reasonable prices. The chicken dishes and the lasagna are good, and the gumbo is also. There are some nice desserts, including a peanut butter pie. If you go in the evening, don't plan on a stroll in the neighborhood.

Wise's Cafeteria, 909 South Jefferson Davis Parkway (488-7811). Open Sunday through Friday from 7 A.M. to 8 P.M. This may look like a run-of-the-mill cafeteria, but locals know you can get some good New Orleans cooking here: red beans and rice, gumbo, seafood, bread pudding. You can't go wrong at Wise's.

NEIGHBORHOOD RESTAURANTS

Small restaurants are scattered all over New Orleans. These are just two: one on the St. Charles Avenue streetcar line and one in Mid City on Canal Street.

Compagno's, 7839 St. Charles Avenue (866-9313). Open Tuesday through Sunday from 10 A.M. to 10 P.M. and Tuesday through Thursday from 2 P.M. to 5 P.M. There is a bar, and there are some tables. What fills them up are a collection of Tulane students, families, and neighborhood regulars. The Italian cooking is good, with fresh-cooked pasta for each order. The fried seafood is excellent, as is the fried chicken.

Mandina's, 3800 Canal Street (482-9179). Open Monday through Saturday from 11 A.M. to 10:30 P.M. Mandina's seems to have an enormous number of regular patrons because it's always crowded and everyone knows each other. There is good gumbo, good fried seafood, and occasional daily specials. Plus lots of cold Dixie to wash it all down.

SANDWICHES

Po' boys, muffalettas, and hamburgers—New Orleans brings the sandwich up to the level of an art form. Taste for yourself.

Bud's Broiler, 5338 Banks Street. Open Sunday through Friday from 11 A.M. to 2 P.M. and from 5 P.M. to 10 P.M., Saturday from 11 A.M. to 10 P.M. There are Bud's Broilers all over town, and if your kids insist on a franchise hamburger for lunch (or you crave one yourself), find a Bud's and enjoy a charcoal-broiled burger with some really good house sauce. There are also hot dogs and a chicken sandwich. You can get soft drinks and beer.

Camellia Grill, 646 South Carrollton Avenue (866-9573). Open daily from 9 A.M. to 1:40 A.M. You sit at a counter, but you get a linen napkin: that's Camellia Grill. If you need a late-night hamburger, or waffle or omelet, you're in luck. Camellia Grill is known and patronized by just about everybody (and they may all be standing in line outside when you arrive).

Central Grocery Company, 923 Decatur Street (523-9851). Open Monday through Saturday from 9 A.M. to 5 P.M. To make a muffaletta sandwich: on a round italian loaf pile olive salad, cheeses, meats, and salami. Result: ecstasy! Visit the Central Grocery for your muffaletta, get a Barq's from the machine, and have a picnic in Jackson Square (hide the can in your brown bag —open containers on the streets are illegal). The Central Grocery Company, a haven of caloric provender, is filled with enticing pastas, spices, dried cod, snails, and all manner of interesting foodstuffs. Sometimes there is a tray of baclava for sale by the slice.

Mother's, 401 Poydras Street (523-9658). Open Monday through Saturday from 6 A.M. to 3 P.M. Everybody from stockbrokers to street cleaners eats at Mother's. Try the Ferdie Special (ham and roast beef) or the Debris (the end slices and trim of roast beef) and get lots of gravy. If you get your sandwich "dressed"—which usually means with lettuce and tomatoes—it comes with sliced cabbage at Mother's. Breakfast and lunch specials are also available.

Parasol's, 2533 Constance Street (899-2054). Open daily from 11:30 A.M. to 2 P.M. and from 5 P.M. to 9 P.M. (closed Sunday and Tuesday). Parasol's is an Irish Channel institution, a "must" stop for all campaigning politicians, and a madhouse on St. Patrick's Day. The service is slow, but the roast beef po' boys are wonderful. Also they sometimes have homemade fudge.

Uglesich's, 1238 Baronne Street (523-8547). Open weekdays from 8 A.M. to 3 P.M. Uglesich is in a drab neighborhood, but the seafood po' boys make it worth an excursion. The oysters are shucked before your eyes and then fried for your sandwich.

SOUL FOOD

Black neighborhood restaurants in New Orleans add a little extra spice to Creole food. These three are good examples.

Chez Helene, 1540 North Robertson Street (947-9155). Opens at 11 A.M. daily. Closes Monday at 8 P.M., Tuesday through Thursday at 11 P.M., Friday and Saturday at 1 A.M., and Sunday at 10 P.M. The service is slow, but the food can be good. The stuffed peppers and potato salad are both well prepared, and the fried chicken can be perfect. The red beans and rice are also tasty.

Dooky Chase's, 2301 Orleans Avenue (822-9506). Open daily from 11 A.M. to 1 A.M. Dooky's is almost a community center, with concert and fight tickets on sale and a crowded bar. The gumbo is great, very peppery. Shrimp Dooky has a remoulade sauce. There are fried seafood platters and stuffed shrimp.

Eddie's, 2119 Law Street (945-2207). Open Monday through Saturday from 11 A.M. to midnight. Fried chicken, red beans and rice, fried seafood, and lots of po' boys, plus a good bread pudding.

ITALIAN RESTAURANTS

Spaghetti and meatballs appear on New Orleans tables almost as often as red beans and rice. There is a lot of good Italian cooking going on here, and you'll find the best at these restaurants.

La Riviera, 4506 Shores Drive (888-6238). Open Monday through Saturday from 5 P.M. to 9:30 P.M. This is a classic Italian restaurant, with a marvelous chef, Goffredo Fraccaro. His prize-winning crabmeat ravioli is delicious. There is freshly made fettucine and all sorts of pasta and veal dishes. Very light and flavorful sauces and a nice, friendly atmosphere.

Mosca's, Highway 90, Waggaman (436-8942). Open Tuesday through Saturday from 5 P.M. to 11 P.M. Take the Huey P. Long Bridge over the river and stay on Highway 90 for 5 miles. The nondescript white café on your left is Mosca's. The servings are huge, the food is ambrosial, and the wait for a table is long, even with a weekday reservation. There is a salad of marinated crabmeat, a wonderful garlicky pan roast of oysters, a broiled shrimp in butter that will leave you with a satisfied smile and a drenched chin, and great roast chicken. Only go to Mosca's with good friends—no one else could stand you with all that garlic.

Pascal's Manale, 1838 Napoleon Avenue (895-4877). Open weekdays from 11:30 A.M. to 10 P.M., Saturdays from 4 P.M. to 10:30 P.M. If you have a lot of patience, you won't mind the interminable wait to get into Manale's. They take reservations—they just don't do anything with them. However, there is an oyster bar for freshly shucked raw oysters, and the barbecued shrimp—dripping with butter and edible, shell and all—is worth waiting for. There are also some pasta dishes.

Toney's Spaghetti House, 212 Bourbon Street (561-9253). Open Monday through Saturday from 6 A.M. to 1 A.M. A Bourbon Street institution, and just recently renovated. Toney's has very good food, a nice tomato sauce, and good stuffed artichokes with garlic, cheese, and bread crumbs. Toney's is good for lunch, too.

SEAFOOD RESTAURANTS

All New Orleans restaurants have seafood on the menu. These are just the best of the informal dining places where seafood is the specialty.

Acme Oyster House, 724 Iberville Street (523-8928). Open Monday through Saturday from II A.M. to 6 P.M. Delicious and consistently good raw oysters. The best ones are tiny and very salty and have a dark spot, supposedly because they are changing sex, as oysters are wont to do. The Acme also has po' boys.

Alonso and Son, 587 Central Avenue (733-2796). Open Monday through Saturday from 9 A.M. to II P.M. This is a neighborhood restaurant, but the fried seafood—shrimp, oysters, fish, soft-shell crabs—is extraordinarily good. There are children's drawings of the entrées on the walls. This restaurant is extremely crowded on Friday nights, which is when most locals decide to go out and eat seafood.

Bozo's, 3117 Twenty-first Street (831-8666). Open Tuesday through Saturday from II A.M. to 10 P.M. Raw oysters, fried seafood, and good boiled shrimp, crabs, and crawfish: Bozo's got them all. This is a large restaurant but has the same neighborhood flavor it did when it was a tiny private club off Broad Street. The move to the suburbs has not changed the kitchen, and the parking is much better.

Bruning's, 1870 Orpheum Avenue (282-9395). Open Monday through Thursday (closed Wednesday) from II A.M. to 9:30 P.M., Friday and Saturday from II A.M. to 10:30 P.M. Well, maybe it's not the best seafood place in town, but Bruning's has a picturesque location, being built out over the lake at West End Park. The gumbo is good. The fried soft-shell crab is delicious. The bar is long, old, carved, and dispenses Dixie. What more could you ask?

Casamento's, 4330 Magazine Street (895-9761). Open Tuesday through Sunday from 11:30 A.M. to 1:30 P.M. and from 5:30 P.M. to 10 P.M. Closes all summer. Casamento's has tiled walls and floors, a tin ceiling, and the healthiest potted plants in town. The oysters are wonderful raw, fried, or in a hollowed loaf of unsliced toasted white bread. There is also a good oyster soup.

ORIENTAL RESTAURANTS

New Orleans has a large number of Chinese restaurants, which vary in quality as the chefs move around. These two restaurants, one Korean and one Japanese, are both tasteful and unique, and have been consistently good.

Genghis Khan, 4053 Tulane Avenue (482-4044). Open daily from 6 P.M. to 11 P.M. Korean food is somewhat similar to Chinese. At least there are egg rolls. Bulgoki, a marinated beef dish, is good, as is the Mongolian hot pot, in which you cook your own meat and vegetables in broth. For lagniappe the owner, a violinist with the symphony, may entertain you with a string quartet.

Shogun, 1414 Veterans Boulevard (833-7477). Open daily from 11:30 A.M. to 2:30 P.M. (except Tuesday and Sunday) and from 5 P.M. to 11 P.M. (except Tuesday). Listen to Japanese Muzak while you watch the tempura cook frying vegetables and morsels of meat. Or choose your own raw fish for sushi or sashimi. Shogun always seems to have lots of Japanese patrons. If you don't use chopsticks, you have to ask for a fork.

FRANCHISES

Believe it or not, New Orleans has two outstanding fast-food franchises. Creole cooking conquers all!

Popeye's Fried Chicken. Popeye's is all over town, and, by now, all over the world. The specialty is peppery hot fried chicken (order it mild if you're timid), and there is also good red beans and rice and perfect light biscuits. The genius behind Popeye's, Al Copeland, puts on a not-to-be-described lavish

Christmas display at his home on Transcontinental Drive at Lake Pontchartrain in Jefferson Parish every December. Just follow the traffic jam.

Mrs. Wheat's Kitchen, 3840 Veterans Boulevard. Mrs. Wheat's has another spot on Veterans Boulevard and more locations planned. The highlight is the Natchitoches meat pie—a half-moon-shaped fried pie with spicy meat stuffing. The salad bar here has an incredible number of ingredients and very good homemade dressings. There are also good soups.

STATEWIDE RESTAURANTS

Don's of Lafayette has a New Orleans branch (the crawfish dinner with several crawfish dishes is the specialty), as does Ralph and Kacoo's of Baton Rouge (whose specialty is catfish and hush puppies). Don's has other branches elsewhere in Louisiana. Both are adequate restaurants, but best at their home base. One New Orleans restaurant has branches in other towns, and it is worth mentioning.

Ruth's Chris Steakhouse, 711 North Broad Avenue (482-9278). Open daily from 11:30 A.M. to 11:30 P.M. Ruth's has two other New Orleans locations and several around the country, but this is the one the politicians frequent. The steak at Ruth's is prime meat, served drenched in butter and sizzling on a platter. Everything else is secondary. If you crave steak, and you're willing to pay for it, go to Ruth's.

DESSERTS

If you have a sweet tooth, you're in luck. New Orleans has some special places that you will love.

Angelo Brocato's, 214 North Carrollton Avenue (486-1465), and on Jackson Square at 513 St. Ann Street. Open daily from 10 A.M. to 10 P.M. Sit at an old-fashioned ice-cream-parlor table and enjoy creamy Italian ice creams, all sorts of *biscotti* (hard, crunchy cookies), and the cannoli—flavored ricotta cheese stuffed into a pastry roll and dipped in pistachios. There is espresso, cappuccino, and all sorts of licorice candy. Don't miss Brocato's.

Croissant d'Or, 617 Ursulines Street (524-4663). Open Wednesday through Monday from 8 A.M. to 5 P.M. Located in a refurbished ice cream parlor that used to hold Brocato's. Go for the fine french pastries and stay to enjoy the marvelously clever design of the shop and patio.

La Marquise, 525 Chartres Street (524-0420). Open Thursday through Tuesday from 9 A.M. to 5 P.M. Croissants and french pastries and just steps from Jackson Square. Buy some and nibble while you watch the pigeons.

Morning Call, 3325 Severn Avenue (885-4068). Always open. The Café du Monde is still at the French Market, but Morning Call (which moved to the suburbs) has a little bit better beignets (square doughnuts) and coffee. You shake your own powdered sugar on the beignets. Don't frequent this place in a black velvet outfit.

Switzerland Bakery, 5722 Magazine Street (899-3692). Open Tuesday through Saturday from 8 A.M. to 5 P.M. Sacher torte, cream puffs, a variety of pastries and breads from the bakery of the former Swiss consul in New Orleans. Pick some up on the way to Audubon Park.

SHOPPING

In New Orleans this is referred to as "making groceries." No one expects you to do your own cooking in New Orleans, but you may want to ship things home, and you might want some special picnic supplies. Here are some suggestions.

Chez Nous Charcuterie, 5701 Magazine Street (899-7303). Open weekdays from 11 A.M. to 6:30 P.M., Saturdays from 11 A.M. to 5 P.M. Good take-out food! Pâtés, cheeses, cold soups, breads, and crackers. Plus main dishes and quiches to take home and heat. This place has saved many an uptown hostess from culinary disaster.

Christian's Foods, 300 South Pierce Street (482-4103). Open

Tuesday through Saturday from 11 A.M. to 6 P.M. Christian's restaurant has a food outlet with sausages, pâtés, salad dressings, bread, fresh fruit ices, and assorted gourmet ingredients.

Creole Country, 512 David Street (488-1263). Open weekdays from 8 A.M. to 5:30 P.M. and Saturdays from 8 A.M. to 5 P.M. Fabulous homemade sausages and hog's head cheese, plus smoked hams. Creole Country has a shop in the Lakeside Shopping Center and one in Lafayette.

Lama's St. Roch Market, 2381 St. Claude Avenue (943-6666). Open Monday through Saturday from 8:30 A.M. to 5 P.M. Some thirty-four public market buildings were built all over New Orleans up to the 1930s. Formerly this housed the stalls of various food sellers who supplied the neighborhood. Nowadays Lama's has seafood—from trout to turtles, red snapper to squid. The best thing, however, is the boiled crawfish. Using their own special blend of peppers and spices they boil the crawfish in giant wire baskets and sell them steaming hot during the spring and early summer. Try them.

Langenstein's, corner Arabella and Pitt streets (899-9283). Open Monday through Saturday from 8:30 A.M. to 6 P.M. This uptown supermarket has everything. They may also help you pack for shipping. They boil their own crawfish, shrimp, and crabs. They bake hams, make soup, daube glacée, hog's head cheese, and pies. Plus they have all the Louisiana cooking ingredients you could need.

NIGHTLIFE

New Orleans does not fold up its sidewalks at sunset. The drinking age is eighteen; there are no Sunday closing laws; and there is a lot going on after midnight.

To find out what's going on: check the newspapers and magazines. The *Times-Picayune* has a daily "Calendar" column and, on Fridays, the Lagniappe tabloid with listings of all entertainment. *Gambit* appears weekly and has full entertainment listings. *New Orleans* and *Louisiana Life* magazines both have entertainment calendars, as does the music magazine *Wavelength*. There are several weekly tourist magazines, too.

The **Greater New Orleans Tourist and Convention Commission** has an Entertainment line at 566-5047. **Ticketmaster,** which handles tickets for concerts and other big events, is at 587-3999. Call to see what's available—they will tell you which outlet is nearest to you. The **Contemporary Arts Center,** 523-1216, keeps a weekly music calendar.

Use good sense when you go out in the evening. If you bring your car, park in a well-lit area near your destination, and obey parking laws (you don't want to be towed away). Don't pick fights, don't walk down dark streets in a strange neighborhood in the middle of the night. Don't let the pretty lady make you buy her champagne in that raunchy joint. In short, use good sense. New Orleans is probably no more dangerous a city than your hometown, but like anywhere else, if you're looking for trouble, you'll find it.

Don't drive when you've had too much to drink. You will go directly to jail.

The listings below include "Nightclubs," a category called "Special," "Clubs with Music," "Bars," "Dance Halls," "Coffee

Houses," and "Country." Not everything in town is listed, but this covers a wide range of entertaining possibilities.

When there is music, there may be a cover charge. When there's a star performer, the cover charge will be higher. The nightclubs and the hotel bars will require dressy clothes.

Remember, this list is only meant to give you a suggestion of what New Orleans has to offer. Just wait till you get your first New Orleans hangover!

NIGHTCLUBS

The Blue Room, Fairmont Hotel (529-7111). Name entertainers daily except Sunday. The Blue Room is a supper club, with a full restaurant menu. Shows at 9 P.M. and 11 P.M.

Duke's Place, Monteleone Hotel (581-1567). The Dukes of Dixieland perform Monday through Saturday atop the Monteleone Hotel.

Pete Fountain's, Hilton Hotel (523-4374). New Orleans' famous clarinetist performs Tuesday through Saturday.

Al Hirt, New Orleans' trumpet man, closed his club at 501 Bourbon Street in 1983. It's likely he will still play here occasionally—check the entertainment listings in the newspapers for him.

SPECIAL

"One Mo' Time," Toulouse Theater, 615 Toulouse Street (522-7852). This long-running show gives a night of 1926 black vaudeville, as performed in New Orleans. The music is authentic, the band is good, and the evening is fun. Don't miss it. Sometimes other New Orleans musical entertainments like this, but focusing on other eras, will appear at the same theater when *One Mo' Time* is not on. Performances Thursday through Sunday at 8:30 P.M.

Preservation Hall, 726 St. Peter Street (522-2238). Nightly from 8 P.M. to 12:30 A.M. Pay $1.00 to sit and listen to traditional jazz. A New Orleans landmark.

The President, Canal Street at the river (524-7245). Board at 8 P.M. for the 9 P.M. shows on Friday and Saturday night. Local and name entertainers, mostly rock. Dance on a riverboat while you cruise New Orleans' harbor.

Tipitina's, Napoleon Avenue at Tchoupitoulas (899-9114). New Orleans and Louisiana entertainers and occasional name stars. Spartan surroundings but mellow atmosphere: jazz, rock, rhythm and blues, Cajun. A little of everything. Go at least once.

CLUBS WITH MUSIC

Blue Angel, 225 Bourbon Street. Renovated surroundings and good jazz. Alternating George Finola and Connie Jones. Closed Sundays.

Famous Door, 339 Bourbon Street. Roy Liberto's Bourbon Street Five and other groups. Nightly.

Jimmy's, 8200 Willow Street. Another uptown club, this one with rhythm and blues, rock, and some New Wave.

Maison Bourbon, 641 Bourbon Street. Clive Wilson's Camellia Jazz Band. Clive, like several other New Orleans musicians, is English. Traditional jazz has always been big in England.

Maple Leaf Bar, 8316 Oak Street. Comfortable old-time bar with jazz, rock, Cajun, and various eclectic music.

Tyler's Beer Garden, 5234 Magazine Street. Uptown jazz club with an oyster bar. Nightly shows at 10 P.M.

BARS

Bayou Bar, Pontchartrain Hotel. Pleasant murals and a good piano player, most recently Tuts Washington.

Nick Castrogiovanni's, 505 South Tonti Street. Not very attractive but popular because of fantastic mixed drinks: try the pousse café, layers of liqueurs.

Chart House, Chartres and St. Ann streets. Sit on the balcony and overlook Jackson Square and have a drink from the bar of this steak house.

The Embers, Bourbon and St. Peter streets. Have a drink in the second-floor lounge of this steak house and hear Bourbon Street music from the balcony.

Esplanade Lounge, Royal Orleans Hotel. A piano player, comfortable chairs, and very good pastry or fancy coffee drinks. Right in the lobby.

Forty One Forty One, 4141 St. Charles Avenue. Large bar, game rooms, Stephen and Martin's Restaurant. Young adult hangout.

Lafitte's Blacksmith Shop, 941 Bourbon Street. Dark, quiet piano bar where the pirate Lafitte supposedly had his local headquarters.

Mystick Den, Royal Sonesta Hotel. Quiet bar with Elario and his guitar.

Napoleon House, 500 Chartres Street. Best bar in town. Somewhat dingy, tiny patio, ceiling fans, classical records for entertainment, and muffalettas if you're hungry. Order a Pimm's Cup: mild punch with a cucumber slice.

Pat O'Brien's, 718 St. Peter Street. Great patio and sing-alongs. Get a hurricane (passion-fruit punch in a hurricane-lamp-shaped glass). You forget how much fun Pat O'Brien's can be.

Rain Forest, Hilton Hotel. High up in the Hilton overlooking the river. A sound and light show simulates a storm in a rain forest. Kids can go here until 5 P.M., and they love it.

Sazerac Bar, Fairmont Hotel. Have a sazerac or a ramos gin fizz. Watching the bartender at work is a real treat. Nice old murals.

Top of the Mart, International Trade Mart Building. Panoramic view of the city and riverfront from this revolving bar.

DANCE HALLS

Munster's, corner Laurel and Lyons streets. Last of the old-time dance halls. Call 899-9109 to be sure a traditional jazz band is playing.

Pat Barberot's Jefferson Orleans North, 2600 Edenborn Avenue, Metairie. Big-band dancing Saturday, Sunday, Wednesday, and Thursday. Best for the ballroom crowd.

COFFEE HOUSES

Borsodi's, 5104 Freret Street. Folk music and poetry reading. **Penny Post,** 5110 Danneel Street. Poetry, folk, bluegrass, "open mike" on Sunday night at 8 P.M.

COUNTRY

WNOE-FM radio has a Country Concert line at 529-1493. Call and find out who is appearing at all the clubs and auditoriums.

ENTERTAINMENT

The concert and performance season in New Orleans lasts from October to May, but there are always some summer attractions.

New Orleans has a symphony, an opera company, and a regular series of traveling Broadway shows. There is an Entertainment line at 566-5047 operated by the **Greater New Orleans Tourist and Convention Commission.**

Ticketmaster of Louisiana, Inc., handles ticket sales for many large events. You can call them at 587-3072 and charge tickets on major credit cards. You can pick up tickets at the box office or at Ticketmaster locations: all D. H. Holmes department stores, Dooky Chase's restaurant, Tulane University, and the Superdome.

The main theaters and auditoriums include the **Superdome,** 587-3768 (large concerts and shows); the **Municipal Auditorium** on North Rampart Street, 522-9106 (circuses and ice shows and some performances); **Saenger Performing Arts Center** on Canal Street at North Rampart Street, 524-0876 (Broadway shows and concerts); **Orpheum Theater,** 129 University Place, 525-0500 (symphony and concerts); and the **New Orleans Theatre of the Performing Arts** on North Rampart Street, 525-7615 (performances).

There are two auditoriums on the Tulane University campus, **Dixon Hall** and **McAlister Auditorium.** Other universities and the **Contemporary Arts Center** also have stage facilities.

The *Times-Picayune* has a daily calendar. *Gambit* is a weekly newspaper with entertainment listings. *New Orleans* magazine and *Louisiana Life* magazine also carry listings, as do many weekly tourist magazines you can find at any hotel desk.

The listings below will give you an idea of what music and drama you might find in New Orleans during your stay.

CONCERTS AND PERFORMANCES

New Orleans Friends of Music (522-2363). Five chamber concerts are given between September and May at Dixon Hall on the Tulane campus. Tickets are available at the door or from DeVille Books, 132 Carondelet Street. This is a series that attracts the most polite audiences in town.

New Orleans Opera Association (529-2278). New Orleans has a resident opera company and brings in name stars for four fall productions running three nights each. Ticketmaster will have tickets.

New Orleans Opera Guild (525-7672). Soloists, music or drama productions, and dance groups of national repute will come to town for productions of the Opera Guild.

New Orleans Philharmonic Symphony (524-2404). The symphony, under conductor Philippe Entremont, has sixteen concerts in its season, each one scheduled on three nights. The orchestra has much improved, and programs have been varied and included interesting new music.

Other musical events in New Orleans include performances by the Musica Da Camera, a medieval and Renaissance group; performances by soloists or opera groups from Xavier University, Dillard University, Tulane University, and Loyola University; and jazz performances at the Contemporary Arts Center. Tulane has a free Music at Midday series at the Newcomb College Chapel on Wednesdays during the school year, and Christ Church Cathedral also has a free concert series during the winter and spring in the cathedral at Sixth Street and St. Charles Avenue on Sundays. The Delta Festival Ballet and the New Orleans City Ballet also perform regularly.

THEATER

Contemporary Arts Center, 900 Camp Street (523-1216). The Contemporary Arts Center has its own season of works by contemporary dramatists, and also playing there are the Dashiki Project Theater (a black group who always have interesting productions), the Off Off Off Broadway Players, Alpha Productions, and occasional plays done by selected directors. The center also has regular film and videotape performances of contemporary works.

Le Petit Théâtre Du Vieux Carré, 616 St. Peter Street (523-5712). The oldest little-theater group in New Orleans has a season of dramas and musicals in their own attractive French Quarter playhouse. Call the box office for tickets. There are children's shows occasionally.

New Orleans Recreation Department, Gallier Hall (524-9278). The NORD theater department puts on musicals in the basement of Gallier Hall and will have summer productions for children and teenagers.

Saenger Performing Arts Center, 143 North Rampart Street (524-0876). The Saenger has a series of Broadway plays by subscription. Sometimes seats are available, and other nonsubscription productions are sometimes scheduled.

Théâtre Marigny, 616 Frenchmen Street (944-2653). This small theater group in the Marigny section below the French Quarter does contemporary drama. One recent project was a Tennessee Williams series.

Universities in the New Orleans area will have theater productions: Loyola, Dillard, Xavier, Tulane, and the University of New Orleans. And one high school puts on musical productions that your kids would love: **Jesuit High School,** 4138 Banks Street, 486-9159.

DINNER THEATERS

Showboat Theatre, Williams Boulevard at the river in Kenner. Equity productions with New York and Hollywood stars and local professionals. Four hundred seats on the *Robert E. Lee* showboat. Dinner available nearby. This will open in the spring of 1984 and is an outgrowth of the old Beverly Dinner Playhouse, which burned down.

Minacepelli's Dinner Theater, 227 Cousin Street, Slidell (888-7000). This family-run theater puts on plays with local actors and combines musical entertainment and good cooking during breaks in the performance.

SUMMER ATTRACTIONS

New Orleans Summer Pops (861-8374). The Pops has popular artists performing, with table seating and drinks available for the audience.

Summer Lyric Theater (865-5269). Summer musical productions at Tulane University. Tulane also has the Tulane Center Stage series of dramas, 865-5361, in the summer months.

LAGNIAPPE

La Trouvaille, Chauvin (594-9503). The Dusenberry family of singers has a Cajun restaurant and weekday lunches, and on the first Sunday of every month you can go there for Sunday dinner and singing entertainment afterward. A real Cajun treat and a nice outing. Reservations are a must, as this is popular, and inexpensive. Go to Houma and take Highway 56 south toward Cocodrie. La Trouvaille is on Bayou Terrebonne. The restaurant closes in July and August.

FREEBIES!

Music, walking tours, booklets, even a cruise—and they're all free!

If you're interested in stretching your vacation dollars, or you had a bad afternoon at the Fair Grounds Race Track, here are some ways to enjoy New Orleans that won't cost a picayune (that's less than a dime!)

1. Make your first stop the **Tourist Information Office** at 334 Royal Street in the French Quarter. The **Louisiana Office of Tourism,** 568-5661, is located here and they are well supplied with maps, brochures, and pamphlets (even in other languages). *River Trails, Bayous and Back Roads* is a 125-page book that covers the entire state with maps, driving tours, hours, and prices of all attractions—a useful and compact guide. The *Birding Tour of Southeast Louisiana* is good for nature lovers. If you wish to write in advance for these materials (or for some on another topic) here is the state office address: P.O. Box 44291, Baton Rouge, Louisiana 70804. Or you can call 1-800-535-8388 for information. The **Greater New Orleans Tourist and Convention Commission** offices are also at the Royal Street visitor center, and they operate a Weekly Events phone line, 504-566-5047 with a recorded message changed on Fridays. You can write the New Orleans tourist commission at 334 Royal Street, New Orleans, Louisiana 70130 for advance information. You'll find they are very helpful, not only about attractions but about lodging, entertainment, and special needs.

2. **Jean Lafitte National Historical Park,** 527 St. Ann Street, 589-2636. The National Park Service of the U.S. Department of the Interior operates a unique multisite national park in the New

Orleans area. In the French Quarter the park office at 527 St. Ann Street on Jackson Square is the starting point for free walking tours led by park rangers. The tours last one and a half hours and topics include "History of the French Quarter," "Jean Lafitte the Pirate," "New Orleans Cemeteries," and "Ghosts and Legends." There is a schedule board in the office and some displays. These tours may not be as scholarly as the ones sponsored by the Friends of the Cabildo through the Louisiana State Museum, but they can be a good introduction to walking and looking in the French Quarter. The cemetery tour, which covers St. Louis Cemetery No. 1, is very good, especially since you should not go into any of the St. Louis Cemeteries alone—the area is too dangerous. The Jean Lafitte tour covers those spots in the French Quarter with which the pirate-smuggler is associated.

The **Barataria Unit** of Jean Lafitte Park can be found on the West Bank of the Mississippi. Cross on the Greater New Orleans Bridge; continue on the West Bank Expressway to the corner of Barataria Boulevard in Marrero. Turn left. This is Highway 45. (The buildings on either side of Barataria Boulevard are Hope Haven and Madonna Manor, children's homes. This is one of the largest groupings of the Spanish Revival style of architecture in the South. The buildings date mostly from the twenties and thirties.) Keep on Highway 45 heading for Lafitte. You will come to park signs designating hiking or canoe trails. The **Bayou Coquille Trail** is a 1.5 mile hike starting on old Indian shell mounds and following a logging road through swampland. The **Ring Levee** hiking trail follows an old levee through a variety of Louisiana terrain and gives you a chance to see a swamp at close hand—even live nutria! Jean Lafitte, pirate or smuggler or entrepreneur, actually frequented this area. You will get a good idea of the richness of Louisiana wildlife by walking here. The **Kenta Canoe Trail** and other canoe trails give paddlers a chance to tour some unspoiled Louisiana bottomland and swamp. Wear mosquito repellent. Picnic tables are available. Highway 3134, a four-lane, will get you to the canoe trail quicker. (There is an intersection shortly after you enter Highway 45.)

Chalmette National Historical Park, another Jean Lafitte unit, covers the site of the Battle of New Orleans, January 8, 1815. There is a marked driving tour of the battlefield and a museum in a more recent plantation house on the grounds. Best time to visit: the weekends nearest and the actual anniversary of the battle. Costumed soldiers, camp followers, Indians, and Kentucky long riflemen demonstrating shooting, crafts, cooking, and other skills of the era make the battlefield come alive each January. To get there simply take Rampart Street in the French Quarter. Head downriver. The street becomes St. Claude Avenue and then St. Bernard Highway.

The Isleños Center, part of Jean Lafitte Park, is on Highway 46, a little over 10 miles below the Chalmette site. This commemorates the Canary Islanders, who settled the area. It is located in an 1850s cottage and has audiovisual displays and an exhibit. The rangers here are local folk who are ready to answer any questions about trapping, fishing, wildlife, etc. Next door is the **St. Bernard Parish Museum,** with more local artifacts in another cottage.

Big Oak Island is an Indian mound, site of an Indian fishing village from 500 to 100 B.C. and also occupied in other centuries. To reach it take I-10 East out of New Orleans and exit at Michoud Boulevard (going toward the river). At the end of Michoud Boulevard you will see signs directing you to the walking trail with information markers. New Orleans' area was filled with Indians before the arrival of Europeans, and Big Oak Island will tell you more about how some early Louisianians lived.

All of the Jean Lafitte National Historical Park sites are free and are open daily from 9 A.M. to 5 P.M. Holiday closings are Christmas Day, New Year's Day, and Mardi Gras Day.

3. **Parades** provide incredible no-cost fun. (That's why they call Mardi Gras "the Greatest Free Show on Earth.") Mardi Gras parades fall in the two-week period before Ash Wednesday and conclude with the massive all-day extravaganza of Mardi Gras. It all happens about six weeks before Easter and the dates vary.

The parade routes will be on the front page of the *Times-*

Picayune/States-Item, and WGSO-AM Radio (1280) will tell you exactly where the lead float is while the parade is in progress. Bacchus on the Sunday night before Mardi Gras is the most lavish, with Endymion on Saturday night being almost as extravagant. Thoth, which begins in the residential neighborhood below Audubon Park, is a good one for children on that Sunday morning—it is not too crowded and the maskers always have lots of "throws." Momus (Thursday night before Mardi Gras), Proteus (Monday night), and Comus (Mardi Gras night) all have flambeaux (flam-BOH), which are huge kerosene torches borne by dancing flambeaux carriers. Walking clubs parade with brass bands early Mardi Gras morning, and these groups along with Zulu (the Zulu Social Aid and Pleasure Club, a black krewe) precede Rex on Mardi Gras Day. The Mardi Gras Indians, black maskers, will be out on Mardi Gras also, usually along North Claiborne Avenue. St. Joseph's Day and St. Patrick's Day have parades, as does the Spring Fiesta. New Orleanians seem to spend a lot of time watching or being in parades. Just follow the local rules: go to the bathroom before you leave home, never park your car on a parade route (there are signs, and the New Orleans Police do tow), and keep yelling "Throw me something, mister."

4. The **free ferry** offers you a cruise on the Mississippi. Just board at the foot of Canal Street at the river. You can take your car or walk. On the other side is the old neighborhood of Algiers Point, an attractive area of much restoration. There is another ferry from Jackson Avenue in the Garden District that goes to Gretna near the Jefferson Parish Courthouse. A ferry provides a quick glimpse of the port of New Orleans: the tankers, freighters, tugs, and barges, and the dredges that constantly scour silt from the river bottom. Also you can see gulls and, in winter, the black and gray-white ducks called dos gris (doh gree, which means "gray back") or lesser scaup. The ferry gives you a sense of the importance of the river to the city, at an eye-level perspective.

5. **Free concerts!** That's right: there's live music almost every

Saturday and Sunday afternoon in Jackson Square or in between the buildings of the French Market on Decatur Street. In addition, Royal Street and the Jackson Square area usually have street musicians and performers (mimes, clowns, jugglers) in action. When they pass the hat, be generous if you feel so inclined. The French Quarter always has music for your ears—even if you just stand outside the bars on Bourbon Street. The calliope on the river tour boat *Natchez* plays every day at 11 A.M. and 2 P.M. and you can hear it in Jackson Square. In the business district there are often lunchtime concerts in Lafayette Square or in front of city hall. The **Archive of New Orleans Jazz** at Tulane University has occasional concerts and seminars or jazz bands on the campus. Check with the archive at 865-6588 for information on any jazz funerals or parades. The archive also sponsors the **Tulane Hot Jazz Classic** in late spring, at the same time as the Jazz and Heritage Festival. The Jazz Classic will have seminars and concerts, and definitely something free. Tulane also has a free classical music series, Music at Midday, during the winter. For more classical music, try **Christ Church Cathedral,** in the Garden District on St. Charles Avenue and Sixth Street. The Cathedral Concert series over the winter months has organists, medieval chamber groups, perhaps even a one-act opera. A scrumptious tea follows. (This is one free event you should pay for: there is a contributions box on your way to tea in the parish hall.)

6. **Free fun on the radio!** WWOZ-FM at 90.7 on your dial is a community radio (nonprofit) station with a unique format and all-volunteer disc jockeys. There is a lot of classic New Orleans jazz (with "Big Mama Rankin"), bluegrass and folk music (with "Hazel the Delta Rambler"), and genuine New Orleans rhythm and blues (with the "Duke of Paducah"). The records are often from private collections, the commentary is great (lots of local artists are interviewed or do their own shows), and there are live broadcasts from **Tipitina's,** the best place to hear live New Orleans rock music, corner Tchoupitoulas Street and Napoleon Avenue. The "Oriental Fox Trot Museum" show highlights pop-

ular music before 1917. WWOZ is such a pleasure to listen to that one anecdote about it is easy to believe: it seems a young Scandinavian couple had come to New Orleans just for the music. When they found WWOZ on the radio they didn't leave their hotel room for a week.

Also on your radio is **WWL-AM,** at 870. On Saturday from 9 A.M. to 6 P.M. and Sunday from noon to 6 P.M. (except for football and baseball games) you will find the "Weekend Live Show" with Frank Davis. Local Chef Paul Prudhomme is a regular visitor; there are live interviews from every fair and event in the surrounding area; and Frank keeps phone callers talking New Orleans: where do you get the best pecans, who makes the best snowballs, how's the fishing at Grande Isle—any question about enjoying New Orleans gets asked and answered. A great way to listen to the local accent and get ideas on different things to do. Also, there are contests with prizes like five pounds of hot sausage, a shrimp net, a muffaletta sandwich.

7. **Finding freebies on your own:** look in the newspapers. *Gambit* is a weekly that costs twenty-five cents and comes to newsstands on Saturdays. *Gambit* has boxes in the French Quarter, so it's easy to find. The inside pages have a calendar of things to do, oriented mostly to young people. The *Times-Picayune/ States-Item* (guess how many mergers it took to get a name that long) is fifteen cents daily and fifty cents Sundays. On Wednesdays the *Picayune* sports section has a "Venture" column by Bob Marshall. This will tell you everything about outdoor activities: bird-watching, hunting, fishing, running, canoeing, etc. On Fridays the *Picayune* has a Lagniappe tabloid with a lengthy calendar of events plus nightclub and concert listings. The "Calendar" section runs as a daily column in shorter form, and on Sundays there is also a "Kid Stuff" column. Sometimes there's a free party with music in Armstrong Park on Rampart Street, or the New Orleans Symphony might be at a shopping center. For the dedicated budget watcher, there is always something going on for nothing (and you can even read the papers for free at the New Orleans Public Library on Loyola Avenue at Tulane Avenue).

8. While it's not exactly in New Orleans, the largest **free country fair** in the nation is held every October in Franklinton, Louisiana. It begins on a Wednesday in late October and runs through Saturday. The **Washington Parish Free Fair** has prize-winning jams, jellies, and pies; quilts and needlework, livestock of all kinds, a flower show, an art show, a hobby and craft show, children's exhibits, and commercial exhibits (such as tractors and mobile homes). It also has the **Mile Branch Settlement,** a collection of nineteenth-century buildings gathered from throughout the parish. Costumed volunteers demonstrate soap making, sugar making, blacksmithing, and basket making. In the kitchen they stoke up a wood stove and serve homemade biscuits and sassafras tea. There's an old schoolhouse and a church, where everyone is invited to join in hymns. Mile Branch Settlement is on the National Register of Historic Buildings and is furnished with donations from local folk. Also on the fairgrounds is an outdoor theater with constant performances, from local dancing schools to an annual Grand Ole Opry star. Every politician in the state shows up; there is a three-hour opening parade on Wednesday morning, and every night there is a full-scale rodeo (admission). Booths serve everything from hamburgers to jambalaya, with some fantastic barbequed chicken as your best bet. No alcohol, but lots of fun anyway. There is also a midway with Ferris wheel and game booths. To get there take the causeway over Lake Pontchartrain, go toward Covington on Highway 190, and turn left on Highway 25 to Franklinton. In an hour and a half you'll be back in the past.

9. **Free museums!** Pinch your pennies while you peruse the past! At Jackson Barracks (on St. Claude Avenue on the way to Chalmette) there is a **Military Museum** in the 1837 powder magazine. Weapons, vehicles, uniforms, and flags fill out a collection that is still growing. Call 271-6262 to make an appointment Monday through Friday between 7:30 A.M. and 3:30 P.M.

The **Middle American Research Institute** collection of Mayan and other Central American Indian artifacts is on the fourth floor (no elevator) of Dinwiddie Hall on the Tulane University

campus. (Fronting St. Charles Avenue is Gibson Hall. Dinwiddie is next to it toward Holy Name Church.) This is a well-
displayed collection of original artifacts and plaster castings.
Tulane has a dig going in the Yucatán and the staff are knowledgeable. There is a book describing the collection you can buy
for $1.00.

Also at Tulane: in the Howard Tilton Library on Freret Street
at Newcomb Place you will find the **Southern Architectural
Archives** housing drawings and scale models from local firms,
exhibits open weekdays from 1 P.M. to 5 P.M. The **William Ransom Hogan Archive of New Orleans Jazz** is also in the library,
as is a fine New Orleans Collection, which sometimes has displays in the Rare Book Room on the fourth floor. The **Newcomb
Art School Gallery** (on Newcomb Place nearer Willow Street)
will have student and faculty work and also the Art Nouveau
crafts and pottery that first gained Newcomb Art School fame.
There are some nice Tiffany windows in the **Newcomb Chapel**
on Broadway near Zimple Street.

The **Historic New Orleans Collection** always has one gallery
open for free viewing at 533 Royal Street. (Use some of the
money you are saving at the fine gift shop.)

The **K & B Sculpture Garden** surrounds the building of the
drugstore firm on Lee Circle. An interesting collection of modern sculpture plus an attractive building make this worth getting
off the streetcar for. Ask inside for pamphlets describing the
items.

The **New Orleans Museum of Art** in City Park has been open
for free on Thursdays. Call 488-2631 to be sure this pleasant
custom continues. This is a first-class art museum with a well-
laid-out gallery system and a good program of support activities.

10. **Don't forget all the parks: Audubon Park** has a jogging
and biking area with no vehicles and a Par Cours series of
exercise equipment along the way. **City Park** is good for joggers and bird-watchers. In Jefferson Parish **Linear Park** runs
along the lakefront for joggers and bikers. You can sit on
the seawall on Lake Pontchartrain and watch the sailboats,

or go to the Moon Walk at Jackson Square and watch the river traffic.

Memories of New Orleans come from things like the scent of jasmine as you pass a patio, the aromas outside restaurants, the bell of the streetcar conductor. So get outside and stroll! "Lagniappe" can mean free, but it mostly means "a little something extra." It's guaranteed to be worth the extra effort.

SPORTS

For years Louisiana license plates have borne the legend SPORTS-MAN'S PARADISE. While this slogan refers to the plentiful fishing and hunting available in the state, it could just as easily apply to almost any other sport: boating, football, tennis, golf, to name a few.

Just one afternoon in the Superdome watching the New Orleans Saints or spending a Super Bowl weekend here can tell you a lot about how sports-mad New Orleanians are.

So don't be fooled into thinking that a vacation in New Orleans means nothing but old buildings and new bars. Whether you like to spectate or do it yourself, New Orleans is a sportsman's area.

HUNTING

The Louisiana Department of Wildlife and Fisheries has nearly 1 million acres in thirty-six wildlife management areas open for public hunting. The hunting season in Louisiana runs from September through February, with an extra April season on wild turkey. Game includes teal, ducks, coots, blue and snow geese, squirrels, deer, gallinules, turkeys, quail, rails, snipe, doves, woodcocks, and rabbits.

Louisiana is on the Mississippi Flyway for migratory fowl, and there are several refuge areas where migratory birds are protected.

If you want to hunt in Louisiana, you will need a license. The basic nonresident fee for a season is $25, and for three consecutive days is $5.00. You need an extra $20 big-game permit.

Residents of Arkansas, Texas, and Mississippi must pay a higher basic fee.

Be warned in advance: it is almost impossible to hunt water-fowl in Louisiana if you do not have a guide. You will need equipment, a boat, decoys, and a good knowledge of Louisiana bayous to begin with.

For small game and land birds you might manage very well. There are eight state wildlife management areas near New Orleans. One, the **Bohemia Wildlife Management Area** in Plaquemines Parish, Highway 39 below East Pointe À La Hache, can be reached by car. The others are accessible only by boat.

There is also an archery season for deer in the state. Enforcement of law is fairly strict, but it is occasionally administered with humor: medical students caught with ducks over the limit a few years back had to work off their sentence at the Audubon Park Zoo on weekends.

For basic information on hunting and licenses write: Louisiana Department of Wildlife and Fisheries, P.O. Box 44095, Baton Rouge, Louisiana 70804. They can supply you with pamphlets and facts on Louisiana hunting, and they may be able to put you in touch with hunting clubs or guides.

Pamphlets you might request include: *A Guide to Wildlife Management Areas* (this gives maps and says which ones have primitive camping facilities), *A Guide to Fishing in Louisiana, Forty Fishing Areas, Coastal Louisiana Charter Fishing Fleet* (this includes all boats that can be chartered for inshore or offshore fishing trips), and the *Louisiana Birding Information Kit* of the Orleans Audubon Society.

Some guides you might contact include: **Paul Wagner,** 504-641-1769, for duck hunting in the Honey Island Swamp area near Pearl River; and **Pascal Townsend,** 504-563-2590, duck hunting and also fishing near Dulac, below Houma.

FISHING

Fishing is big business in Louisiana. Commercial fishermen go after shrimp, oysters, catfish, trout, and almost anything else that swims, so you know there's plenty to be caught.

A nonresident fishing license costs $6.00 for a year or $3.00 for seven consecutive days. You do not need a license to fish with a pole or catch crabs with a net. If you are under sixteen or over sixty, you can get a free permit to hunt or fish from the Louisiana Wildlife and Fisheries Department.

Within the city limits of New Orleans the fishing is good (Orleans Parish extends into Lake Pontchartrain and Lake Catherine). In fact, there used to be a City Limits Tarpon Club, for people who caught their tarpon in Orleans Parish. Some of the heaviest tarpon caught in the state—the top one weighing in at 198—have been taken inside New Orleans limits, when the tarpon come into the brackish lakes in the fall.

There is no limit on your saltwater catch in Louisiana. There are lots of good things to catch, too: channel bass (called redfish), pompano, flounder, sea trout, croaker, sheepshead, and drum. In the Sargasso rips in the Gulf—where the Mississippi River meets the Gulf—you will find sailfish, marlin, tuna, wahoo, and dolphin, while in the open Gulf you can catch Spanish mackerel, king mackerel, bluefish, bonito, cobia, red snapper, tarpon, barracuda, and shark.

Freshwater fish include black bass (called green trout), striped bass, walleye, yellow bass, crappie (called "sac-à-lait," which means, roughly, "bag-of-milk"), sunfish, and catfish.

You can fish in New Orleans at both **Audubon Park** (where it is free and nothing is provided) and **City Park** (where you must buy a permit). City Park has an annual bass tournament, so lagoon fishing can be really good.

You will see people fishing and crabbing all along the lakefront (Lakeshore Drive, along Lake Pontchartrain). The lake has a seawall, and there are benches and picnic tables and shelters—all very clean and attractive—along the shore.

You can also fish and crab along **Paris Road.** This road runs from the river to the lake, across the bottom of New Orleans. It begins at Chalmette and ends at Hayne Boulevard and Lake Pontchartrain. There are boat launches and a bayou next to Paris Road.

Under the **Seabrook Bridge**—over the Industrial Canal at Lake Pontchartrain—the fishing and crabbing are often good, and there is a free boat launch into Lake Pontchartrain.

For a nice country outing with some sport involved, you might buy some chicken necks and crab nets (any hardware or sporting goods store or Schwegmann's Supermarket) and take Highway 90 on the West Bank and then Highway 45 to Lafitte. There is a public park, **Rosethorne Park,** with picnic tables, boat launch, and a spot to throw your nets in right off the highway to Barataria. Continue on the highway to the Barataria Tavern restaurant. Cross the bridge next to it and stop at the country store. There are picnic grounds and a crabbing area (for $2.00 a car) across from the store. The outhouse is primitive; the piers are rickety, but it's very quiet and peaceful, and if the crabs are running, you'll fill a bushel basket in no time.

There are fishing rodeos every year in Louisiana, usually beginning in July. These are three- and four-day events based in little towns on or near the Gulf. You register and then fish. If your fish is the biggest, you win a trophy. The fishing rodeo at Grand Isle is perhaps the best-known Louisiana event. There is also a fishing rodeo in Gulfport, Mississippi.

If you want to charter a boat for deep-sea fishing, you can do it at Empire (about 60 miles) and Venice (about 70 miles) or at Grand Isle (about 120 miles), where there is also surf fishing and surf bathing. In Grand Isle contact **Captain Tim Sebastian,** 504-787-2750, a fishing boat charter captain. If Captain Sebastian can't take care of you, he'll refer you to someone else.

Fishing charter boats cost far over $100 a day and up. They can accommodate up to about six people. Bait and tackle are usually furnished, and your fish can be cleaned for you to take home. The charter boats go out in the Gulf to the blue water and the oil rigs, where the big ones are. For speckled trout fishing there is a guide from **Sportsman's Paradise** in Cocodrie, **Stu Scheer,** 504-594-2414.

For information on big-game fishing and accommodations where the river meets the Gulf, write the Louisiana Department of Wildlife and Fisheries.

Accommodations—motels or cabins for rent by the day—are available in all the towns where the charter boats dock. Grand Isle has a camping ground on the beach.

No matter where you are in Louisiana, if there's water around, somebody is fishing in it.

BOATING

With all that fishing going on, you know there have to be a lot of boats. And there are: from pirogues (PEE-rogues) to yachts.

Pirogues are dugouts, sometimes made from hollowed-out cypress trees and sometimes from fiberglass. In **Lafitte** (take the bridge across the Mississippi River, get on Highway 90, and turn left on Highway 45) there are pirogue races every year. Check at the **Tourist Information Office,** 334 Royal Street, for dates. The pirogue races also feature music, a beauty contest, and lots of cold beer. **Slidell** also has races on Bayou Liberty.

The **Southern Yacht Club** in New Orleans is the second oldest in the country and has been known to produce Olympic gold medalist yachtsmen. The newer **New Orleans Yacht Club** is providing good competition. Sailing on Lake Pontchartrain is more exciting than you might think. The lake is very shallow and inclined to be choppy. Squalls can blow up almost anytime. Nevertheless, there are regattas going on all year. Between Christmas Day and New Year's Day the Sugar Bowl Regatta draws sailors from all over the country. To watch the sailboat races just drive along Lakeshore Drive and park.

If you want to bring your own yacht to New Orleans, write the **Harbor Master,** Municipal Yacht Harbor, 401 North Roadway, West End, New Orleans, Louisiana 70124. They may be able to accommodate you.

To see the marina area, take the Pontchartrain Expressway (get on at Lee Circle) to the West End Boulevard exit, go to the junction with Robert E. Lee Boulevard, go one block, and take the next left on Lake Marina. The marina with its rows and rows of beautiful boats and its fancy boathouses is worth a trip. If you continue on the road by the marina, you will come to West End —the western end of the lake, where all the good seafood and crab restaurants are, and the **Municipal Yacht Harbor.**

You can launch your own boat on a sand beach next to the **Seabrook Bridge,** also on Lake Pontchartrain but at the other end. Just keep going straight on Pontchartrain Boulevard until you have to turn right on Lakeshore Drive, and continue on to the Seabrook Bridge.

There are other boat launches in and around New Orleans. You can find one by the Municipal Yacht Harbor at West End, on Paris Road, or at Fort Pike (take Highway 90 East toward Slidell). Or you can bring your boat with you and launch it in any of the bayous and lakes below New Orleans.

Check with the Louisiana Department of Wildlife and Fisheries about boat licensing regulations or call the **U.S. Coast Guard,** 589-6183.

You might want to watch a blessing of the shrimp fleet in Morgan City. Check with the **Tourist Information Office** at 334 Royal Street for the date. They always have a calendar of state events.

If you want to rent a boat, you can. Charters are locally available from the **New Orleans Sail Club,** 525-3206, either bareboat or with crew. Be sure and keep your radio on: when they say small-craft warnings around New Orleans, they mean it.

OUTDOOR LAGNIAPPE

The swampland and forests of Louisiana have an incredible beauty, and no visit to New Orleans should be complete without at least a glimpse of the outdoors.

A good place to start is the **Louisiana Nature Center.** The

Nature Center is located just off the I-10 Read Road exit, at 11000 Lake Forest Boulevard, 246-9381. There are hiking trails through various terrain and changing exhibits, plus films and a "discovery loft" with all sorts of hands-on displays for kids: shells, insects, snakeskins, etc. The Nature Center has a regular outings program and lectures on things like edible wild plants or gathering mushrooms. At times they even do a "Flora and Fauna of the French Quarter" walking tour. Be sure and call them while you are here.

The **Orleans Audubon Society** has a **Bird Alert** phone number, 504-246-2473. They will tell you about interesting sightings and coming programs and outings.

The **Sierra Club** publishes a *Trail Guide to the Delta Country,* which is available in bookstores or by writing the Sierra Club, 111 South Hennessey Street, New Orleans, Louisiana 70119. This is a must for canoeing or hiking on your own, and there is information on float trips down nearby scenic rivers, bicycling, and even skydiving. You can call the Sierra Club at 504-455-0882.

If you are not prepared for an extensive outing, at least visit the **Audubon Zoo,** where there is a special "Louisiana Swamp" exhibit.

When Louisiana's state bird, the brown pelican, is dying out because of pesticides, you can guess that the **Ecology Center,** 482-8760, and all conservationist groups have a fertile field for work in the state. If you are ecology-minded, you'll want to find out what's going on.

For general bird-watching, Louisiana is an ideal spot. Because of its position on the Mississippi Flyway, Louisiana has a large number of species recorded in the state (over four hundred). In New Orleans the parks are usually filled with birds, especially in the area around the Popp Fountain, far in the back of City Park.

Avery Island, below New Iberia, has a world-famed bird sanctuary, featuring roosting platforms for snowy egrets and other egrets and herons. Watching the birds come in to roost at sunset is really an experience. For a small admission you can also see the gardens on Avery Island, where the famous Tabasco sauce is made and where there is a salt mine, too.

Grand Isle is a good place to watch for migrating birds in early spring and fall.

By writing the **Louisiana Office of Tourism,** P.O. Box 44291, Baton Rouge, Louisiana 70804, you can get a booklet on bird-watching in Louisiana. Or you can call them out of state, 1-800-535-8388.

There are two stores dealing with canoes and camping equipment: **Delta Wilderness Outfitters,** 504-835-1932, 1817 Veterans Memorial Boulevard, Metairie; and the **Canoe and Trail Shop,** 504-488-8528, 624 Moss Street, on Bayou St. John in New Orleans. Both of them have extensive equipment, and they also have regular trips and outings.

Do not forget the "Venture" section in the *Times-Picayune/States-Item* on Wednesdays. Bob Marshall is a good outdoor writer, and he has a regular list of everything that's going on in town, and nearby.

On Thursday nights from 6 P.M. to 7:40 P.M. Frank Davis has an outdoor show on WWL-AM radio, and if you want to call and ask him a question, he'll certainly try to answer it. His "Weekend Live Show" on the same station also will let you know what's going on outdoors.

New Orleans now has many runners, and there are regularly scheduled races including the **Mardi Gras Marathon** (it usually is run on the Lake Pontchartrain Causeway bridge), and the **Crescent City Classic** in the spring. There are two Par Cours in town, with exercises and simple equipment at spots along a running path. One is in Linear Park, on the lakefront levee of Jefferson Parish near the causeway. The other is in Audubon Park.

Paul Wagner, 504-641-1769, in Slidell, does guided tours of the Honey Island Swamp as well as duck-hunting and fishing trips. Out of Houma the **Terrebonne Swamp and Marsh Tours,** 504-879-3934, will tour you through swamp and marshland and perhaps introduce you to an alligator.

The canoe and hiking trails of **Jean Lafitte National Historical Park** are on the West Bank of the river. Take Highway 90 to Highway 45, and you will see the park signs. This is a good introduction to the Louisiana swampland, and it is free. The trails close at 4 P.M. in winter and 5 P.M. in summer. Another nearby swamp hike is the **Honey Island Swamp Nature Trail,** off Highway 59 near Pearl River, at the Honey Island exit.

FOOTBALL

New Orleans loves football. The New Orleans Saints professional team may not be champions yet, but it's not because their fans don't think they're the greatest. And for exciting football with nail-biting fourth quarters, you just can't beat the Saints. The halftime shows are spectacular, especially when they feature the top-notch marching bands from two Louisiana schools: Grambling State University and Southern University.

To see the Saints play, write New Orleans Saints, 1500 Poydras Street, New Orleans, Louisiana 70112. Or call 504-587-3664. However, there are so many season-ticket holders that it's tough to get a choice seat.

The Saints play in the Superdome on Poydras Street. Tulane's team, the Green Wave, plays there, too, and has improved in recent years.

Grambling State University and Southern University meet for the **Bayou Classic** at the Superdome. Write Louisiana Superdome, P.O. Box 50488, New Orleans, Louisiana 70150. The Battle of the Bands at the dome the night before is spectacular.

Every New Year's Day the **Sugar Bowl** is played at the Superdome. You can purchase tickets by writing the Mid-Winter Sports Association, 510 International Building, 611 Gravier Street, New Orleans, Louisiana 70130. The bowl game plus the Sugar Bowl basketball tournament—between Christmas Day and New Year's Day—and sailing and tennis matches result in capacity crowds, so get tickets early.

New Orleans is near enough to Baton Rouge to get to an

L.S.U. game. The L.S.U. Tigers are almost always in contention in the Southeastern Conference.

GOLF

The highlight of the golf season in New Orleans is the annual **New Orleans Open,** the **U.S.F.&G. Golf Classic,** scheduled on the professional golfers' tour every spring. The tournament is held at the Lakewood Country Club in Algiers. To get there, cross the Greater New Orleans Bridge over the Mississippi—the bridge near Canal Street—and just follow the arrows leading you left. Tickets are available at the gate or by writing U.S.F.&G. Golf Classic, 925 Common Street, Suite 875, New Orleans, Louisiana 70112. The course is attractive with moss-hung oak trees, but the sun may be very hot—be sure to bring a hat.

Golf is a year-round sport in New Orleans and about the only thing that keeps some enthusiasts off the courses is a torrential downpour or a hurricane. There are several courses available to the public. They are, naturally, less crowded during the week.

Audubon Park. Audubon Park has a golf club inside the park grounds, and the public can play there for a fee. No reservations are allowed, except on weekends for members only. To get there, go up Magazine Street past the park to Walnut Street and turn right. You will reach the clubhouse in three blocks (it will be on your right).

City Park. City Park has four eighteen-hole courses open from daylight to dark. For reservations on weekends only call 283-3458. Fees differ from course to course. To reach City Park go out Esplanade Avenue (the bottom of the French Quarter) until you reach the park entrance. The golf courses are inside the park to the right.

Pontchartrain Park. Pontchartrain Park has an eighteen-hole course that is open weekdays from 7:30 A.M. to dark, weekends from 5:30 A.M. to dark. There is a lesser fee for senior citizens. Call 288-0928. To get there, take Broad Street (it crosses Canal Street about a mile from the French Quarter) to Gentilly Boulevard (almost a continuation of Broad Street) to Chef Menteur Highway (that's the same road as Gentilly Boulevard), and turn left on Congress Drive. The address is 6514 Congress Drive.

Brechtel Golf Course. Brechtel Golf Course is operated by the city of New Orleans in Algiers, and has a nine-hole course. To get there go over the Greater New Orleans Bridge and take General de Gaulle Drive (to your right) to Behrmann Place and turn right (at the Exxon station). You will pass the golf course in half a mile. No reservations are necessary.

Plantation Golf Club. Plantation Golf Club has an eighteen-hole course. To get there take the Greater New Orleans Bridge and turn right at Terry Parkway (the first red light), then left on Holmes Boulevard and right on Behrmann Highway, and you'll find the course in 1 mile.

There are many country clubs in and around New Orleans, all with golf courses. You might check to see if your club has reciprocal privileges here. Military personnel may be able to play at the eighteen-hole course at the Naval Air Station in Algiers.

Golf is just one more reason why you'll like New Orleans. Be sure and bring your clubs.

TENNIS

The **New Orleans Lawn Tennis Club** is one of the oldest in the country, and good tennis players can always be found in New Orleans amateur ranks. The city operates a tennis program through the New Orleans Recreation Department. There are many private courts, and schools and colleges keep courts, too. Tulane University has even been known to give an athletic scholarship to a female tennis star.

Between Christmas Day and New Year's Day the Mid-Winter Sports Association hosts the Sugar Bowl Tennis Invitationals. A series ticket is available at the gate or in advance from the association, 510 International Building, 611 Gravier Street, New Orleans, 70130.

City Park. City Park has fifty-four courts, of various composition. During the summer the courts are lit until 10 P.M. Night rates are higher. There are no advance telephone reservations, but you can buy your tickets early if you like.

Audubon Park. Audubon Park has ten courts renting in the daytime and not open at night. Get your tickets at the park administration office in front of the zoo entrance.

SWIMMING

Contrary to what you might think, there is no ocean beach in New Orleans. But there is the salt water of Lake Pontchartrain. There are protected swimming areas along the lakefront (you will notice the signs). Sad to say, Pontchartrain is sometimes polluted. The pollution notices are usually on the front page of the *Times-Picayune.*

Besides the swimming pool at your hotel or motel, there are public pools throughout the city.

You can also swim in Lake Pontchartrain from the beach at **Fontainebleau State Park.** Go across Lake Pontchartrain on the causeway and veer right toward Lacombe for the park entrance.

For surf bathing you can go to **Grand Isle,** where the Gulf of Mexico comes in sizable waves, or to the **Mississippi Gulf Coast** at Biloxi or Gulfport, where the beach is white but the water is shallow and rather listless.

RACING

The Fair Grounds Race Track is the third oldest in the nation, but racing in New Orleans goes back further than that. Before the Civil War the thoroughbreds of Louisiana were famed, and the Metairie Race Course—now covered by Metairie Cemetery —was known all over the country.

The Fair Grounds has 101 days of racing every year, beginning on Thanksgiving Day. Whether it's because of the French heritage or what, New Orleans takes to the races.

The clubhouse and entrance are Victorian and charming, but

the pari-mutuel windows are strictly Damon Runyon. The races start weekdays at 1:30 P.M. and Saturday at 1 P.M.

There is a grandstand admission fee and an extra charge for the clubhouse. The food at the Fair Grounds is worth the clubhouse admission. The corned beef, the turtle soup, and gumbo are very good. The clubhouse is air-conditioned, and there are closed-circuit television sets, so you don't even have to walk down to the track to see the races.

Highlights of the racing season are the **New Orleans Handicap** and the **Louisiana Derby** in March. Every card has at least one race for Louisiana-bred horses only.

When the Fair Grounds is closed, **Jefferson Downs** is open for night racing April through mid-November. Post time is 7:15 P.M., Tuesday through Saturday. Jefferson Downs also has a clubhouse and is located in Jefferson Parish off Williams Boulevard near Lake Pontchartrain.

There is another racetrack in Louisiana: **Evangeline Downs** in Lafayette. Sometimes Evangeline has races for quarter horses, speedy mounts that specialize in quarter-mile races only. Since Evangeline Downs is in Cajun country, the announcers say "Ils sont partis" instead of "They're off."

If you want to ride yourself, there are horses for hire at the stables in Audubon Park and City Park.

MISCELLANEOUS

You can watch or play almost any sport you can think of in New Orleans. There are even ice skating rinks, at the Plaza shopping center on Read Road and Lake Forest Boulevard, and on Clearview Parkway near the Huey P. Long Bridge.

Professional boxing is offered from time to time at the Superdome, the Municipal Auditorium, or the St. Bernard Civic Auditorium in St. Bernard Parish on Judge Perez Drive.

Several hotels, such as the Fairmont and the Hilton, have their own tennis courts. The Rivercenter offers tennis and racquetball at the Hilton.

Be sure and find out if any clubs you belong to have reciprocal membership agreements with clubs in New Orleans. The tennis, yacht, and athletic clubs as well as country clubs may honor an out-of-town membership and let you use their facilities. If you expect to do that, be sure you have your current membership card with you. Some ladies' exercise franchises—such as Shape Spa—have a similar arrangement. Check with your hotel or motel to see if they offer any guest passes.

If you don't get out and get some exercise while you're in New Orleans, it's your own fault. After that good Creole food you'll wish you had.

SIGHTS TO SEE

Listed here are those parks, gardens, homes, and museums that are open to visitors throughout the year. For Spring Fiesta and for occasional fund-raising events other houses may be on tour, but these attractions are regularly available.

PARKS, GARDENS, OUTDOORS

Audubon Park, St. Charles Avenue from Exposition Boulevard to Walnut Street. Audubon Park has it all: tennis courts, a jogging path with Par Cours exercise stations, a golf course, a stable with horses for rent, play equipment for the kids, picnic shelters, lagoons. The Audubon Zoo is one of the best in the country, with beautifully designed walkways, moated enclosures, and a miniature train ride. There is also a Riverview pavilion. The zoo is open (for admission) from 9:30 A.M. to 5 P.M.

City Park, Esplanade Avenue at Bayou St. John. The **New Orleans Museum of Art** plus tennis courts, riding stables, canoes and paddle boats for rent, golf courses, a bocce court, the **New Orleans Botanical Gardens** (weekend afternoons by admission) plus lots of oak trees and shady picnic spots along the lagoons (which are well stocked with fish). A children's museum is planned.

The New Orleans area has lots of parks (including a **Linear Park** jogging path along Lake Pontchartrain in Jefferson Parish and **LaFrenière Park** in Jefferson, which hosts an annual Fall Medieval Fair), but City Park and Audubon Park are the most easily accessible and are well used.

Fort Pike State Commemorative Area, Highway 90 East of

New Orleans. This fort was first constructed after the War of 1812. There is a small museum (for admission) in the fort buildings, ramparts to walk on, good fishing and crabbing along the shoreline, and a picnicking and boat-launch area. **Fort Macomb,** nearby, is also a State Commemorative Area.

Jean Lafitte National Historical Park. This wide-ranging park includes: a display area on St. Ann Street at Jackson Square with free walking tours of the French Quarter; hiking and canoe trails in the swampy terrain off Highway 45 on the West Bank; the **Isleños Museum** on Highway 46 in St. Bernard Parish (commemorates the early Canary Islanders who settled the area; next door is the **St. Bernard Parish Ducros House Museum**) and the **Chalmette Battlefield,** where the Battle of New Orleans was fought, with later plantation house and extensive displays and historical markers. **Big Oak Island,** off I-10 in New Orleans East, is an early Indian archaeological site. Jean Lafitte Park locations are all free, open daily from 9 A.M. to 5 P.M. (earlier for trails in winter).

Louisiana Nature Center, 11000 Lake Forest Boulevard. Walks through Louisiana swampland, an imaginative display area, full schedule of films, programs, and outdoor expeditions. The Nature Center will give you a real idea of what New Orleans was like before the city was constructed. Children will especially like the **Discovery Loft,** where they can pick up and touch all manner of things: bird skeletons, shells, etc. Open (for admission) Tuesday through Sunday.

Longue Vue Gardens, 7 Bamboo Road (488-5488). A private estate with eight acres of formal gardens, walkways, and fountains. Regular programs of interest to gardeners and weekend performances in the gardens. Plus: a forty-six-room mansion with extensive collections of decorative art. A must for the serious gardener. Open (for admission) Tuesday through Sunday.

HOUSES

Beauregard House, 1113 Chartres Street (523-7257). The home of the late novelist Frances Parkinson Keyes and once the residence of Civil War General P. G. T. Beauregard. Built in 1826. Open (for admission) Monday through Saturday from 10 A.M. to 3 P.M.

1850 House, 523 St. Ann Street. Part of the Louisiana State Museum complex, this Pontalba row house is decorated in mid-nineteenth-century style. Open (for admission) Tuesday through Sunday from 9 A.M. to 5 P.M.

Gallier House, 1132 Royal Street (523-6722). Architect James Gallier, Jr.'s, own nineteenth-century home. Beautifully and accurately restored with well-informed guides, audiovisual material, gift shop. Open (for admission) Monday through Saturday from 10 A.M. to 4:30 P.M.

Hermann-Grima House, 821 St. Louis Street (525-5661). Restored 1832 mansion belonging to the Christian Women's Exchange. Cooking demonstrations also. Open (for admission) weekdays (closed Wednesday) from 10 A.M. to 3:30 P.M., Saturday from 10 A.M. to 3:30 P.M., and Sunday from 1 P.M. to 4:30 P.M.

Longue Vue, 7 Bamboo Road. The forty-six-room mansion at Longue Vue Gardens contains displays on the decorative arts, in this house built and decorated in the late 1930s, early 1940s. Open (for admission) weekdays from 10 A.M. to 4:30 P.M., weekends from noon to 4:30 P.M.

Madame John's Legacy, 632 Dumaine Street. Late eighteenth-century house, part of Louisiana State Museum complex. Open (for admission) Tuesday through Sunday from 9 A.M. to 5 P.M.

Merieult House, 533 Royal Street. The Historic New Orleans Collection is housed in a complex of buildings including this 1792 town house. Extensive art and document collection. Also, the "hidden house" that was the home of General and Mrs. Kemper Williams, decorated in the 1940s and 1950s, in

New Orleans fashion. If you are interested in interior decorating, see Longue Vue and the Williams house. Open (for admission) Tuesday through Saturday from 10 A.M. to 4:45 P.M.

Opera Guild House, 2504 Prytania Street. This antebellum Garden District house is the only mansion open for regular tours in that area. Small collection of opera memorabilia. Open (for admission) weekdays from 1 P.M. to 4 P.M.

Pitot House, 1440 Moss Street (482-0312). This 1799 West Indies–style plantation house was moved from nearby to this site and restored by the Louisiana Landmarks Society. Open (for admission) on Monday and Thursday.

Spring Fiesta Townhouse, 826 St. Ann Street. This town house dates from the 1840s with twentieth-century renovation work and some Victorian furniture. Open (for admission) Monday and Thursday from 11 A.M. to 3 P.M. The **Spring Fiesta,** 581-1367, has nineteen days of tours of homes and gardens beginning the Friday after Easter.

Sun Oak, 2020 Burgundy Street (945-0322). A small 1836 cottage in the Faubourg Marigny. Carefully restored. Relics from archaeological dig in the backyard are displayed. Open (for admission) Monday through Saturday at various hours or by appointment.

MUSEUMS

Archbishop Antoine Blanc Memorial, Ursuline Avenue at Chartres Street. The **Old Ursuline Convent,** dating from 1745, and the **Our Lady of Victory** (once St. Mary's Italian) Church. Now holds archives of the Roman Catholic Archdiocese of New Orleans. Tours on Wednesday at 1:30 P.M. and 3 P.M. for donation.

Cabrini Children's Museum, 1218 Burgundy Street. A doll collection in a Creole cottage. Open weekdays from 1 P.M. to 6 P.M., Saturdays from 9:30 A.M. to 5 P.M. Part of New Orleans Recreation Department.

Contemporary Arts Center, 900 Camp Street (523-1216). Galleries of contemporary art exhibits and regular programs of drama, music, movies, and videotapes. Open Tuesday through Saturday (by admission to galleries) from noon to 5 P.M. Other events by ticket.

Confederate Museum, 929 Camp Street (523-4522). Oldest museum in town. Relics of the Confederacy. Interesting to Civil War buffs. Open (for admission) Monday through Saturday from 10 A.M. to 4 P.M.

Historic New Orleans Collection, 533 Royal Street. Ten galleries of art and documents on early New Orleans, imaginatively displayed, plus the eighteenth-century **Merieult House** and the town house of the founder of the collection, General Kemper Williams. One gallery is always open for free. Extensive gift shop. Open (for admission) Tuesday through Saturday from 10 A.M. to 4:45 P.M.

Historical Pharmacy Museum, 514 Chartres Street. Collection of old drugs and apothecary's materials in an old drugstore. Open (for small admission) Tuesday through Saturday from 10 A.M. to 5 P.M.

K & B Plaza, Lee Circle at St. Charles Avenue. The Virlane Foundation collection of modern sculpture is located on the surrounding plaza and inside the K & B Building. Free. Not to be missed by art aficionados: has some of the best stuff in town.

Jackson Barracks, 6400 St. Claude Avenue. Inside this attractive nineteenth-century army barracks (now part of the Louisiana National Guard) the 1837 powder magazine has a large military artifacts collection. Call 271-6262 for appointment weekdays from 7:30 A.M. to 3:30 P.M.

Kenner City Museum, Third and Minor streets, Kenner (468-7200). This museum honors the late Sheriff Frank Clancy of Kenner and also has a collection on the history of this Jefferson Parish town. Nearby is a small restored area, railroad station, and community theater. Museum open Saturdays from 10 A.M. to noon, other days by appointment.

Louisiana Maritime Museum (581-1874). A fine collection of ship's models, lighthouse equipment, documents, art, ships' flags, everything pertaining to the maritime industry. Open daily (for admission) from 10 A.M. to 5 P.M. Presently located at 130 Carondelet Street.

Louisiana State Museum, Jackson Square. The **Cabildo** and the **Presbytère** are the two buildings flanking the St. Louis Cathedral and both hold collections of the Louisiana State Museum, plus traveling shows. The Folk Art Collection is on St. Peter Street in the Jackson House. The **Arsenal,** next door, houses volunteer fire-fighting equipment. **Madame John's Legacy** on Dumaine Street is an eighteenth-century house. The 1850 House in the Pontalba Apartments is decorated as a mid-nineteenth-century home would be. The Old U.S. Mint, at Esplanade Avenue and Decatur Street, holds the Louisiana Historical Center of research documents, the New Orleans Jazz Museum collections, a Mardi Gras exhibit, and the Amistad Research Center with black documentation. Louisiana State Museum buildings are open (for admission) Tuesday through Sunday from 9 A.M. to 5 P.M.

Middle American Research Institute, Tulane University. The M.A.R.I. galleries showcase early Latin American Indian art and artifacts. Located on the top floor of Dinwiddie Hall on St. Charles Avenue. Open weekdays from 9 A.M. to 4 P.M.

Musée Conti, 917 Conti Street. Wax museum, usual dioramas, Cyclops monster at end. Substantial admission. Open daily from 10 A.M. to 5:30 P.M.

New Orleans Museum of Art, City Park (488-2631). Open (for admission) Tuesday through Sunday from 9 A.M. to 5 P.M. Thursdays are free. Good art museum, collection ranges through various centuries. Especially nice rooms furnished and decorated in Louisiana and Federal style. Photography collection. Regular program of films, lectures. Museum shop. Café for lunch. Regular traveling shows (such as the King Tut exhibit).

Ursuline Museum, 2635 State Street (866-1472). Artifacts of the Ursuline nuns including a letter from Thomas Jefferson, handcrafts. Open by appointment on Tuesday and Thursday mornings. A small donation is requested.

TOURS—SIGHTSEEING

You can tour New Orleans in any number of ways. Here are some that will give you a good sample of what's available. Except for the Jean Lafitte Park tours, there is a fee involved for all of these. Call and check the prices so you won't be surprised.

WALKING TOURS

Friends of the Cabildo, 701 Chartres Street (523-3939). Walking tours of the French Quarter at 9:30 A.M. and 1:30 P.M. There is a fee, but it goes toward upkeep and the acquisitions fund of the Louisiana State Museum. Well-trained and knowledgeable guides. Starts from the Cabildo at Jackson Square.

Heritage Tours (949-9805 or 566-7592). English professor Kenneth Holditch and Cynthia Ratcliffe offer a literary tour of the French Quarter: where all those authors lived and worked, what buildings figured in what books. Tours throughout the city can be arranged. Scholarly and good-humored.

Jean Lafitte National Historical Park, St. Ann Street at Jackson Square. The National Park Service has free French Quarter walking tours, with themes such as "Cemeteries," "Jean Lafitte," "Haunted Houses." Drop in the office and see what's offered. Each lasts about one and a half hours.

Louise S. McGehee School, 2343 Prytania Street (561-1224). Group tours of Garden District homes by trained tour guides (usually students' mothers) are a fund-raising activity for this girls' school. Access to Garden District homes not usually open. Call and see if you can get in a tour while you're here.

Preservation Resource Center, 604 Julia Street (581-7032).

This nonprofit organization works to help reclaim and restore New Orleans' old buildings. Tours (on foot or with transportation) emphasize architecture and preservation. Call for appointment, or drop in to see their office in the Julia Row 1830s town house block.

Spring Fiesta, 529 St. Ann Street (581-1367). Annual nineteen-day home and garden tour schedule begins the Friday after Easter.

BOAT TOURS

"Bayou Jean Lafitte," Toulouse Street Wharf near Jackson Square (586-8777). The New Orleans Steamship Company has a selection of boats touring New Orleans' waters. The *Bayou Jean Lafitte* takes a Bayou Cruise daily.

"Cotton Blossom," foot of Canal Street (586-8777). A cruise up to the riverfront landing at the Audubon Zoo begins at 10 A.M., 12:45 P.M., and 3 P.M. The boat returns after each trip, so you can wander around the Audubon Zoo and return to Canal Street later.

"Creole Queen," foot of Poydras Street (529-4567). New Orleans Paddlewheels, Inc., operates this lush tour boat for two cruises daily, at 10:30 A.M. and 1:30 P.M., touring the harbor.

"Natchez," Toulouse Street Wharf (586-8777). The *Natchez* stern-wheeler takes a harbor cruise for two hours at 11:30 A.M. and 1:30 P.M. On Friday and Saturday nights at 6:30 there is a two-hour dinner cruise with a buffet and the Tulane Jazz Band. Fun for the kids.

"President," foot of Canal Street (586-8777). Saturday-night dance cruises with rock bands or other popular groups. Some Friday-night special entertainment also. Board at 8 P.M.; cruise the river while you dance from 10 P.M. to midnight.

"Voyageur," foot of Canal Street (523-5555). Louisiana Cruises, Inc., operates this tour boat, which takes a Bayou Cruise from 10 A.M. to 3 P.M. daily with a stop at the Chalmette Battlefield and a Harbor Cruise for two hours at 3:30 P.M. with another stop in Chalmette.

CARRIAGE TOURS

Gay 90's Carriages, Inc. (943-8820). Carriages pulled by horses or mules park at Jackson Square and at Royal and St. Louis streets. A half-hour tour is $6.00 for adults, $3.00 for children under twelve. This work is very hard on the animals in the summer. If you must take one of these tours, at least pick a carriage drawn by a mule. They are hardier animals. (Mules are the ones with really long ears sticking out of their straw hats.)

Old Quarter Tours (944-0446). This carriage tour company's vehicles are at Jackson Square. They say they use only mules in the summer. Adults $6.00, children under twelve $3.00 for a half-hour tour.

BUS TOURS

The Greater New Orleans Tourist and Convention Commission at 334 Royal Street has a directory called the *Visitors' Guide,* which you can pick up or write for. Inside are listings of all the tour services that have joined the commission. All tour companies in New Orleans must have licensed guides. Because the licensing test is becoming progressively more difficult, the guides are getting better and better (at least none of them are telling that old story about the *A* (for "Almonester") and *P* (for "Pontalba") initials entwined in the cast-iron balconies of the Pontalba Buildings being there for the A&P stores).

If you must make arrangements for a large group, you might consider first approaching the **Friends of the Cabildo, Louise S. McGehee School,** and the **Preservation Resource Center.** They are all nonprofit organizations, and you may get entrée into some private homes and buildings not usually shown. They can also probably deal with any foreign-language needs you might have.

Otherwise, for foreign-language guides, check with the New Orleans Tourist and Convention Commission.

These are two large companies that have regularly scheduled tours. There are several others, and your hotel may have suggestions on the ones they deal with.

Grayline of New Orleans, 108 University Place (525-0138). Buy tickets and get picked up at major hotels. Daily three-hour tour of the entire city at 9:30 A.M. and 1:30 P.M. The Plantation Tour leaves at 10 A.M. and visits Oak Alley and Houmas House. The Nightclub Tour (except Sundays) begins at 8:30 P.M. and visits the Top of the International Trade Mart, the Blue Angel and the Blue Room, ending at 12:30 A.M. Spanish and French guides available.

Southern Tours, P.O. Box 13008, New Orleans, Louisiana 70185 (486-0604). Pickup at major hotels (you may be picked up before the tour begins; be sure to check the pickup time with your hotel or the tour companies). Three-hour city tours at 9 A.M. and 2 P.M. include a walk in Jackson Square. Nightclub tours at 9:15, every night but Sunday. Visits the **Blue Room,** the **Blue Angel,** and the **Café du Monde** coffee stand at the French Market. Plantation Tours daily at 10 A.M. for **Houmas House** and **San Francisco.** (Lunch will not be included on the Plantation Tours, but they will probably stop at Lafitte's Landing or the Cabin on the West and East banks of the river near the Sunshine Bridge.) Foreign-language tours in French, Spanish, German, and most other languages can be arranged.

SOUVENIRS

Naturally you are going to want something to take home as a remembrance of New Orleans, and probably you have someone at home who is expecting or deserves a present. Most likely neither one of you would be satisfied with a tacky ashtray, so here are some gift ideas.

Food. How about some local coffee? Luzianne makes a good coffee and chicory, and Community Coffee has a very good dark roast. Add to that some of Paul Prudhomme's Cajun Magic spice mixes or Tony Chachere's Creole Seasoning, and some Wild Pecan Rice from Konriko, some Zatarain's Crab Boil or Fish Fry mix, maybe some Camellia Red Beans. Don't forget Tabasco sauce. Get some pralines from Aunt Sally's Praline Shop in the French Market, where you can watch them being made. You can do your grocery shopping in the French Quarter at the A&P on Royal and St. Peter streets or at Puglia's, 1100 North Rampart Street. There is a Schwegmann's on St. Claude Avenue at Elysian Fields Avenue and, for the fanciest variety, try Langenstein's, uptown corner of Pitt and Arabella streets.

Perfume. Hové Parfumeur, 824 Royal Street, will suggest a scent especially for you, or you can choose from several local varieties.

Music. Take home New Orleans jazz on records or tapes. Two record shops with extensive collections are **Smith's Record Shop,** 2019 St. Charles Avenue, and **Leisure Landing,** 5500 Magazine Street. Many musicians will have records on display in the clubs where they are playing.

Posters. Collecting Jazz Festival posters is a New Orleans occupation. There are posters for other local and state festivals and even one for the World's Fair. **De Ville Books** at 132 Carondelet Street will have posters, as will **A. L. Lowe** frame shop, 1126 South Carrollton Avenue. **Pro-Creations,** 225 North Peters Street, produces the Jazz Festival posters and many others. They may have the best prices.

Art. New Orleans has many serious working artists, and if you are a collector, you should get to know their work by visiting galleries. Here are some suggestions: the **Academy Gallery,** 5256 Magazine Street; the **Bienville Gallery,** 1800 Hastings Place at Magazine Street; **Galerie Simonne Stern,** 2727 Prytania Street; **Gasperi Folk Art Gallery,** 831 St. Peter Street; **Tilden-Foley Gallery,** 933 Royal Street; and the **Sandra Zahn Oreck Gallery,** 529 Wilkinson Row.

Antiques. The best and most expensive antique shops are on Royal Street: **Manheim Galleries,** 409 Royal Street, and the **Waldhorn Company,** 343 Royal Street. **M. S. Rau,** 630 Royal Street, has lots of Victorian bric-a-brac. **As You Like It,** 3929 Magazine Street, always has flat silver. Magazine Street has many, many antique shops. If you really want to look at antiques, take a day just for Magazine Street.

One New Orleans antique phenomenon is **Morton's,** 701 Magazine Street. Morton's has a store as well as the largest antique auction gallery in the South. If you know furniture and like auctions, you might do very well at Morton's. Remember, if you are bidding against dealers, you can afford to pay more for things than they can—you don't have to think about a markup. You can find Louisiana furniture and art at Morton's, as well as silver.

Don't forget the **Flea Market** on weekends at the far end of the French Market.

Museum shops. Museum shops in New Orleans are good places for souvenirs. You will find Louisiana Indian baskets, loofah vegetable sponges, vetiver (an aromatic root to store with your linens), records, books, calendars and datebooks, children's bonnets and dolls, facsimile Louisiana Confederate money, and all sorts of other choice things. Try the shop at the **Presbytère**

on Jackson Square, the **Historic New Orleans Collection,** 533 Royal Street, the **Gallier House,** 1130 Royal Street, and the **Hermann-Grima House,** 818 St. Louis Street.

Tacky ashtrays. If you really need ashtrays with NEW ORLEANS written on them, or a little man leaning on a signpost that says BOURBON STREET, or a T-shirt with NEW ORLEANS printed on it, there is a Woolworth's on Canal Street near Bourbon. They have a huge selection, and they are definitely not a fly-by-night operation. They've been there for years. (They also have reasonable prices.)

WHAT TO READ

One good way to get the feeling of New Orleans is to read about the city before you get here.

A Confederacy of Dunces by John Kennedy Toole is the classic New Orleans comic novel. A prizewinning hit, the book came out long after the author had committed suicide, despondent that his book had been turned down so many times. His mother persevered and, with the help of Walker Percy, got it published.

Walker Percy lives across Lake Pontchartrain, but his novel *The Moviegoer* is good New Orleans reading. Also try *The House on Coliseum Street* by local author Shirley Ann Grau. Frances Parkinson Keyes's *Crescent Carnival* and *Dinner at Antoine's* are old New Orleans favorites.

A Hall of Mirrors by Robert Stone is a good New Orleans novel, and *All the King's Men* by Robert Penn Warren is the best fictionalization of Huey Long's rise.

Here is a list of some worthwhile nonfiction about New Orleans: *New Orleans Jazz: A Family Album* by Edmond Souchon and Al Rose; *Storyville, New Orleans: Being an Authentic Illustrated Account of the Notorious Redlight District* by Al Rose; *The French Quarter: And Other Stories About New Orleans* by Herbert Asbury; *Voodoo in New Orleans* by Robert Tallant; *Frenchmen, Desire, Good Children* by John Chase; and *A Short History of New Orleans* by Mel Leavitt. Historians writing presently about New Orleans include Leonard Huber and Charles L. "Pie" Dufour.

A fantastic series of books on the architectural history of the city has been done by the Friends of the Cabildo. Actually, the publication of these books was the main reason behind much of the recent restoration work in some offbeat neighborhoods. The volumes include *The Lower Garden District, The American Sector, The Cemeteries, The Creole Faubourgs, The Esplanade Ridge, Faubourg Tremé and the Bayou Road,* and one being done presently on part of the uptown residential section. City Park, Metairie Cemetery, and Jefferson Parish have also been subjects of recent pictorial history works.

If you have a special interest in geology, you might like *A Tour Guide to the Building Stones of New Orleans* by Edward S. Slagle.

There are three authors of Louisiana children's books you might look for: Mary Alice Fontenot with her Clovis Crawfish series, Jim Rice with his Gaston the Alligator series, and Berthe Amoss's *The Chalk Cross* and *The Witch Cat.*

Two short novels on the Cajun country are in *Marshland Brace* by Chris Segura, and Mary Lou Widmer has a romance, *Night Jasmine,* set in New Orleans.

Books make nice souvenirs. The shop at the **Presbytère** of the Louisiana State Museum on Jackson Square and the shop at the **Historic New Orleans Collection** at 533 Royal Street will have a good selection of histories. Other bookstores you might check are **DeVille Book Store,** 132 Carondelet Street; the **Maple Street Book Shop,** 7529 Maple Street and at the **Rink** on Prytania Street at Washington Avenue; and the **Little Professor,** 1000 South Carrollton Avenue. **Doubleday Book Shop,** 633 Canal Street, and **B. Dalton,** 714 Canal Street, will have extensive collections. For out-of-print New Orleans books try **Bayou Books,** 1005 Monroe Street in Gretna.

THE WORLD'S FAIR

The 1984 Louisiana World Exposition's running dates—from May 12, 1984, to November 11, 1984—are just the apex of the fair's effect on New Orleans.

The renovations along the city's riverfront cover land that was once either barren or occupied by little-used warehouses. Whatever else the World's Fair, as it is usually called, does for the city, it has widened the developed area of the central part of town.

The fair site covers eighty-two acres. The **Great Hall**—which will become the New Orleans Convention Center—covers fifteen acres. Throughout the site are lagoons and watercourses. The theme of the exposition is "The World of Rivers . . . Fresh Water as a Source of Life."

As in other World's Fairs, many of the structures are temporary. That doesn't mean they can't be fanciful. In the middle of the exposition site is the Wonder Wall, created by the official architectural firm of August Perez and Associates as well as architect Charles Moore. The Wonder Wall winds for twenty-three hundred feet, with water flowing in front of it and through it. It expresses all sorts of architectural styles and has lights and music from traveling musicians, and concessions for food, and even video games.

The main gates of the fair, and a large arch at the foot of Canal Street, will have huge river gods and goddesses. Visitors can enter from Girod Street at South Front Street, from Erato Street (where the main parking lots will be), and at Poydras and South Front streets.

Right along the river is the **International Pavilion** with exhibits from foreign countries, an amphitheater seating fifty-one hundred people (this is where major stars will appear and where tickets will be necessary), the **United States Pavilion** (with a special movie made for the exposition), and the view of the river where the Tall Ships will dock.

Inside the main gate is the Great Hall, where the Louisiana State exhibit will trace the history of Louisiana from prehistoric times.

Both lagoons, with boats to ride on, and a monorail will carry visitors through the Great Hall. Or they can walk. Other states and corporations have displays here. There will even be an oil rig, on the fair site, plus a business and marketing center for visitors' use.

Some buildings will serve as bridges between the Great Hall and International Pavilion. The bridges are necessary because the Public Belt Railroad tracks, which serve the port, are in the middle of the fair site.

The theme of water is carried on throughout the site, and there is a theater for water shows, or **aquacades.**

There will be a tent where jazz and gospel music will be played twelve hours a day. There will be floating stages, parade floats, and strolling musicians and entertainers. There are rides such as a water flume and Ferris wheel. There is a **Women's Pavilion** and an Afro-American exhibit, "I've Known Rivers."

Nightly fireworks displays, laser displays, a daily circus, plus Louisiana musicians, cooks, and craftsmen at work; there should be something to see every minute.

There is even a walking cartoon character, a pelican, which will remind you even more of Disney World.

Probably the best thing to see is the exhibit at the **Vatican Pavilion.** Since the Vatican has one of the world's finest art collections, a sampling of it here has to be worth seeing. The Archdiocese of New Orleans actually bought the land the Vatican Pavilion stands on. That is what you might call a serious investment.

There are a **Children's Theater** series, plans for a **Youth Symphony Orchestra,** even a nightclub for the "official beer,"

Miller's. Plus, there are T-shirts, posters, and just about any other kind of souvenir for sale. And, in the fairgrounds are countless concession booths and restaurants. Considering the fact that Louisiana food, in general, is pretty good, the concessionaires are better than average.

Actually the Louisiana World Exposition celebrates the one hundredth anniversary of the first New Orleans World's Fair, the 1884–5 Cotton Exposition. The Historic New Orleans Collection location on Tchoupitoulas Street during the World's Fair is the site of a display of some of their extensive collection of Cotton Exposition memorabilia, and, with the New Orleans Museum of Art, an exhibit of nineteenth-century American paintings of rivers, streams, lakes, and waterfalls.

If you want to write for tickets, the address is Louisiana World Exposition, 805 South Front Street, New Orleans, Louisiana 70130. Tickets are priced at about $15 per adult per day and do not include food or major shows in the amphitheater. The fair opens at 10 A.M. and pavilions close at 10 P.M. Grounds and attractions remain open until 1 A.M.

Parking is provided near the Erato Street entrance. (Erato Street runs just about under the Greater New Orleans Bridge upramp.) A simpler solution might be to park your car at the Superdome and take the shuttle bus (thirty cents) on Poydras Street to the fairgrounds. This would be best in the daytime.

Travel agents have package arrangements for the World's Fair, and the larger hotels may provide shuttle service. The site is within fifteen blocks of most of the French Quarter and business district, so it is convenient to many hotels.

Several million visitors are expected to go through the fair. After closing day, the Convention Center will remain, as well as much of the renovated warehouse area. The area right on the docks, by the river, is being developed into entertainment areas for after the fair's closing, so whenever you get to the fair site, there will still be something to see and something to entertain you.

INDEX

Note: The principal page references under entries are in *italics*. Streets and avenues are listed alphabetically under "Streets" and "Avenues." Boulevards, drives, squares, etc., will be found under their first names.

A&P, 86, 87, 284, 286
Absinthe House, 74
Academy Gallery, 287
Academy of the Sacred Heart, 109
Acadian House Museum, *186–87*
Acadians. *See* Cajuns
Acme Oyster House, 46, *83*, 239
Airline Motors Restaurant, *164*
Airports, 155, *204–5*
Albania Plantation, *189*
Algiers, 120, 231, 256, 271, 272
A. L. Lowe frame shop, 287
Alonso and Son, 239
Amistad Research Center, 94, *281*
Amite, 194
Amtrak, *205*
Andouille, 13, 164, 165, 233
Andrew Jackson Hotel, *211*
Angelo Brocato's, *241–42*
Anglo-American Museum, *180*
Annunciation Square, 133, *134*
Antique shops, 60–62, 101, 194, 287
Antoine's Restaurant, 44, 84, *226–27*, 227
Archbishop Antoine Blanc Memorial, *72–73*, 110, 279
Architectural Archives, Southern, 80, *112*, 160
Ardillo's, *194*
Armstrong Park, 9, 32, 35, *79–80*, 82, 258
Arnaud's Restaurant, *83*, 227
Arsenal, *54*, 86
Arsenal Museum, *179*
Art galleries, 101, 287
Art museums, 54, 71, 112, *152–53*, 179, 260, 280, 281, 292
Art school, 112
Asphodel Plantation, *193*
As You Like It, 287

Atchafalaya Swamp, *187*
Audubon Park, 7, 98, 107, 111, *113–14*, 260, 264, 269, 271, 273, 274, 276
Audubon Pilgrimage, *192–93*
Audubon Place, 112, *115*
Audubon Zoo, 9, *114*, 263, 268, 276, 283
Aunt Sally's Praline Shop, 58, 286
Auto Lockup, *201*
Avenue Plaza Hotel, *217*
Avenues of New Orleans
  Bienville, 80
  Carrollton, 108, *115–16*
  City Park, 153
  Claiborne, 82, 108, 116, 172
  Elysian Fields, *138–39*
  Esplanade, 59, 68, *92–94*, *147–50*
  Howard, 123
  Jackson, 96, *102*, 107, 136
  Louisiana, 96, *106*
  Loyola, 117, *126–27*
  Magnolia, 104
  Melpomene, 132
  Napoleon, 133
  North Claiborne, 30, 192, 256
  Orleans, 192
  Orpheum, 154
  St. Charles, *27–29*, 33, 60, 95, *98–99*, 107, *108–15*, 124
  St. Maurice, 140
  Tulane, 111, 126
  Washington, 28, *104–5*, 136
  See also Streets of New Orleans
Avery Island, *185*, 193, *268–69*
Avondale Shipyards, *171*

Balls, 197
  Carnival, *25–27*, 82, 121, 191, 208
Banks, 60–62
Barataria, 143, 265

Barataria Tavern, 195
Barataria Unit, 254
Barq's soft drink, 21
Bars, 246–47
Baton Rouge, 22, 157, 169, 177–82, 241
Bayou Bar, 45, 46, 218, 246
Bayou Barataria, 70, 75, 195
Bayou Books, 290
Bayou Classic, 270
Bayou Coquille Trail, 254
Bayou cruises, 120, 283
Bayou Folk Museum, 198
Bayou Jean Lafitte, 57, 283
Bayou Lafourche, 157, 172–76, 199
Bayou Road, 147, 150–51, 290
Bayous
  description of, 157
  pirogue of, 195, 266
Bayou St. John, 2, 89, 147, 150–51, 269
Bayou Segnette State Park, 225
Bayou Teche, 183–84
Bayou Terrebonne, 252
Beauregard Hotel, 217
Beauregard House, 278
Beauregard Square, 79
Beignets, 19, 242
Belle Alliance, 173
Belle Helene, 168
Berdou's, 46, 234
Beverly Dinner Playhouse, 252
Bienville Gallery, 101, 127, 287
Bienville House, 215
Big Oak Island, 255, 277
Biloxi (Miss.), 130, 273
Blue Angel, 40, 46, 246, 285
Blue Room, 245, 285
Blue Stores, 69
Blythewood, 194
Board of Trade Plaza, 122
Boating, 154–55, 266–67
Boats, tour, 57, 114, 120, 143, 205, 283–84
Bocage, 167–68
Bogalusa, 192
Bohemia Wildlife Management Area, 263
Bonnet Carré Spillway, 157, 164
Books on New Orleans, 289–90
Borsodi's, 248

Boston Club, 29, 119, 121–22
Bottinelli Place, 154
Boudin, 13, 233
Bouligny, 232
Bourbon House, 75
Bousillage, 189
Bozo's, 239
Breakwater Drive, 155
Breaux Bridge Crawfish Festival, 194–95
Brechtel Golf Course, 272
Brennan's Restaurant, 46, 62, 226–27
Broadway Café, 115
Brocato's, 46, 56
Brooks Brothers, 208
Broussard, 188
Broussard House, 188–89
Brulatour Court, 63
Bruning's Restaurant, 45, 154, 239
Bucktown, 154
Bud's Broiler, 236
Burgundy Inn, 215
Burnside, 167
Burtheville, 107
Bus, 206
  tours by, 284–85
Business district, 117–28
  hotels in, 216–17, 219–20

Cabildo, the, 53, 60, 86, 281
  See also Friends of the Cabildo
Cabin, the, 166, 285
Cabrini Children's Museum, 77, 279
Café des Émigrées, 91
Café des Réfugiés, 91
Café du Monde, 44, 57, 58, 242, 285
Café Pontalba, 57
Café Sbisa, 232
Cajun cooking, 11, 22, 70, 231, 252
Cajuns (Acadians), 4, 160, 173, 175–76, 186–87, 192, 197, 199, 290
  film on, 184–85
  music of, 195, 197, 246
Calendar of events, 190–200
Camelia Grill, 46, 236
Cameron, 196
Camping, 146, 198, 224–25, 269
Camp Parapet, 160–61
Canal Place, 117

Candy, 58, 111, 184, 286
Canoe and Trail Shop, 269
Canoe trails, 254, 268, 270
Caribbean Room, 46, 228
Carnival Season, 24–27
Carol apartment building, 230
Car rental, 206
Carriage tours, 284
Carrollton, 107, 108, 115–16, 160
Carville, 168, 169
Casa Hové, 86
Casamento's, 240
Castillo's Mexican Restaurant, 83
Cast iron, 55, 61, 65–66, 68, 81, 103, 104, 121
Catahoula, 187–88
Catfish, 234, 241
Causeway Boulevard, 160
Celestial Knights, 25
Cemeteries, 80–82, 104–5, 150, 153–54, 155–56, 198, 254, 290
Central Grocery Company, 45, 236
Centroplex Auditorium, 179
Chalmette Battlefield, 45, 142–44, 255, 283–84
Chalmette Slip, 143
Chamber of Commerce, 206
Charenton, 160
Charity Hospital, 111, 202
Chart House, 44, 246
Chateau Motor Hotel, 215
Chateau Orleans, 223
Chaurice, 13
Chauvin, 252
Chez Helene, 237
Chez Marcelle, 188
Chez Nous Charcuterie, 242
Children's museums, 77, 153, 189, 277, 279
Children's theater, 251
Chinese restaurants, 240
Christ Church Cathedral, 99, 250
Christ Episcopal Church, 174
Christian's, 230
Christian's Foods, 46, 242–43
Christian Women's Exchange, 85, 278
Churches and cathedrals
    Business District, 123, 126, 128

Downtown, 140
French Quarter, 52–53, 72–73, 78, 279
Garden District, 99, 100, 102
Irish Channel, 133, 135–36
in other places, 151, 164, 166, 174, 186, 193
Uptown, 109, 111, 112, 250
Church of St. John the Baptist, 126
Church of the Immaculate Conception, 128
Church with the Lighted Steeple, 109
Citibusiness, 226
Citizen's Bank, 61
City Park, 46, 148, 152–53, 192, 260, 264, 268, 271–74, 276, 290
Civic Center, 126–27
Clancy's, 232
Clinton, 193
Clothes, shopping for, 208–9
Coffee houses, 208
Coliseum Place Baptist Church, 133
Coliseum Square, 129, 132–33
Columns Hotel, 213
Commander's Palace, 45, 98, 228
Compagno's, 235
Concerts, 112, 122, 181, 195, 250
    free, 256–57
Confederate Memorial Museum, 123, 280
Congo Square (former name), 35, 79
Congregation Gates of Prayer, 154
Contemporary Arts Center, 25, 43, 123, 191, 244, 249, 250, 251, 280
Convent, 165–66
Corn Stalk Hotel, 211–12
Cottage Plantation, 193
Cotton Blossom, 114, 120, 283
Country Concert line, 248
Courthouses, 62, 83, 115
Covington, 126, 191–92, 194
Crabs, 13–14, 228, 234, 254–65
Crawfish, 16, 18, 194–95, 241, 243
Creole cooking, 11–23
Creole cottages, 77, 139, 149
Creole Country, 23, 46, 243
Creole House, 54
Creole Queen, 283

Creoles
  Americans and, 5, 6
  definition of, 4–5
Crescent City, Krewe of, 29
Crescent City Classic, 269
Croissant d'Or, 242
Crozier's, 46, 230
Cruises. See Tour boats
Cypress Grove Cemetery, 154

Dancing, 247–48
  Greek, 69
  performances of, 154, 174, 250, 283
  on side-wheeler cruise, 120, 195, 246
  See also Balls
Danna Center, 110
Dashiki Project Theater, 251
Daube, 12–13
Dauphin Orleans Hotel, 215
Days Inn, 221
Delachaise Marching Club, 28
Delacroix Island, 145
De La Ronde Oaks, 144
Delcambre Shrimp Festival and Fair, 196
Delgado Community College, 153
Delmonico's, 234
Delta Festival Ballet, 250
Delta Queen, 205
Delta Wilderness Outfitters, 269
Dental treatment, 202
Department stores, 80, 119
  See also Shopping
Derbigny Plantation, 171–72
Des Allemands, 167
Designers Anonymous, 209
Destrehan, 161–64
De Ville Books, 250, 287, 290
D. H. Holmes department stores, 119, 208, 249
Didee's, 181
Dillard University, 250, 251
Dinner theaters, 252
Dinwiddie Hall, 112, 259–60, 281
Discount stores, 209
Discovery Loft, 277
"Dixie," origin of, 61
Dixon Hall, 112, 249, 250

Docville, 145
Dollhouse, 115
Doll museums, 77, 189, 279
Donaldsville, 157, 172, 173
Dooky Chase's, 237, 249
Doubleday Book Shop, 290
Downtown, 138–40
  meaning of term, 118
Drinks, 21–22
Drugstores, 24-hour, 202
Dry cleaning, 209
Ducros Museum, 145, 277
Dueling Oaks, 152
Duke's Place, 245
Dutch Gardens, 193

Easter, 155
Ecology Center, 268
Eddie's, 237
Edgard, 164
Edward Douglass White House, 175
1850 House, 56, 278
Elks Place, 126
Elmwood, 161
Elmwood Shopping Center, 209
Elton, 160
Embers, The, 44, 247
Emergencies, 201–3
Empire, 196, 265
Endymion, 29, 256
English Turn, 2, 146
Entertainment, 249–52
Esplanade, 57, 148–50, 290
Esplanade Lounge, 45, 247
Evangeline Downs, 274
Evans Creole Candy Factory, 58
Evergreen, 170
Exchange Alley, 83
Exchange Place, 121
Exercise, 260, 269, 275, 276
Exposition Boulevard, 113

Fair Grounds Race Track, 40, 150, 195, 198, 273–74
Fairmont Hotel, 219, 245, 274
Fairview-Riverside park, 225
Fall Medieval Fair, 276
Famous Door, 246

Farmers' Market, 59
Fast-food franchises, 240–41
Faubourg Marigny, 138–39, 279
Faubourgs, 290
  definition of, 138
Faubourg Ste. Marie, 95–96
Feet First, 209
Felicianas, the, 193
Felicity, 170
Felix's Restaurant, 83
Ferries, 164, 165, 168, 169, 256
  free, 58, 120, 136, 256
Festa d'Italia, 127
Filé, 18, 19, 58
Film Buffs' Institute, 110
Firemen's Cemetery, 154
Fishing, 145, 174, 264–66
  rodeos of, 196, 265
Flambeaux, 31, 256
Flea Market, 59, 287
Float trips, 194, 268
Folk art, 54, 198, 281, 287
Folsum, 194
Fontainebleau State Park, 225, 273
Food of New Orleans, 11–23
  festival of, 195–96
  at Mardi Gras, 33
  as souvenirs, 286
  See also Restaurants
Foreign-language guides and tours, 284–85
Foreign Relations Association, 123
Fortier Gallery, 71
Fort Jackson, 199
Fort Macomb, 277
Fort Pike, 267, 276–77
Fort St. Charles, 93
Forty One Forty One, 247
France, New Orleans and, 1–4, 35
Franklinton, 197, 259
Freedman's Bureau, 133
Free things to do, 253–61
French Market, 9, 19, 58–59, 69–70, 285
French Opera House, 74, 100
French Quarter, 10, 45, 48–94, 282, 286
  hotels in, 215–16, 218–19
  jazz in, 40

map of, 49
  at Mardi Gras, 30–31
French Quarter Maisonettes, 212
Friends of the Cabildo, 44, 53, 54, 93, 282, 284, 289–90

Galatoire's, 44, 73, 226, 228
Galerie Simonne Stern, 287
Gallier Hall, 29, 124, 251
Gallier House, 44, 67–68, 278, 288
Gambit, 43, 244, 249, 258
Garden District, 45, 95–106, 107, 228, 279, 282
  history of, 5, 95–97
Garden District Marching Club, 28
Gardens, 154, 185, 186, 193–94, 276, 277
Gasperi Folk Art Gallery, 287
Gautreau's, 232
Gayarré Place, 149, 151
Gay bars, 73
Gem Bar, 61
Genghis Khan, 240
Gentilly Boulevard, 147, 150, 151
Geoscience Museum, 180–81
Germans, the, 5, 100, 130, 135, 140, 166–67
Gino's, 181
Godchaux store, 119, 208, 209
Golden Meadow, 196
Gondolas, 207
Gonzalez, 195, 196
Gourmet shops, 23, 286
Grace Episcopal Church, 193
Grambling State University, 270
Grand Isle, 196, 265, 266, 269, 273
Grand Route St. John, 150, 151
Grayline of New Orleans, 285
Greater New Orleans Bridge, 8, 57–58, 293
Greenville, 107
Green Wave, 111, 127, 270
Greenwood Cemetery, 154
Gretna, 136, 230, 231, 234, 256, 290
Grillades, 12
Guesthouses, 211–14
Guidebook, streetcar, 108
Gumbo, 17, 18–19, 58, 233
Gus Mayer (store), 119

Hale Boggs Federal Buildings, 125
Hammond, 194
Harvey Canal, 120, 121
Hastings Place, 101
Haunted House, 68
Hedgewood Hotel, 99, 213
Heritage Day Festival, 194
Heritage Museum Village, 186
Heritage Tours, 282
Heritage Trail, 153
Hermann-Grima House, 85, 278, 288
Hermitage, 168
Hilton and Towers Hotel, 220, 245, 274
Historical museums, 53, 63, 93–94, 180, 260, 280, 292, 293
Historic districts, 118, 129
Historic New Orleans Collection, 44, 63, 278, 288, 290, 293
Hodges Gardens, 193–94
Holt Cemetery, 154
Holy Name of Jesus Church, 111
Holy Name School, 109
Holy Rosary Church, 151
Holy Trinity Church, 140
Honey Island Swamp, 263, 269, 270
Hope Haven, 254
Horseracing, 198, 273–74
Hospel Factory Outlets, 209
Hotels, 210–11, 214–20, 222
Hot Jazz Classic, 39, 195
Houmas House, 167, 285
House tours, 67–68, 71, 85, 89, 97–99, 139, 151–52, 154, 166, 183–84, 186–88, 194, 197, 199, 278–79
Hové Parfumeur, 286
Howard Tilton Memorial Library, 80, 112
Huey P. Long Bridge, 16, 171
Hurstville, 107
Hyatt Regency, 219
Hymel's Restaurant, 166, 167

Iberville at Canal Place, 219
Indians (black clubs), 30, 32, 33, 148, 192, 256
Indians (native Americans), 58, 62, 147, 160, 167, 177, 181, 185, 255
Indulgence, 100, 232–233

Industrial Canal, 110, 140–41, 155, 265
Instant Care Center, 202
International Hotel, 219
International House, 123
International Trade Mart Building, 58, 117, 120, 247, 285
Irish Channel, 96, 129–37, 192
Iron. See Cast iron; Wrought iron
Iron Theater, 88
Isleños Center, 45, 144–45, 255
Italian Open Golf Tournament, 192
Italian Piazza, 10, 127, 192
Italian restaurants, 238–39

Jackson Barracks, 141–42, 259, 280
Jackson Brewery, 57
Jackson House, 54
Jackson Square, 2, 44, 48, 50–59, 86, 257, 284
   map of, 51
Jambalaya, 17, 195, 196
Jazz, 34–41, 57, 58, 75, 86, 126, 134–35, 184, 192, 245–46, 250, 289, 292
   archive of, 39, 112, 260
   festival of, 40, 150, 195, 286–87
   history of, 35–36, 79, 148
   at Mardi Gras, 28, 29, 32, 37
   museum of, 39, 80, 94, 281
   shopping for, 286
Jean Lafitte National Historical Park, 44, 45, 56, 81, 142, 253–55, 270, 277, 282
Jefferson City, 107, 276
Jefferson College, 165
Jefferson Downs, 274
Jefferson Parish, 107, 115, 148, 160, 172, 241, 256, 260, 290
   Mardi Gras in, 24, 28
Jimmy's, 246
Jonathan, 229
Julia Row, 10, 223, 283
Jungle Garden, 185, 193

K & B Plaza, 125, 260, 280
Katz and Besthoff (K & B) Plaza, 125, 260, 280
Kenner, 161, 204
Kenner City Museum, 161, 280
Kingsley House, 134–35, 137

Kisatchie National Forest, 198
Kolb's, 27
Konriko Rice Mill and Company Store, 17, 184–85, 286
K-Paul's Louisiana Kitchen, 45, 70, 226, 230–31
Krauss Department Store, 80, 119, 208

Lacombe, 160, 231
La Cuisine, 234
Lafayette, 22, 96, 107, 114, 173, 191, 197, 241, 274
Lafayette Cemetery No. 1, 104–5
Lafayette Square, 117, 119, 124–25
La Fête, 196
Lafitte (city), 120, 143, 195, 265, 266
Lafitte Guest House, 212
Lafitte's Blacksmith Shop, 75, 247
Lafitte's Landing, 172, 285
Lafourche Parish, 160
LaFrenière Park, 276
Lake Catherine, 264
Lakefront Airport, 155, 205
Lake Maurepas, 2
Lake Pontchartrain, 2, 82, 89, 118, 147–48, 154–55, 225, 264–67, 273
Lakeshore Drive, 154–55, 264
Lakeside Shopping Center, 209
Lake Verret, 174
La Maison Duchamp, 186
La Marquise, 242
Lama's St. Roch Market, 243
Lamothe House, 212
Langenstein's, 23, 46, 243, 286
Laplace, 45, 164
La Provence, 231
La Riviera, 238
La Salle Hotel, 222
LaSalle Parish, 160
La Trouvaille, 252
L'Auberge Hotel and Guest House, 222
Laurel Valley Plantation, 176
Lee Barnes Cooking School, 23
Lee Circle, 27, 107, 118, 125, 154
Leisure Landing, 286
Le Pavillon Hotel, 216
Le Petit Salon, 86

Le Petit Théâtre du Vieux Carré, 86, 251
Le Richelieu Motor Hotel, 215
LeRuth's, 45, 229
Liberty Monument, 120
Libraries, 39, 63, 80, 93–94, 109–10, 112, 127, 258
Linear Park, 260, 269, 276
Livaudais plantation, 96, 99
Lombard plantation, 140
Longfellow-Evangeline State Commemorative Area, 186–87
Longue Vue Gardens, 45, 154, 193, 277, 278
Loreauville, 186
Louis XVI (restaurant), 229
Louisiana Arts and Science Center, 179
Louisiana Cotton Festival, 197
Louisiana Gulf Coast Oil Exposition, 197
Louisiana Historical Center, 93, 281
Louisiana Jockey Club, 150
Louisiana Landmarks Society, 151, 152
Louisiana Maritime Museum, 121, 280–81
Louisiana Military History and State Weapons Museum, 142
Louisiana National Guard, 141
Louisiana Nature Center, 45, 267–68, 277
Louisiana State Capitol, 177, 178–79, 193
Louisiana State Museum, 44, 53, 54, 56, 86, 90, 93, 278, 281, 282
Louisiana State Supreme Court, 127
Louisiana State University (L.S.U.), 177, 178, 180–81, 198, 271
Louisiana Yambilee Festival, 197
Lower Garden District, 96, 129, 290
Loyola University, 107, 110–11, 250, 251
Lyons Carnival Organization, 28

McAlister Auditorium, 112, 249
Madame John's Legacy, 90, 278, 281
Madewood, 174
Madonna Manor, 254
Magnolia Lane, 172

Magnolia Mound Plantation, *179–80*, 193
Mahogany Hall, 80
Maison André, *231*
Maison Bourbon, *246*
Maison Chartres, *212*
Maison de Ville, *86*, *212*
Mandina's, *235*
Manheim Galleries, *287*
Manresa, *165–66*
Maple Leaf Bar, 46, *246*
Maple Street Book Shop, *290*
Maps
    French Quarter, *49*
    how to get, *206*
    Jackson Square, *51*
    plantation tour, *161–62*
Mardi Gras, *24–33*, 58, 74, 82, 101, 119, 121–22, 126, *191–92*, 208, 255–56
    guide to, 27
    jazz at, 28, 29, 32, 37
    museum of, 94, 281
    official colors of, 31, 95
    song of, 31, 32
Mardi Gras Fountain, 155
Marie Antoinette Hotel, *215*, 229
Marigny Triangle, 139
Marina, *154–55*, *166–67*
Marksville, 160
Marquette House International Hostel, 222
Marriott Hotel, 220
Marshall's, 209
Martha Washington Oak, 114
Marti's, *233*
Maurice's Bistro Room, 46, *231*
Meat Market, 59
Medical treatment, 202
Melrose, *198*
Memorial Tower, *180*
Merieult House, 63, *278–79*, 280
Messina's Restaurant, 83
Metairie Cemetery, *153–54*, 273, 290
Metairie Road, 148, 153
Middle-American Research Institute, 112, *259–60*, 281
Mid-Winter Sports Association, 270, 272

Mike Anderson's, *181*
Mile Branch Settlement, *197*, 259
Milneberg, 148
Milton H. Latter Memorial Library, *109–10*
Minacepelli's Dinner Theater, 252
Mintmere, *188*
Mississippi Flyway, 180, 262, 268
Mississippi River, *57–58*, 114, 143, 187
    boats on, 57, 114, 120, 143, 205, 246, *283–84*
    bridges over, 8, *57–58*, 136, 157, 161, 164, 293
    English Turn in, 2, *146*
    museums of, 121, 179
    See also River Road
Mrs. Wheat's Kitchen, *241*
Monkey Hill, 114
Monteleone Hotel, *61*, *218*, 245
Moon Walk, 44, 57, 261
Morgan City, 196, 267
Morning Call, 242
"Morro Castle," 92
Morton's, *287*
Mosca's, *238*
Motels, *220–21*
Mother's Restaurant, 118, *236–37*
Mount Hope Plantation, *180*
Muffaletta sandwich, 236
Municipal Auditorium, 9, 31, 35, 79, 82, 233, 249, 274
Municipal Yacht Harbor, 266, 267
Munster's, *247*
Musée Conti, *281*
Museum of Natural Sciences, *180*
Museums, *259–60*, *279–81*
    archaeological, 112, *259–60*
    art, 54, 71, 112, *152–53*, 179, 260, 280, 281, 292
    Bowie, *197*
    children's, 77, 153, 189, 277, 279
    Confederate, 123, 280
    decorative arts, 154
    folk, 54, 198, 281
    furniture, 152
    glass, 153
    historical, 53, 63, *93–94*, *180*, 260, 280, 292, 293

house, 67–68, 71, 85, 89, 97–99, 139,
151–52, 154, 166, 183–84, 186–88,
194, 197, 199, 278–79
jazz, 39, 80, 94, 281
maritime, 121, 280–81
military, 142, 179, 199, 259, 277, 280,
282–83
pharmacy, 70, 280
photography, 153, 281
plantation, 159, 165, 167–70, 174, 176,
179–80, 193
religious, 110, 279, 281
rural life, 178, 186, 259
of St. Bernard Parish, 144–45,
255
science, 180–81
sculpture, 125, 260, 280
voodoo, 88–89
Music, 34–43, 120, 174, 194, 250
Cajun, 195, 197, 246
at Mardi Gras, 32–33
shopping for, 286
See also Concerts; Jazz
Mystick Den, 247

Napoleon House, 44, 46, 70, 247
Napoleonville, 173–74
Natchez, 57, 283
Natchez Pilgrimage, 193
Natchitoches, 198–99
Newcomb Chapel, 112, 250
Newcomb College, 105, 112, 250
New Iberia, 17, 183–89
New Orleans Botanical Gardens, 276
New Orleans Convention Center, 291,
293
New Orleans County Club, 154
New Orleans International Airport,
204–5
New Orleans Jazz and Heritage Festi-
val, 40, 150, 195, 286–87
New Orleans Jazz Museum, 39, 80,
94, 281
New Orleans Museum of Art, 46, 102,
104, 149, 152–53, 260, 276, 281
New Orleans Public Library, 127, 258
Nicholls State University, 176
Nick Castrogiovanni's, 246

Nightclubs, 40, 245, 246
tours of, 285
See also Striptease clubs
Noble Arms Inn, 212
Nottoway, 157, 169
Nutria, 199, 254

Oak Alley, 157, 169–70
Oak and Pine Alley, 187
Oakley House, 193
Off Off Off Broadway Players, 251
Old Pentagon Barracks, 179
Old Quarter Tours, 284
Old Spanish Custom House, 151
Old U.S. Mint, 39, 93, 281
Old Ursuline Convent, 69, 72–73, 91,
279
Old World Inn, 213
Olivier Guest House, 212–13
Opelousas, 197
Orleans Ballroom, 87–88
Orleans Parish, 155, 172
Orpheum Theater, 122, 249
Our Lady of Guadaloupe church, 78
Our Lady of Victory church, 72–73,
279
Our Mother of Perpetual Help Chapel,
100
Outdoors equipment, 269
Oyster Festival, 194
Ozanam Inn, 123

Palmer Park, 116
Parades, 255–56
See also Mardi Gras
Parasol's Bar, 137, 237
Parc d'Orleans I and II, 224
Paris Road, 265, 267
Parks, 260–61
St. Bernard's State, 145–46, 225
Park View Guest House, 214
Pars Cours, 260, 269, 276
Pascal's Manale, 238
Pat Barberot's Jefferson Orleans
North, 248
Pat O'Brien's, 21, 46, 86, 247
Patout's, 188
Penny Post, 248

Père Antoine Alley, 54–55, 65
Perseverance Hall, 79
Pete Fountain's, 220, 245
Pharmacy museum, 70, 280
Piazza d'Italia, 10, 127, 192
Pilottown, 199
Pirate's Alley, 53–54, 65
Pirogue Races, 195, 266
Pitot House, 151–52, 279
Place d'Armes, 2, 50
    See also Jackson Square
Place d'Armes Motor Hotel, 216
Planetarium, 115
Plantation Golf Club, 272
Plantation tours, 157–76, 193, 285
Plaquemines Parish, 1, 145, 263
    Orange Festival in, 199
Police and Fireman's Chapel, 78
Pompano, 16, 227, 228, 231, 234
Pontalba Apartment Buildings, 52, 55–
    56, 284
Pontchartrain Hotel, 45, 217–18, 228,
    246
Ponchartrain Park, 271–72
Port of New Orleans, 57–58, 117, 138,
    256, 292
Posters, shopping for, 286–87
Presbytère, 54, 281, 287–88
Preservation Hall, 40, 45, 46, 86, 245
Preservation Resource Center, 126,
    282–83, 284
Prince Conti, 216
Pro-Creations, 287
Provincial Motel, 216
Prytania Park Hotel, 214
Public Belt Railroad, 292
Puglia's, 286
Puppetorium, 57

Quadroon Balls, 87

Rail travel, 205
Rain Forest, 247
Ralph and Kacoo's, 241
Ramada Hotel, 220
Rayne Memorial Methodist Church,
    109
Red Stores, 59, 69

Reimann House, 80
Religious orders, 3, 109, 110, 115, 128,
    135–36, 141, 165
Reserve, 164–65
Restaurants, 226–42
    guides to, 226
Ring Levee hiking trail, 254
Rink shopping center, 100, 290
Riverbend area, 209
Riverboat Travel Park, 224
Rivercenter, 274
Rivergate Exhibition Hall, 25, 120, 121,
    195–96
River Road, 45, 108, 157, 159–76
    Christmas bonfires on, 159, 199–200
Riverside Museum, 179
Rivertown, 161
Rockery Inn, 142
Rocky and Carlo's, 144
Roman Candy Wagon, 111
Roosevelt Hotel, 21
Roosevelt Mall, 152, 153
Rosa Park, 110
Rosedown, 193
Rosethorne Park, 265
Rouselle's Restaurant, 164
Royal Lafayette, 218
Royal Orleans Hotel, 45, 63, 84, 218–
    19, 247
Royal Sonesta Hotel, 219, 247
Rural Life Museum, 178
Ruth's Chris Steakhouse, 241

Sabin's Fine Foods, 181–82
St. Alphonsus Church, 135, 136, 137
St. Anna's, 134
St. Anthony's Garden, 54, 65, 87
St. Bernard Civic Auditorium, 274
St. Bernard Parish, 45, 138, 144–45
    Mardi Gras in, 28
    museum of, 144–45, 255, 277
St. Bernard State Park, 145–46, 225
St. Charles Guest House, 214
Saint Charles Hotel, 218
St. Charles Inn, 214
St. Elizabeth's, 133–34
St. Francisville, 192–93
St. Joseph (home), 170

St. Joseph Cemetery, 136
St. Joseph's Abbey, 126
St. Louis Cathedral, 50, 52–53, 65, 165
St. Louis Cemetery No. 1, 65, 80, 81–82, 254
St. Louis Cemetery No. 2, 81, 82
St. Louis Cemetery No. 3, 150
St. Louis Hotel, 63, 83, 84, 216
St. Louis Plantation, 169
St. Martin of Tours Church, 186
St. Martinville, 173, 186
St. Mary's Assumption, 135–37
St. Mary's Dominican College, 115
St. Maurice Church, 140
St. Michael's Church, 166
St. Patrick Cemetery, 154
St. Patrick's Church, 123
St. Peter and Paul Church, 140
St. Roch Campo Santo, 155–56
St. Tammany Parish, 160
St. Thomas Housing Project, 129
St. Vincent's Infant Home, 133
Saks Fifth Avenue, 119, 208
Salt mine, 185, 269
Sam's Women's Apparel, 209
Sandra Zahn Oreck Gallery, 287
Savoir Faire, 233
Sazerac Bar, 247
Schwegmann's Supermarket, 23, 46, 265, 286
Seabrook Bridge, 265, 267
Seafood restaurants, 239–40
Seven Oaks, 171
Shadows on the Teche, 183–84
Shape Spa, 275
Sheraton New Orleans, 220
Shipyards, 171
Shogun, 240
Shopping, 208–9 80, 119,
  for books, 290
  for groceries, 242–43, 286
  for souvenirs, 286–88
Sisters of the Holy Family, 88
Showboat Theater, 252
Slidell, 192, 166
Smith's Record Shop, 286
Solo's, 209
Soniat House, 213
Soulé College, 102

Southern Architectural Archives, 80, 112, 260
Southern Athletic Club, 104
Southern University, 270
Southern Yacht Club, 266
Souvenirs, 286–88
Spanish Fort amusement park, 99, 147
Spanish Plaza, 120
Spanish Trail, 147
Sports, 262–75
Sportsman's Paradise, 266
Spring Fiesta Townhouse, 279
State parks, 145–46, 224–25
Steamboat Houses, 141
Steamboats. See Tour boats
Stephen and Martin's Restaurant, 247
Storyville, 7, 36–37, 80, 151, 289
Streetcar Named Desire, 60, 69, 138
Streetcars, 60, 108, 114, 117–19, 125, 132–33
Streets of New Orleans
  Adele (former name), 129
  Baronne, 128
  Barracks, 72, 92, 93
  Basin, 80–82, 127
  Bienville, 83
  Bourbon, 46, 48, 73–75
  Broad, 85
  Broadway, 115
  Burgundy, 77, 80, 139, 140, 279
  Calliope, 136
  Camp, 123–24, 132, 133
  Canal, 27, 33, 58–60, 68, 70, 98, 117, 119–22, 148, 291
  Carondelet, 98, 118
  Chartres, 52, 60, 70–73, 83, 84, 140, 141, 278
  Clio, 132–33
  Coliseum, 100–101, 104, 132, 133
  Common, 132
  Conery, 105
  Constance, 135, 137
  Conti, 80, 83
  Craps (former name), 77, 138
  Dante, 116
  Dauphine, 60, 76, 129
  Decatur, 50, 52, 57, 68–70, 93, 122, 138

Delery, 141
Desire (former name), 60, 69, 138
Douglass, 141
Dryades, 126
Dublin, 116
Dumaine, 66, 90–91, 278
Egania, 141
Eighth, 105
Eleonore, 107
Erato, 293
Euterpe, 133
Felicity, 96, 107
First, 103
Fourth, 104
Freret, 111, 115
Gallatin (former name), 70
Galvez, 151
Governor Nicholls, 72, 91–92, 147
Gravier, 123
Harmony, 106
Hospital (former name), 72, 91
Iberville, 61, 82–83
Joseph, 107
Josephine, 135
Hulia, 126
Leda, 150
Lowerline, 107
Madison, 71
Magazine, 96, 101, 111, 113, 122, 132, 134, 287
Marigny, 139–40
Market, 135
Moss, 151–52, 279
Mystery, 151
Nayades (former name), 95, 98
New Custom House (former name), 82
North Peters, 68
North Rampart, 9, 122
Oak, 116
Orange, 133
Orleans, 65, 82, 87–88
Philip, 102
Piety (former name), 138
Poydras, 9, 10, 117, 127, 192
Prytania, 97, 99–100, 104, 132, 133, 279
Race, 132
Rampart, 35, 78–80, 82, 147

Royal, 21, 48, 59, 60–68, 139, 278, 287
St. Ann, 52, 55, 81, 88–89, 278, 279
St. Ferdinand, 140
St. Louis, 70, 80, 84–85, 88, 278
St. Peter, 52, 55, 57, 75, 80, 86–87, 88
St. Phillip, 59, 88, 91, 148
Sauvage, 150
Second, 103
Seventh, 105
Sixth, 105
Tchoupitoulas, 113, 127, 132
Third, 103–4, 137
Toledano, 107
Toulouse, 74, 85–86
Tremé, 80
Ursulines, 91
Walnut, 113
Webster, 107
Wilkinson, 71
See also Avenues of New Orleans
Striptease clubs, 48, 73
Sugar Bowl, 191, 199, 270
Sugar House, 216–17
Summer Lyric Theater, 252
Sun Oak house, 87, 139, 279
Sunshine Bridge, 157, 166, 172
Superdome, 9, 111, 127, 191, 249, 270, 274
Swimming, 113, 146, 273
Swenson's Ice Cream, 56
Switzerland Bakery, 242
Synagogues, 109, 154

Tangipahoa River, 194
Taxicabs, 207
Tchoupitoulas Plantation Restaurant, 170–71
Tennis, 272–73
Terrebonne Parish, 160
Terrebonne Swamp and Marsh Tours, 269
Texcuco, 166
Theaters, 40–41, 86, 122, 124, 249, 251–52
early, 87
first movie, 121

Théâtre Marigny, 251
Theatre of the Performing Arts, 9, 79, 82, 229, 233, 249
Thibodaux, 175
Thoth, 256
Ticketmaster, 27, 244, 249
Tiger Stadium, 180
Tilden-Foley Gallery, 287
Tipitina's, 43, 45, 46, 246, 257
Toney's Spaghetti House, 238–39
Top of the Mart, 247, 285
Toulouse Theater, 41, 245
Tour boats, 57, 114, 120, 143, 205, 283–84
Tourist information, 25, 61, 97–98, 123, 183, 190, 197, 206, 244, 249, 253, 266, 269
    in Baton Rouge, 177–78, 190
    on hotels, 210
Touro Infirmary, 109
Touro Synagogue, 109
Tours, 282–85
    boat. See Tour boats
    bus, 284–85
    carriage, 284
    of homes. See House tours
    of plantations, 157–76, 193, 285
    of swamps, 263, 269
    walking, 44, 53, 56, 126, 161, 254, 268, 182–83
Trailer parks, 224
Translators, 123
Tremé, 148, 290
Trinity Episcopal Church, 102
Tulane University, 39, 80, 107, 111–12, 195, 259–60, 272, 281
    entertainment at, 249–52
    Green Wave of, 111, 127, 270
Turkish bath, 104
Tyler's Beer Garden, 246

Uglesich's, 237
Uncle Sam Plantation, 166
Union Passenger Terminal, 127, 205, 206
U.S. Custom House, 68–69, 120, 121
University of New Orleans, 155, 251

University of Southwestern Louisiana, 114
University Place, 122
Upperline, The, 233
Uptown, 107–16, 118
    hotels in, 217–18
Uptown Apparel Company, 209
Uptown Inn, 214
Uptown Izzy's, 209
Uptown Square, 115, 208
Ursuline Museum, 110, 281

Vendetta Alley, 71
Venice, 265
Versailles (restaurant), 229–30
Vieux Carré, 48
Vieux Carré Commission, 92
Villa Covento, 213
Ville Platte, 197
Virlane Foundation, 125, 280
Vitascope Hall, 121
Voodoo, 5, 70, 78, 87–89, 147–48, 289
Voodoo Museum and Gift Shop, 88–89

Waggaman, 238
Waldhorn Company, 287
Walgreen's Drugstore, 61
Walking tours. See Tours
Warwick Hotel, 217
Washington Artillery, 57
Washington Parish Free Fair, 197, 259
Washington Square, 139
Washing Well, 209
Wax museum, 281
West Bank, 28, 45
West End, 45, 154–55, 239, 267
White Castle, 157, 168, 169
"White League," 120–21
Whole Food Company, 150
Willy Coln's, 230
Windsor Court, 217
Wise's Cafeteria, 235
Wisner Boulevard, 153
Witches Closet, 91
Woodhouse Row, 223
Woolworth's, 288

World's Fair (1984), 9, 10, 117, 207, 286, 291–93

World's Industrial and Cotton Centennial Exposition (1884), 7, 35, 105, *113*, 293

Wrought iron, *61*, 71, 86

Xavier University, 250, 251

Yachting, 154–55, *266–67*

Yellow Bowl, *188*

YMCA International Center, 222

Zatarain's mixes, 286

Zemurray Gardens, 194

Zoo at Audubon Park, 9, *114*, 263, 268, 276, 283

ABOUT THE AUTHOR

CAROLYN KOLB was born June 29, 1942, in New Orleans. With her parents, Mr. and Mrs. J. H. Goldsby, Jr., she moved to Bogalusa, Louisiana, and graduated from high school there. She returned to New Orleans to enter Newcomb College of Tulane University and graduated in 1963 with a degree in English.

She married Kenneth Carlton Kolb, a New Orleans native, in 1964 and since that time they have lived in New Orleans, where he owns an advertising and public relations agency.

Carolyn Kolb is a former reporter on the City Desk of the *Times-Picayune,* a former New Orleans correspondent for Reuters, Ltd., British news agency, and was for two years director-curator of the New Orleans Jazz Museum. She has written numerous magazine articles and has advertising and public relations experience, as well as having a Louisiana real estate broker's license.

The Kolbs and their children, Pherabe and Kenneth, and Smokey the cat live in uptown New Orleans.